From Dreamer to Dreamfinder

A Life and Lessons Learned in
40 Years Behind a Name Tag

Ron Schneider

ISBN: 978-0-9854706-1-6

Published by Bamboo Forest Publishing
First Printing: July, 2012

Visit us Online at:
www.bambooforestpublishing.com

Table of Contents

Foreword

Author's foreword

Introduction

Afterword

Appendices

Acknowledgments

FOREWORD BY LARRY NIKOLAI

I have had the great fortune to know Ron Schneider for 35 years. We started work at Magic Mountain's Spillikin Corners on the same fateful day in 1977 and spent the next three years together entertaining the guests in that sadly lost (but fondly remembered) slice of Southern California theme park history.

I say "entertaining the guests" – actually I was running the old time tintype photo shop while Ron was constantly wandering through, disrupting the operation in his boisterous Professor Spillikin persona. We both recognized kindred Disney fans in each other and fell into an easy friendship of shared hopes for a future where we would finally leave the temporary blissfulness of Spillikin and move on to bigger things.

Ron made the first move to a bigger thing and finally landed at the *Golden Horseshoe Revue* at Disneyland. He was kind enough to invite my wife and me to the Disneyland 25th anniversary employee open house, and here I got my first glimpse of backstage at the park – all the geeky things I had wanted to see since I was a kid. It was here we saw *two* Pecos Bills face off on the Horseshoe stage – Ron and his idol, Wally Boag.

On another evening we visited C.L. Womphopper at his Wagon Works and were treated to a personal message broadcast over the restaurant paging system: "We have a phone call for Mr. and Mrs. Nikolai – the babysitter wants to know where you keep the fire extinguisher!" And on our first trip to EPCOT Center a couple of years later we were treated to a backstage audience with Dreamfinder himself, complete with the little purple dragon that I've come to know and love.

And yet, after reading this thoroughly entertaining memoir, I realize I don't know Ron as well as I thought – he's done so many things in the intervening years that I was not aware of. I've known and enjoyed many of the shows he has worked on – without ever knowing he was involved!

Ron has worked and walked with many theme park legends, and I dare say he is one himself. This guy *is* themed show entertainment personified, and this book proves it.

Larry Nikolai
March 27, 2012

AUTHOR'S FOREWORD

The spark that inspired what follows has been with me a long time.

As a young man I collected books and manuals about Disneyland and amusement parks, but they were all about the parks *in general*; historical records, picture books, souvenir guides... filled with facts and dates and lovely color photography, but not much else.

The few authors who wrote about the parks critically were either dismissive or glowing in their praise. And sociological studies were filled with psychobabble and muted warnings of the imminent arrival of – well, Disney's 'Next Gen' Technology is being installed as I type this, so I guess there was something to their paranoia after all.

But I never found anything that addressed my area of interest – live themed entertainment. It fell to me to apply my own performance training to the jobs I got and find out where the two meshed and clashed.

There can be no argument that – when it comes to the wide variety of jobs I've had and the challenges I've faced – I've been outrageously lucky. I was born in Southern California in September of 1952, greatly increasing the odds that I would be, as I was, in attendance on Disneyland's first day of regular operation.

I was the perfect age to open and grow with Magic Mountain, and used that experience to make me the perfect candidate for Universal Studios and Disneyland in 1980... and so on throughout my life.

Of course there was more involved than timing; there was the very human instinct to 'follow my bliss'. The love of theater, of performing, of magic and puppetry and Disneyland drove me from a young age to acquire the knowledge and experience I'd need when I was finally presented with those opportunities.

The final thing I would need to realize my dreams was the people... the wonderful friends, family and fellow performers, competitors and collaborators, teachers and employers who would cheer me on, boost me up, tutor and challenge and give me a break. And in that, I was unendingly lucky.

As I went along from job to job I kept recognizing patterns in the work, both my own and that of the talent around me. I discovered principles that made the stuff we did work (or not work) and I kept thinking, "I'm going to have to write that down some day".

It's the nature of theme park entertainment that what we do seems easy, light and frivolous... and most of it is. Because it's 'Disney' or 'fantasy' or 'childlike', it's sometimes tough to think of it as art, as something that can contain infinite subtleties and can be used to move a sophisticated audience. This is the dichotomy that has fascinated me these past four decades.

So here's the story of what I did and what I learned and how. If you've ever lost your heart to a theme park performance... or dreamed that you could live and work in that Magic Kingdom... or had a yen to push the envelope of interactive entertainment... or just wondered what it's like to live with a mischievous purple dragon, then "Hello, there! So glad you could come along..."

For Katie Marie

"It starts when we're kids, a show-off at school,
Making faces at friends, you're a clown and a fool;
Doing pratfalls and bird calls and bad imitations,
Ignoring your homework, is that dedication?
You work to the mirror...
You're getting standing ovations!" –

-From *The Muppet Movie*, lyrics by Paul Williams
and Kenny Ascher

"You are never given a wish without also being given
the power to make it come true. You may have to work
for it, however."

-From *Illusions*, by Richard Bach

INTRODUCTION

The Earl of Sandwich restaurant in Downtown Disney makes a great Thanksgiving Special: turkey, gravy, stuffing, mayo and cranberry sauce on a toasted roll. I nearly choke on mine when my Disney pal Matt says, "We want to bring back the Dreamfinder."

I cough, collect myself, and ask, "Who is 'We'?"

"D23, the Official Disney Fan Club, is planning a weekend in May of next year to celebrate Walt Disney World's 40th anniversary. The finale will be a concert of music from the parks starring Richard Sherman; we want Dreamfinder and Figment to honor Richard and surprise the D23 Members by showing up to sing *One Little Spark* with him."

I gotta admire his guts. "A brilliant idea. It will never happen."

✳ ·. ·. ✳ . ·. ✳ ·. ·.
✳

May 15th, 2011

My best friend Josh and I cut through the crowd trying to act casual

– in spite of being the only people at the D23 Event who have arrived with luggage; a suit bag, a wig box and a large blue sack.

At last we make it to the dressing room, tucked in a distant corner of the Contemporary Resort Convention Center. We drop our bags and make sure everything looks as innocuous as possible.

We head in the back way to the ballroom. For the past few days this space has been filled with thousands of rabid Disney Fans attending speeches and presentations about Walt Disney World (WDW), its history, its future and the people who made it happen. Just now, though, the room is sealed tight for this rehearsal. It's the only chance the performers will get to run through tonight's concert in the actual space before the doors are opened in less than two hours.

I recognize Denny Zavett, long-time featured talent on the Empress Lilly Steamboat, and several retired Kids of the Kingdom looking impossibly young and fit. There are dozens of Cast Choir members and musicians and a squadron of Disney Stage Techs swarming over the space, setting up lights and mics for the coming event.

Matt greets me and introduces me to the Stage Manager – one of the few people who know what we're up to. He gives me my mic pack and sits me down to wait for my chance to rehearse.

On stage, Disney Historian Tim O'Day is by the grand piano, watching over Richard Sherman: one half of the team behind *Mary Poppins* and decades of Disney music. They spot me from the stage and wave.

At last they're wrapping up their review of the songs Richard will share. They've done this dozens of times; the rehearsal has been, more than anything, a chance for them to coordinate their patter with the media that will fill the huge screens onstage. I'm guided to my spot off right as the crew cues up the video that will introduce my bit with Richard, a rarely seen video of the 1983 dedication of the Journey Into Imagination ride.

I stand in place, bathed in the light coming from the screen towering beside me. This is a clip I've never seen... that's me, much younger and thinner, climbing out of a carriage, as nervous as I've ever been and facing the press, the public and the executive boards of Walt Disney Productions and Kodak for the first time. As my cue to step onstage approaches I hear myself in the video singing *One Little Spark* to a pre-recorded track twenty-eight years ago:

Two tiny wings, eyes big and yellow,
Horns of a steer, but a lovable fellow...

The video sound cuts out and my mic goes live as I stroll onstage, singing the new lyric I've written for this occasion in the voice originated by Chuck McCann, inspired by Frank Morgan and recreated by me since 1982:

He is my best imaginary friend,
And just like that we're back again!

There is a gasp from everyone in the room as they hear that voice for the first time since the original Journey Into Imagination closed in 1998. I'm in my own clothes – no blue suit, no curly red beard and no dragon – but everyone is looking at me with wonder as, with a rush of emotion, they realize the Dreamfinder is back.

It's a moment that catches everyone, especially me, by surprise. Those involved in our little scheme knew we'd create a sensation among the fans, but we hadn't expected this reaction from the cast at rehearsal.

We finish the run-through and hurry back to the dressing room just as they start letting the crowd in. The performers backstage are swapping stories of where they've been and what they've done since leaving Disney. Pictures of grandchildren (!) are shared between Kids of the Kingdom and everyone reminisces about stage shows and commercial shoots back in the '70s and '80s.

So on with the suit. Not the original, but a clever recreation. Damn, I've put on weight since I was measured for it months ago. Then the rouge and lipstick. I flash back to the parade in Miami where I met the Burger King, another corporate mascot sporting a red beard and wig; we compared notes on shades of lipstick and brands of spirit gum.

The mustache next. This is the only part I have to glue on. Then the beard, held in place by elastic straps that are covered by the wig. Folks always want to know why I would shave my own beard for the job, never realizing that if I used my real beard as Dreamfinder I'd have had to sleep with my face in curlers every night. No, thank you.

Finally the hat and coat and there he is on my left again; the little purple demon who could take my mind off my itchy face even while causing my thumb to cramp up. We look at each other as we always did. He silently greets me and I tell him what's going to happen – Figment's reaction to any new experience is always the same: he curls himself into my chest until I can pry his head out to where he can see what's happening; then he's fine, like any curious child who just happens to have orange horns and scales.

I and my entourage of Josh and my costumer, make our way through the kitchen to the space behind the stage. I can hear Richard Sherman out front explaining the genesis of *There's a Great Big Beautiful Tomorrow*. Matt is at his post, supervising the projections; he flashes me an excited smile. The Cast Choir is seated nearby and as I hurry past they quietly react to seeing Figment and I together; strange, since I can't imagine many of these young people would be old enough to remember who we used to be.

We stretch out in the VIP lounge, used by the guest speakers that day; it's just us now. Josh plays stage mother, running around to check our time, fetching me water and taking pictures. For the most part I've switched over to the reflective mood I used to maintain between sets as Dreamfinder in the '80s. It just seems natural at this moment to sit as I used to at the make-up mirror, thinking about the job and the years and the road that brought me back here. To this place, with That Dragon...

Chapter 1
SPARKS OF INSPIRATION

On July 17th, 1955, the Schneider Family of Inglewood, California – Arthur, Beatrice and their children, Ronnie and Lisa – join America in watching the live broadcast of Disneyland's grand opening... a jumble of live performances, technical glitches and breathless promotion.

The next day we step into history, attending the first day of operation for Walt Disney's dream. Along with my maternal Grandmother Yolande, we present our pass at the front gate and are among the first members of the paying public to experience Main Street, U.S.A., Adventureland, Frontierland, Fantasyland and Tomorrowland (what there is of it).

Except we haven't paid; the family business, Air Comfort Company, has installed the air conditioning in the few real buildings that comprise the 1955 Magic Kingdom, so a small white pass with the date stamped in red gets us through the gates today.

A few memories of that visit persist: The long drive through the orange groves to Anaheim... Having my picture taken poking my head through a poster board featuring Pluto licking the face of a small cowboy, my happy smile shaded by a ten-gallon white cowboy hat that juts out from the drawing...

For lunch we duck into a saloon in Frontierland. A pretty waitress takes our order, then delivers it just as the room goes dark. Seated near the back of the house, I'm completely focused on my food and pay little attention to the loud and brightly-lit something-going-on at the other end of the room.

The only other memories of that day belong to My Sainted Mother, who recalls remarking, "Everything's lovely; it's a shame it'll all be run-down and dirty in a year." And a family tradition is born when I fall asleep in the back seat of the car on the way home.

In the years that follow, my fascination with Disneyland is nurtured by Disney's Sunday night TV shows. I have no patience for the action serials – *Davy Crockett* or *Johnny Tremain* – or the nature specials; but if there's animation on that week, or best of all a feature on the park, I'm glued to that screen. Walt Disney seems to this young mind to be a wizard, giving me a personal tour of his workshop.

TV is my playground in the '50s. True, the selection isn't nearly as vast as we enjoy today, but the box is alive with friends... living beings who love and appreciate me just as I am.

Every morning there is *Captain Kangaroo* with Mr. Green Jeans and the Treasure House gang. Every afternoon there are Engineer Bill and Sheriff John and Chucko (the Birthday Clown) and Bozo (the regular Clown) and Paul Winchell (with Jerry Mahoney and Knucklehead Smiff) and Tom Hatten (my favorite of the afternoon hosts: he shows the old Popeye cartoons)!

Everything changes when The Mouse premiers. My TV Friends all shift time slots, backing away as if to avoid getting creamed. *The Mickey Mouse Club* is pure spectacle. Engineer Bill and Sheriff John always spoke to me as a friend; Mickey's Gang seems to shout their sincerity, playing to a huge invisible audience. Can't they see I'm the only one here? And there aren't nearly as many segments about Disneyland as I hope for.

Saturday mornings are a special treat: first, there's Shari Lewis, with Lamb Chop and Hush Puppy. Shari's ventriloquism is wonderful, but then so is the way she smiles and moves with her pony tail and her eyes and – let's not get ahead of ourselves, young fella.

Then from Television City in Hollywood, *The Magic Land of Allakazam* with magician Mark Wilson, his lovely assistant Nani Darnell and Rebo, the Magic Clown. They have a huge studio audience cheering and applauding Mark and Rebo and Nani... I begin to wish I had a studio audience.

Instead, I have the next best thing – Loving Parents. My dad is an accomplished musician – a bugler in the army, he played horn in bands around Southern California and still loves to sit in with musical groups in clubs around L.A. And my Mom who does all she can to make my dreams come true.

Because of her I get to be a featured guest on the *Engineer Bill Show* and sit in the grandstand at *Bozo's Big Top* and get to visit Television City in Hollywood and watch from the front row as Mark Wilson appears at center stage, stepping magically from a pile of empty boxes to start his broadcast.

Also because of Mom – by the time I'm eight years old we've moved to Cheviot Hills, midway between MGM and 20th Century Fox Studios. And I've got my own magic act and my own puppet stage and my marionettes and my deluxe Jerry Mahoney ventriloquist dummy... and an invisible studio audience that lives in my backyard.

One more early influence from TV...

My school chums share with me their passion for old comedy. The works of Laurel and Hardy, W.C. Fields, and The Marx Brothers become our gospel and we study their texts and rhythms and temperaments religiously.

It helps that we reside in the very area where they made a living. I attend a screening of one of Robert Youngson's anthologies of early comic films at the Meralta Theater in Culver City, then step outside onto the very streets where Stan and Ollie made them. My sister Lisa gets a job at a movie theater in Beverly Hills where Groucho Marx, bored with the film he's come to see, comes out to the lobby to flirt with her. Another friend and I watch Fred Astaire get into his Rolls-Royce one afternoon in Westwood and execute a terrible tandem 'buck and wing' for him as he drives by.

In those years KHJ-TV presented *The Million Dollar Movie*, repeating one particular film every night of the week, and twice on Saturdays and Sundays. Here's an opportunity to carefully study one film, to consider every aspect of a performance... and to tape record and memorize the best parts. The week their featured film is *The Jolson Story* starring Larry Parks as the World's Greatest Entertainer, I watch every broadcast. Then comes *The Court Jester* and *The Errand Boy*...

Al Jolson, Danny Kaye and Jerry Lewis... I learn their every comic bit, every patter song, every nuance of their performances. At this point it's probably for the best that my only audience is of the invisible-and-imaginary variety.

But eventually – one way or another – I'm going on the stage.

By the time I'm fourteen, I've been acting in local plays and skits and making amateur films with my neighborhood friends. And I've been trying to break into the school plays at Palms Junior High School, but I'm too much of a stereotypical nerd to be cast in anything substantial.

During my last year in Junior High, though, Palms gets a new drama teacher. I've found that just about everyone has had one teacher who made a difference in their life; and if you're especially lucky you might have had more than one.

Alan Roy Josefsberg is just starting his teaching career. His father is Milt Josefsberg (a legendary comedy writer/producer in the golden age of radio and TV) but Alan is just a scared kid himself – only ten years my senior – focused on trying to convince the school board that he's an accomplished musical comedy director (he isn't).

My chubby, nerdy self follows Alan around after school for days telling him how talented I am. I'm not sure if I was right or just pathetic, but he takes pity on me and casts me as Captain Hook in *Peter Pan*, his first school production; in fact he gives me the lead in all four shows he does that year.

I loved Alan Josefsberg... still do, in fact. We only have that one year together as teacher and student – the next year I start at Hamilton High School in West Los Angeles – but for years afterward I will drop by Palms Jr. High to hang out with my friend and watch him direct the shows at Palms.

Alan gives me the two most valuable things you can give a young artist: confidence and experience. We stay close through the years and I cherish our friendship till the end of his days. If you have teachers who gave you more than just a grade, let them know.

Determined that my future lies on a stage somewhere doing God-knows-what, I start casting about for all the acting experience I can find. I spend a couple of years with L.A. County's Summer Musical Program for Youth. Our talented Stage Manager is Peter Bloustein, a real professional who tolerates my relative inexperience and becomes a fast friend. When Peter reveals in 1970 that he works days in the Entertainment Division of Disneyland, I make enough of a fuss that he invites me to join him one night while he calls the technical cues for Tomorrowland's new summer musical, *Show Me America*.

No one in my family is surprised that I'm so enthused about this chance to watch a Disney stage production from the tech booth. For years before I met Alan or Peter, someone else had been subtly influencing me, teaching and encouraging. I may never have met him, but when Walt Disney died on the morning of December 15th, 1966, I started thinking about how Walt had been there all through my youth and the tremendous impact he'd had on me and the world.

And the next time I visit Disneyland I see the place through new eyes...

✳ ⋅ ✳ ⋅ ✦ ⋅ ✳ ⋅
✳

I grow up at a time when the Disneyland parking lot runs right up to the ticket booths and Main Street Station. We could walk to the Main Gate, with festive music and the 'Voice of Disneyland', Jack Wagner, drifting across the pavement and feeding our excitement. "There are many ways to visit Disneyland," Jack announces... but I know of only three.

Either my parents bring us (after months of "When can we go to

Disneyland?")... or the annual YMCA Summer Camp field trip... or (after the divorce) as a treat on one of Daddy's weekend visits. Unused 'A' thru 'E' tickets from previous visits are retrieved from Mother's dresser to supplement the new books, then reluctantly, thoughtfully surrendered at the entrance to each attraction. The very act of handing a precious 'E' ticket to the ride attendant inspires my rapt attention to every detail of the adventure that follows.

On my first visit after Walt Disney's passing, though, I find myself frustrated by the usual race from ride-to-ride. About mid-afternoon I ask Dad if I can go off by myself for a while, and wind up sitting on a bench in Town Square watching people. Walt used to do that, too – though I don't know that yet.

Something about sitting here in his park after Walt Disney is gone makes me contemplative. I remember hearing once that he had a secret apartment somewhere in Town Square. I look around, imagining how cool it would be to live here, to work here. Everyone walking past seems so happy, the music is so catchy... the performer in me wants to jump up and start singing.

The setting reminds me of a movie my folks had taken me to months before in Beverly Hills, called *The Music Man*. A wonderful fast-talking salesman named Harold Hill mesmerizes the people in a small Midwestern town, just like the one I'm sitting in. That night I fell in love with Harold Hill and with musical comedy. In the weeks that followed I learned all the songs from *The Music Man*, including Harold's patter song, *Ya Got Trouble* (though I couldn't understand some of the old-fashioned lyrics). And now the feeling comes over me as I sit in Town Square watching the passing 'Citizens of Main Street' that I could jump off this bench and start: "Friends, either you're closing your eyes to a situation you do not wish to acknowledge..."

The irresistible feeling of being onstage, immersed in this total theatrical setting, overwhelms me. I jump up and start strolling up the street toward Sleeping Beauty Castle, stepping in time to the music coming from the buildings around me. For an instant I'm self-conscious; could the other people be staring at my little parade?

I take a moment to glance around and notice others similarly parading up Main Street, letting the music carry them along. Ordinary folks are keeping time with the tunes, inspired to lose themselves in the turn-of-the-century fantasy Walt created. This place has made performers of us all, taken us out of our normal lives and generated a playful mood where we can move and think and feel like characters in some grand show, with new adventures just down the street to share and conquer.

Reaching Disneyland's Central Hub, I have to sit down again. My mind is filled with one thought: Disneyland is theater. A greater, grander form of theater than any I'd ever seen or considered, because the audience is on the stage telling the story. No, <u>living</u> the story. In that moment, Disneyland becomes as much of an obsession for me as puppetry or magic or acting. I have to learn how this miracle came to be, how it works and where I might fit in.

I vividly recall the moment in 1993 when I first signed on to the Internet and typed 'Disneyland' into the search engine. There weren't 1% of the Disney sites we have today – but I was dazzled by the amount of information even then. I felt like I'd come home.

In 1967, on the other hand, there is nothing but Disney's own product, and all they'll tell a hungry Disneyphile about their operation in Anaheim is it's 'The Happiest Place on Earth'. Thanks for the help, guys.

My early efforts to learn about the park consist mainly of buying postcards; and it's the cards that yield my first real insight.

I buy a short stack of cards on each trip, or the long fold-out sets spotlighting various lands or attractions. Back in my room – former home to galleries of artwork featuring The Beatles or the *Batman* TV show – the walls are now stripped bare except for one giant map of the Magic Kingdom, drawn by Disney artist Sam McKim. Under that map I sit at my desk, laying out my treasure trove of postcards for examination...

And that's when I make my first amazing discovery! In every picture the skies above Disneyland are perfect; blue and sunny with lovely white clouds everywhere. But there's something funny about these clouds. In a postcard picture taken facing west into Frontierland, the clouds are absolutely identical to the clouds in another picture looking east into Tomorrowland. No, not just identical... they're the <u>same</u> clouds!

Sorting carefully through my collection, I piece together a field of fluffy white clouds too big to be contained on any one postcard. It dawns on me that somewhere there exists one giant slide of generic white clouds, portions of which are used in Disneyland postcards to generate these images of 'The Happiest Place on Earth' I've been studying.

I feel simultaneously cheated – and fascinated. It's my first lesson in crafting Theme Park Magic out of a real world environment.

One Saturday, I hop a bus to the Main Library in Downtown Los Angeles and spend the day in their archives, hunting down and printing out everything they have about the park's history, going all the way back to construction and opening. And I take every opportunity to visit the park. If a friend is going with their family, I invite myself along. Whenever I meet an out-of-towner who'll be visiting Disneyland for the first time, I offer my services as tour guide.

I start writing letters to the Company asking questions about the operation. After seeing a Walt Disney Productions' stockholder report at a friend's house and marveling at the text and pictures within, I send off a request for back issues dating from the time of Disneyland's opening. All my letters are answered with warm tidings and corporate denials – 'proprietary information' I'm advised.

I try writing letters with a more scholarly tone, claiming to be a UCLA student studying tourism and writing a paper of some sort. Jackpot! I get my stockholder reports and other fascinating brochures and press releases. In this manner I start creating my library of notebooks on Disneyland... and a reputation among my friends and family as being The Guy Who Knows The Park. But my real theme park education is only now about to begin.

Chapter 2
DAVE SMITH, THE ARCHIVES, AND WALLY BOAG (1970)

By 1970 I've spent so many months staring at the words 'Disney' and 'Disneyland' that I pride myself I can pick out the letters 'D-i-s' in a page of newsprint without really trying.

One day I happen to open a copy of *Variety* ('The Bible of Show Business') and a tiny article catches my eye announcing the formation of the Disney Studio Archives. I immediately send off a personal note of congratulations to the newly-appointed Keeper of Disney History, former UCLA Librarian David Smith. A few days later I get a note from Dave, inviting me to come and visit; I'm on the phone before the note hits the floor.

Walt Disney Studios in 1970 is every inch what I'd seen on TV: the park-like setting, the quaint street signs, the '40s architecture reflecting some historic idealist's vision of the future. The mood is very different from other studios I've visited: the industrial 20th Century Fox complex, the expansive MGM factory or the tram-riddled Universal Studios lot. It really does look like a college campus, and the people strolling by seem a lot nicer.

In the Animation Building the hallways are lined with artwork from the animated classics. I'm especially delighted by a series of small dioramas I recognize from the August 1963 *National Geographic*, the issue featuring a profile of Walt Disney, wherein Mickey Mouse explains the animation process to Mr. G.O. Graphic.

At last I reach Dave's office at the very end of the top floor. The fellow who greets me and shakes my hand could have come straight from Central Casting, so perfectly does he embody the bookish librarian you might find in a live action Disney film of the '50s. Young Dave Smith turns out to be an enthusiastic guide who shares his new digs and their precious contents as if welcoming an old friend.

As Dave is explaining that this office used to belong to Walt's secretary, my eyes are sweeping the room... and immediately land on a large wooden hutch near the door, all blond wood and glass shelves. There, sitting in a pile on the middle shelf, I spy a stack of animation cels – the actual cels from *Steamboat Willie*.

With Dave's blessing (and close supervision), I pick one up off the top of the pile and ask about the water spots; he tells me he'd found them stored under a leaky pipe. If he hadn't found them, these priceless drawings might have been irreparably damaged or lost forever. In that moment I became one of the first of untold billions of Disney Fans who would, in the decades to come, thank God for Dave Smith.

From that point, I'm treated to an exhilarating, detailed tour of the nascent Walt Disney Archives. Since Dave has only recently started collecting and organizing these objects, he appears almost as amazed at what he shares with me as I am. And the fact that I'm one of the first-ever visitors to the operation means that everything is just sitting there; nothing is locked away behind glass or stored in faceless cabinets. The sense of Disney History that surrounds me is overpowering.

In the center of the room is a rolling wardrobe cart on which hangs Guy Williams' Zorro costume, Fess Parker's Davy Crockett outfit and (Holy of Holies!) Annette Funicello's Mouseketeer sweatshirt. Next to the cart stands a weathered Audio-Animatronic figure of President Abraham Lincoln, the original that had debuted at the New York World's Fair in 1964.

Laid out in a row under the heavily-shaded windows are the storybooks that had introduced the animated features *Snow White and the Seven Dwarfs*, *Cinderella* and *Sleeping Beauty*... each magnificent book as regal and rich as they ever appeared on film. The pages are real parchment, the titles and artwork drawn by the animators, real jewels set into the book covers. Next to them is an assortment of original concept art for *Peter Pan* and beside that are Walt Disney's personal scrapbooks.

The collection spills out of Dave's office to fill another storage space and a room beyond that – which Dave casually informs me was Walt Disney's working office. I see too much to remember it all… but the best is yet to come.

Dave opens another door and I step into Walt's formal office. In the four years since his passing this room has only been dusted; nothing has been changed or moved. I circle the desk, admiring the awards, the miniatures, the baby grand piano, the toys and gifts, the huge black and white aerial view of my Anaheim obsession.

I'm suddenly struck with an over-powering urge, the kind no man can resist… so I ask Dave where the bathroom is. I fully expect to have to go back out into the hall to use the men's room, but he points to an adjacent door and I step into Walt Disney's personal bathroom. I would have known it anywhere… the wallpaper is covered with small graphics of antique steam trains. Humbled, I take a seat.

After my moment of private reflection, Dave offers me a tour of the studio backlot. He patiently walks me through the old *Zorro* sets and past the house from *The Love Bug* before we stop in the studio theater to watch the post-production crew mix the sound for a scene from *Bedknobs and Broomsticks*. We wind up at the front gate and as we shake hands I innocently inquire where he is off to next. He tells me, "The Studio recently approved British author Richard Collier to write the official biography of Walt. I've arranged a screening of *Peter Pan* for him, as it's the only Disney film he's never seen."

"Really?" I ask. "Got room for one more?" Next thing I know, I'm back on the top floor of Animation in Walt's private screening room, sitting in his over-sized leather chair with an ashtray nearby. Behind me Richard Collier sits at a lighted desk, taking notes as we watch the 16mm studio print of Walt Disney's *Peter Pan* (This was long before there were immaculately restored DVD's in everyone's home collection; in 1970 a 'studio print' is something everybody in the studio uses when they need to watch a film, and it looks like hell).

I've visited the Studio Archives four or five times since and two things always happen: I get a warm welcome from my friend Dave and I'm impressed at how the place has grown. Today there's off-site storage and climate-controlled rooms, public areas and private offices, reading rooms and staff everywhere – all of it thanks to that young man who shook my hand in 1970. Dave is the first Cast Member to make me feel like I belong in the Company. Because of his generous spirit, I have touched and been touched by Walt Disney's magic. And his plumbing.

The Disney Fan Community owes a large debt of gratitude to Dave Smith and his people; I know that because I tried being a Disney Fan before there was an archive.

Now that almost everything that's been written about Disneyland is available online or through Amazon, every ride soundtrack is on CD and every attraction is on YouTube, it's no great challenge to become an 'authority' on the history of Disneyland. It wasn't always that way. There used to be a lot more legwork involved.

Disneyland marketing would put copies of Vacationland *magazine in every hotel lobby in Anaheim and it always had at least one good article about the park or one of its attractions. And of course the* Disney News *magazine came out quarterly, mailed to the home of every member of the Magic Kingdom Club.* Disney News *articles were filled with behind-the-scenes photos and hard facts and numbers about the shows and attractions. I memorized every issue.*

But the best were the rare Sunday nights when the Wonderful World of Color *would do a feature on Disneyland and WED Enterprises. We didn't have a VHS recorder back then so there I sat with my tape recorder microphone pressed to the TV speaker, eager to catch every syllable Walt shared about his plans for Anaheim or the New York World's Fair. How strange years later to watch the same shows on DVD and to be reminded of the visuals that went with the soundtracks I had memorized years before.*

In the '70s I'd prepare for a trip to The Park by buying ten rolls of black and white Kodak Instamatic film, several blank cassettes and a few packs of Kodak Super 8mm movie film. I'd ride the Disneyland Railroad with one arm in the air, holding my cassette recorder up close to the overhead speaker.

I collected Disneyland sugar packets, since they had tiny color photographs of the attractions printed on them. I'd buy postcards and spend hours arranging them in the order one would encounter each view during a typical day in the park. (I always rode the train around the park once then walked down Main Street, turning right into Tomorrowland and proceeding counter-clockwise.)

I'd be sure to visit every shop at least once looking for any new print souvenirs, post cards, picture books or maps and jealously grabbed up every parking lot receipt, front gate brochure and promotional hand-out.

While we're reminiscing, my favorite lunch was to be had at Captain Hook's Galley aboard the Jolly Roger in Fantasyland. A bowl of the clam chowder (same recipe used at the Blue Bayou!), a Hot Tuna Burger, an orange soda and a cup of their great fruited gelatin (I heard they used fruit juice instead of water), all enjoyed in the shade of the palm trees in Skull Rock Cove. So quiet and cool it was hard to believe I was just a few feet from the orbital frenzy of the Mad Tea Party.

And I had a Juice Ritual that I always observed. First, a glass of apple juice in the Main Street Market House, then a glass of grape juice from the Welch's Grape Juice stand in Fantasyland, then a glass of pineapple juice from the Dole Stand at the Enchanted Tiki Room and finally a glass of fresh-squeezed O.J. from Adventureland's 'Sunkist, I Presume'. Eventually I added a New Orleans Square Mint Julep to the routine, along with a fritter.

(By the way I hold the distinction of having had the last glass of grape juice served at the Welch's Stand. As they were closing the Old Fantasyland in 1982, I stopped in and asked for a drink but the man told me they weren't selling the grape juice anymore. When I expressed my disappointment he said he'd check in the back to see if there was any more syrup and – Walt be praised! – came back with one last glass of the precious purple punch.)

One day in the summer of 1970 some high school friends and I decide to try to do everything in Disneyland in just one day. On a dash through Frontierland I spy open doors in a corner building – the Golden Horseshoe Saloon. I'd run past the place many times on my way to the rides, but couldn't remember ever going in; this day seemed like the perfect opportunity.

I have no way of knowing that I'm about to encounter one piece of Disney History that will change me and my goals forever.

We sit at a table down front as the old-style projection screen squeaks down from the rafters. A series of quaint slides provide a preshow, with comic announcements and a sing-along. When the houselights dim three musicians down front strike up a spirited overture and we're off. Right away, I'm struck with the atmosphere of the place — the jewel box theater with its architectural details, authentic bar, waitress costumes, Remington-style paintings and the collection of steer horns adorning the walls. Even the words 'Pepsi-Cola' embroidered on the plush curtain are in an ornate font that softens their anachronistic impact. The band itself – piano, trumpet and drums – are a rather somber lot, who go about their business as if it really is just a business.

For someone accustomed to theme park shows, this is a revelation. Nothing in this room draws attention to itself as 'wholesome' or 'childish'. There is no overweening Disney gloss to the place, no one insisting that I loudly proclaim that I am having fun. It's as if I've left a Synthetic Atmosphere and stepped into the Real World of 1871.

Four truly beautiful saloon dancers take the stage ('Milly, Tilly, Molly and Polly' as the song goes) to sing and dance a welcome, flirting and waving as if we're dusty pioneers on payday, looking for female companionship and a respite from the trail. They then introduce, "Our boss – all the way from St. Lou – Slue Foot Sue!"

A truly magnificent-looking lady (this is Betty Taylor) in a beaded gown herds 'her girls' safely off stage and announces that she's 'Looking for a Big City Beau'. She sings as she ventures into the house to charm the children, flirt with fathers and focus her attentions on one embarrassed, balding cowpoke. She introduces "the boss of this Golden Horseshoe" and out skips the happiest, friendliest 'boss' you can imagine (Fulton Burley). The only way to explain this guy is: he's happy in his work. He sings an old Irish tune, *Clancy Lowered the Boom*, punctuating the verses with old jokes and geniality.

The dancing girls return for a romantic production number performed by Betty and Fulton, and as the lights fade out and the applause reaches its peak – shots ring out! And my life changes.

The first time I see Wally Boag he's standing in the middle of the Horseshoe in a long coat that looks like it had been cut from an old couch. The derby on his head is pushed back and he's toting a large carpet bag in one hand and a raised six-shooter in the other. "Here I am, your Avon Man!" What strikes me about this isn't his suit or sudden entrance: it's his attitude. This man is totally at ease. Even apathetic. Every other comic I've ever seen tried to charm the audience, to make an impression. Here is a guy who acts as if <u>we</u> are the ones who suddenly appeared around <u>him</u>... and we're five minutes late.

It turns out he's a traveling salesman. After swapping some friendly 'digs' with the 'boss', he takes the stage and starts peddling his wares: a bottle of Pepsi, a deck of trick cards, a rubber chicken. Every item, every line, everything this guy does gets a laugh. Obviously what I'm watching is an authentic vaudeville act, polished to perfection over a long, long run.

He produces a set of four animal balloons that seem to defy the laws of physics, inflating forwards, backwards and in sections. He swaps them about, making an elephant, a rabbit and a dog from the same four balloons. He whips out a set of bagpipes and plays it for laughs, He does an eccentric dance. Then, just when you think he's run out of tricks, he takes off his toupee, proclaiming, "It's so hot in here today!"

The whole time he's onstage I'm laughing... and I'm not alone. Everyone's laughing – small children, young couples and grandparents. Wally dances off stage to a big round of applause, then returns one minute later with the others to perform a brilliant musical comedy sketch as Pecos Bill.

As funny as everything has been up to now, nothing prepares me for 'Pecos Bill'. This routine, I learn later, had grown over the previous fifteen years from a simple bit into a masterpiece of musical invention, ensemble comedy and razor-sharp timing. The centerpiece is the moment when Fulton pretends to slug Wally and knocks out a few of his teeth. Then he spits out a few more. Then a lot more. And they just keep coming and coming and coming until everyone's in stitches.

By the time the show ends I'm certain of three things: 1) I'll be returning to the Golden Horseshoe; 2) Wally Boag is my new hero; and 3) someday I'm going to be just like him.

Chapter 3
CALARTS, WED AND MY FIRST DISNEY JOB (1970-71)

As a high school student, I'm only interested in subjects that are theater- or performance- related. One history teacher understands this and lets me turn my report on the Aleutian Islands into a *Batman* TV script. For a Civics class I present my report on the American Nazi Party portraying a party recruiter; the predominantly Jewish class are simultaneously amused and alarmed – but I get an 'A'.

Still I barely have a 'C' average (except in Drama where I always get an 'A' with little effort), so I know my grades aren't going to get me into college; and I'm not interested in taking any further classes not related to acting. I need to find a place exclusively focused on theater, where I can get in on talent (and chutzpah) alone.

Amazingly, Walt Disney's California Institute of the Arts is opening the year after I graduate from Hamilton High! I send for the school catalog and am amazed to receive an arts and crafts project: a set of silvery cardboard boxes that I have to assemble, each covered with information on the different majors offered – Film/Video, Music, Art, Critical Studies, Theater and Dance. The text emphasizes that CalArts is primarily a graduate school (not a problem, I had just 'graduated' from high school, hadn't I?) and, since the tuition is totally out of my family's reach, I apply for an acting scholarship. That's right… I'm unqualified AND broke!

Inspired by the school's promise that students can set their own course of study (and looking for someplace to study musical theater and theme parks), I show up at auditions and do a crazy monologue from Arthur Kopit's *Oh Dad, Poor Dad, Mama's Hung You in the Closet and I'm Feelin' So Sad* for Sergei Tschernisch, a Dean of the School of Theater. Not only am I accepted to the School of Acting, but I get the scholarship!

Since the campus in Newhall isn't ready, school is held in Villa Cabrini, an old campus in the San Fernando Valley. The place is strewn with magnificent old eucalyptus trees and variously described as an ex-nunnery or a former police training facility.

Nothing in my limited experience has prepared me for what I find at CalArts that first year – socially, academically or (ahem) chemically. The first gathering of the student body is held in a large general-purpose room. That is to say, I think it's large – I can't see the far wall for all the cigarette, incense and reefer smoke in the air.

My first day of acting training starts bright and early with a session of T'ai Chi, which everyone except me seems intimately familiar with. I finally sit down under a nearby tree and wait for someone to either: 1) come over and ask me why I'm not participating; or 2) explain to me what's going on. No one does either.

Next, we gather in the gymnasium and are told to roll around on the floor and pretend the ceiling is crashing down on us. I roll around, waiting for insight or direction. The next day we're told to go away and come back in thirty minutes as one of the Seven Deadly Sins. I take the bus back to the dorm and crawl into bed; I am Sloth.

The dormitory, it turns out, is the best part of CalArts for me. Since the Newhall dorms are no more ready for occupancy than the rest of the campus, the residents are temporarily housed on the top floor of the Men's Wing of Zelzah Hall, across the street from San Fernando Valley State College. This is a circular affair, one long third floor hallway wrapped around an open courtyard. On this floor the CalArts students are paired off by sexes in a dynamic blend of artists, animators, film makers, musicians, actors, dancers and assorted creative misfits from all across the U.S.

The atmosphere is electric – with something new and fascinating happening at all hours. I'm awakened from a dead sleep one night by a terrific pounding and whooping only to find a square dance with live music in the hall just outside my door. Brilliant charade tournaments are conducted... and I spend some evenings seated on the floor, listening outside the room of a concert harpist who practices for hours each night.

At first I'm afraid I'll have nothing to contribute to the party, until it becomes known that I'm somewhat of an authority on Disneyland and the life of Walt Disney. Turns out everyone there is a Disney Fan; it's part of what attracted them to the school in the first place. I become the go-to guy for insight and trivia – not to mention guided tours of the park.

Having given up hope of ever connecting with the school's theatrical curriculum, I avail myself of the opportunities offered elsewhere. I audition for Music Department Dean Marni Nixon and am assigned a vocal coach to study singing, and I attend animation and film study screenings. One showing of Disney's 1951 *Alice in Wonderland* turns out to be particularly memorable; surrounded by the appreciative CalArts audience I am made aware for the first time of the large number of drug references in both the animated film and Lewis Carroll's original stories.

One day a presentation is scheduled in the General Room: Robert Hicks of WED (today known as WDI, for 'Walt Disney Imagineering') will speak on Disney's plans for the proposed Mineral King Resort. I find the plans and graphics terribly exciting; not so my schoolmates. They get very loud and critical of the project, believing that the Company is planning to desecrate the land with a wholly inappropriate 'Disneyland in the Wilderness'. They refuse to listen to WED's plan to design, build and operate the resort in a conscientious and responsible manner, and afterward Mr. Hicks is left trying to put a good face on what has been, for him, a disappointing afternoon.

As the audience files out, I step up and shake Robert's hand. "Don't let 'em get you down," I tell him. "Remember, everyone told Walt that Disneyland would be a spectacular failure." He's grateful for the sentiment and, after we talk awhile about my interest in the Company, he invites me to come and visit him the next week at WED Enterprises in Glendale.

I meet Robert Hicks in the WED Enterprises lobby off Flower Street around lunch time. In the fall of 1970, WED is totally preoccupied with next year's opening of Walt Disney World. When you look at the pre-opening publicity for WDW, any pictures you see of work being done on the Audio-Animatronic figures and attractions were probably taken at WED around this time. You'll be looking at exactly what I saw in-the-synthetic-flesh on that day.

Robert opens one door and I see an artist painting the dioramas intended for the *One Nation Under God* film segment of *The Hall of Presidents*. Next door, foam replicas of the Presidents' heads are being painted to be used on their wardrobe dummies.

Around another corner I ran smack into Henry, master of ceremonies of the *Country Bear Jamboree*. You've no doubt seen the picture of Henry in his little stage as he's being programmed by the Imagineers? Well, here he is, running through his routine silently for hours on end, part of the test and adjust process.

Through a black drape we step into an immense open space, more like a factory floor than a sound stage. There is a raised platform running down the middle of the room with computer consoles on top and hundreds of feet of cable running out from under. The computers are rigged to revolve, so they can work their magic on either one of the two massive stages that flank them.

On one side there is a giant blue drape backing a multi-level playing area, where stand all of the major Disney animated characters in Audio-Animatronic form, with Mickey Mouse at center, dressed in his formal best. This is the cast of the *Mickey Mouse Revue*, ready to be programmed for their debut in Florida. And facing Mickey and the Gang from across the room is every American President from George Washington to Richard Nixon, the cast of Liberty Square's upcoming The Hall of Presidents.

Finally I get to see the giant scale model of the whole of Walt Disney World, with its assortment of hotels, many of which would never be built. As we stand there Robert announces he has to leave for a meeting and starts walking me toward the lobby. We pass an open door marked 'WED Library', and somehow I convince him to run off and leave me there for the afternoon. I spend two glorious hours leafing through documentation of various projects, including a file drawer full of ideas from an early brainstorming session for The Haunted Mansion.

When I get back to the dorm there's a message waiting for me from Herbert Blau, Dean of the School of Theater. The next day in his office he asks me why I haven't been attending any theater classes. I tell him that there didn't seem to be anything in those classes that pertained to my interests; that I came to CalArts to study musical theater and theme parks. Herbert explains, "Musical theater is dead."

I ask him, "Then where did Walt Disney get $75 million to build this school?"

We agree that my continued presence at CalArts would be inadvisable (especially since he is revoking my acting scholarship), so I move back home to Mom.

It occurs to me that while I was away at college I had turned eighteen and am at last old enough to apply for a job at Disneyland! Showing up at the Casting Office, I fill out a preliminary application and sit down for an interview with Disney Casting Representative Leon Duty. I tell him my story and how much it would mean to me to work at Disneyland.

Leon says they're hiring temp people to work in Parade Issue through the coming Christmas season – handing out costumes for that year's edition of *Fantasy on Parade*. Hardly a creative position, but I don't care – I'm going to be a Disneyland Cast Member!!

Until I tell Leon that I don't own a car; Company rules state that every Disneyland employee must have reliable transportation. Leon says, "I can't hire you, Ron. I'm sorry." I tell him I understand the Disney principle of presenteeism (the expectation that employees will be present at work under all conditions), and that this job means the world to me. God bless him, Leon sees I'm sincere and hires me anyway.

As a personal favor, Leon schedules me for a day in the Disney University 'Traditions' class – several hours of videos, games and lectures on the Company's history and philosophy – something usually reserved for newly hired full- and part- time Cast Members. Our instructor, Chris Ridgway, greets me at the door with a stack of Disneyland manuals and in-house publications, saying, "Leon Duty asked me to give you these." (I don't have the heart to tell him I already have them all in my collection at home).

Once the job starts, Mom loans me her car for the duration and every day I report to an old fashioned circus tent set up backstage where the cast dresses and the parade costumes are stored. I must seem a bit of a dork to the folks I work with, being so happy to be doing this simple job.

There are two parades a day. For me the great part of the job is the two hours between collecting the costumes from the noon parade and handing them out for the show at five o'clock. There is all of backstage Disneyland to explore… and I make the most of it.

One day I discover the maze of tunnels around and under New Orleans Square and Pirates of the Caribbean. A small employee cafeteria downstairs sports a mural of cartoon racing cars with Mickey Mouse taking the lead while in the car behind him Snoopy shakes a frustrated fist. The racing theme must have inspired the name of the place… the employees call it 'The Pit'.

Years later, park management redecorates and renames the place the D.E.C. (pronounced 'Deck') – for 'Disneyland Employee Cafeteria'. Their thinking is 'The Pit' has a negative connotation, implying that the food is sub-par… which it definitely isn't. But old habits die hard and everyone still calls it 'The Pit'.

I buy a sandwich and look around for someplace to sit, but the place is packed. I take a walk around the tunnel with my drink and sandwich, trying different doors. Finally I wind up sitting on the stairs of a Caribbean port town, watching a crowd of pirates across the way dunk the Town Mayor into a well. No one in the passing boats thinks to turn and look in my direction.

Another day I find a door in the administration building that opens directly into the Disneyland Railroad's Primeval World diorama. I step past a silent volcano where a Stegosaurus and a T-Rex are frozen in place and up to a desert watering hole where a few Gallimimus have gathered for a drink. Suddenly everything starts moving at once. The steam train has entered the building! Luckily, I'm near a boulder just big enough to hide behind until it has passed.

Over that Christmas season I make similar sojourns into the backstage areas of The Haunted Mansion, Submarine Voyage, Carousel of Progress and Club 33, learning everything I can about how the park works; the more I see, the more I want to be a part of it all. My first theme park job – even though it's backstage and totally devoid of Pixie Dust — turns out to be everything I could have hoped for.

And of course I can barely bring myself to cash my first Disneyland paycheck.

Chapter 4
MAGIC MOUNTAIN AND MAJOR (1971-72)

May of 1971 will see the premiere of a new attraction north of Los Angeles in the city of Valencia – Magic Mountain. Here's a chance to be on the opening crew of a brand new park… Maybe even to work out front with the guests!

The casting bungalow in the parking lot is full-to-bursting with applicants and staff, but I quickly make it known that I will be an invaluable asset to the organization. After all – haven't I worked at Disneyland?

I'm assigned to the opening crew of Grand Prix, Magic Mountain's version of Disneyland's Autopia. I get my first theme park costume: blue trousers and cap and a short sleeve white shirt with a Chevron company logo. I even get my first name tag! The outfit is designed to make me look like a gas station attendant, but I don't care; I actually take a moment to stare proudly at myself in the mirror.

All my life I've gotten a thrill walking the grounds of an unopened park as the finishing touches are going in. All efforts are focused on turning these acres of reality into something definitely unreal. Deadlines loom, sod is laid, everyone's sweeping and painting and getting their bearings in their new jobs.

Groups of new hires are guided through on orientation tours, lakes are filled, ride vehicles delivered and tested, executive and custodian work side-by-side with an eye on the ticking clock. Everyone dresses, eats and rests together in a city of makeshift trailers (since the employee facilities will be the last bit to be finished).

The experience of working as a team to get a new attraction up and running brings people together as nothing else can, and this feeling is a valuable asset. The pride a Cast Member takes in their new home translates into a sincere concern for the guest experience.

It is easy to destroy this feeling: all you have to do is ignore it. It will last only if it is recognized and nurtured by the people in charge. The Disneyland cast maintained this feeling for decades after opening. I will always be grateful that I had a chance to work at Disneyland under the original regime, however briefly.

Strange as it sounds, my new job at Magic Mountain occasions my return to the CalArts dormitories! The brand new campus is finally complete – and located just two freeway exits from Magic Mountain. Since I don't own a car I elect to spend my first summer working at The Mountain and living in the CalArts dorms (which have rooms for rent through the summer months), hitchhiking down the road to work.

Every morning is an adventure as I take my place at the rarely-used freeway entrance by the college, a desert-like setting where I often imagine I'll be discovered weeks later, my bleached bones rotting in the California sun, my thumb still pointing northward.

Magic Mountain has been built by the Newhall Land and Farming Company in the hope that it will draw new business and residents to the area and raise property values. The man running things is Doc Lemmon, who fifteen years prior had overseen operations for the opening of

Disneyland.

Throughout the training, much is made of our following in the Disney tradition of quality guest service. But – as often happens with a new project on this scale – the powers that be have their hands full putting out fires, so we front-line employees are left to our own devices when it comes to handling the guests.

The Grand Prix crew quickly settles into the routine of running the attraction. We become proficient at controlling the guests' arrival back at the load area, preventing collisions and even riding the moving vehicle like a surfboard on its return to the load area (NOT a safe and sane way to run the place, but a great show for waiting passengers).

Early one morning our first driver is an elderly woman who can barely make it into the car. I help her over the side and strap her in… and she shoots out of the station like a bat out of hell! The 'governor' (which keeps the car running at a maximum speed of eight miles an hour) had not been engaged, so she's tearing around the track at about 30 mph. Our foreman runs out onto the track trying to catch and stop her while the rest of us stand awestruck at departure.

The foreman never did catch up with our Hot Rod Granny, who pulls into the station laughing like a school girl. Naturally, she asked if she can "go around again!"

My favorite spot in the rotation is working the turnstile, greeting guests and making small talk with those at the front of the line. I become adept at keeping the load area safely filled with the next round of passengers, averaging 600 people an hour.

About a month after opening, there's this guy making the rounds of the attractions installing sound systems in the queue lines and microphones by the turnstiles. Suddenly I'm not just talking to the guests at the front of the line; I have a captive audience of 150. Folks waiting twenty minutes to ride have nothing to amuse themselves but each other… and me!

Like I said, I've long before this memorized all the ride spiels from my beloved Disneyland, so I start adapting material from the Keel Boats, the Jungle Cruise and the Golden Horseshoe. But as I gain confidence I start to ad-lib my own stuff and soon I have enough original material to comfortably fill that twenty minute wait.

There are a lot of opportunities for overtime that summer, so after a shift at Grand Prix, I take my show on the road. Eventually I've developed original material for the queues at the Gold Rusher coaster, the Log Jammer, Spin Out and Eagle's Flight. And soon I'm delighted to discover that the daytime ride operators are starting to use my material.

One afternoon I notice that our turnstile counter is ready to turn over, marking the arrival of our 10,000th guest. I notify our foreman and together we scrounge up some scrap lumber to pound together a 'racing trophy'. I scrape '10,000th Grand Prix Driver' on the side with a nail and stain the wood using an oil slick on the floor of our maintenance garage. An air filter on top serves as an ornament. And we mock up a simple ceremony for the little girl from Saugus, who gets to take two 'victory laps' around our little corner of the Magic.

One other wonderful thing about working that first summer at The Mountain is the management decision to invest heavily in live name entertainment. Al 'Grandpa Munster' Lewis is paid to hang around the Children's Play area in the afternoons, for some reason I've never been able to understand. Every afternoon there's a live variety show in the 3,000 seat Showcase Theater hosted by some wonderful talent, including my favorite local radio hosts Al Lohman and Roger Barkley, Jim Backus as Mr. Magoo and Edgar Bergen with Charlie McCarthy.

Night shows at the Showcase Theater feature some top name Vegas Acts: Pat Boone and his Family, Frank Gorshin, Phyllis Diller, Sonny & Cher, and – my favorite – the legendary Jimmy Durante. I'm usually front row center for these performances. On Gorshin's closing night, I sneak backstage to shake his hand and mention I've caught his act seven times. "You probably know this stuff better than I do," he remarks.

I reply, "I open here next week with your material."

At the end of Magic Mountain's debut summer, the park throws a huge party to show their appreciation to the opening crew. They unveil a plaque (still standing at the park entrance) that has all our names on it.

The management team has bravely offered to personally operate the park's major attractions for the party, so us hourly employees have run of the place. The gang from Grand Prix has always amused ourselves with a plastic squirt bottle in our ride maintenance area, so we decide to raid one of the custodial supply closets and, armed with half a dozen water-filled bottles, we set about dousing folks from the other rides (especially those who had pulled in higher hourly capacity numbers than we did)!

The entire Mountain soon deteriorates into a massive water fight. At one point we have the head of operations pinned down on the second floor load area of the Gold Rusher coaster. I'm dousing him pretty good when he grabs a plastic cup from a nearby railing and hurls its contents in my face; he then screams, "OH NO!", since he'd just wasted a perfectly good cup of vodka just to get revenge on a lowly Grand Prix employee. I walk away, smiling and smacking my lips.

Being a seasonal park, Magic Mountain goes to a weekends-only schedule in September and I move into an apartment in Culver City. I get a job at the local Sears Service Center handling customers and scheduling service calls, a position I find oddly satisfying. Again, I'm running my own show, working to put a smile on the guest's face.

Meanwhile on the east coast, Walt Disney World opens and I grit my teeth, frustrated that I'm not there. Maybe someday.

As summer 1972 approaches, I spy a small article in the L.A. Times revealing plans for Magic Mountain's second season. Among the new additions will be a Children's Animal Farm and Petting Zoo featuring an 'Old Man of the Mountain, who will sit on the porch of his cabin telling stories to children while surrounded by affection-trained animals.' I race back to that Casting Bungalow with the article in hand and present myself as the object of their search.

Sure enough, when I'm interviewed for the storyteller job it becomes apparent that the blurb in the Times had contained everything anyone knew about this new character. Human Resources has no idea what the job will entail or how to fill it. When the interviewer asks me what experience I've had, I only have to brag about my spieling experience of the previous summer and the job is mine.

My first day on the job I'm told to report to Africa, U.S.A., a remote spot in the hills north of Magic Mountain where the Raffill family trains wild animals for use in movies and television. (Stewart Raffill is still a film producer, writer and director.)

I meet my new boss, Frank Lamping, who tells me to go stand in the middle of a large field of tall grass and wait. Soon Frank comes bumping along in a pickup truck with a camper shell on the back. He opens the back door and standing inside is Major – a full-grown African lion. I'm frozen in place… As a child the only animal I hadn't been afraid of was Jacques, the family poodle.

Frank explains, "Major has just finished a film for Disney, *Napoleon and Samantha*. He was captured fully grown twelve years ago… We figure that makes him about twenty-five years old; or 125 in lion years. But he's still very strong and has all of his teeth and claws."

Frank leads Major out of the truck by a heavy chain fastened loosely around the big cat's neck and brings him straight over to me… and this immense lion comes over and rubs right up against my leg. For a second I'm afraid he'll knock me over… then I realize that this is a show of affection (on a Major scale)! "Major's the Raffill family's personal pet. He's been affection trained so he loves people." Frank runs me through some of the basics of working with Major while the big pussy cat sits and acts nonchalant.

We send Major about his business and head over to Nudie's Western Outfitters in the San Fernando Valley where I'm fitted for a buckskin 'Mountain Man' outfit. Then it's back to Magic Mountain to check out progress on the Animal Farm itself.

Frank shows me around the big red barn that will be our center of operations. Everything's behind glass so guests can see how the farm operates. Major will have his own stall and there's a full kitchen and nursery for newborns… and a brand new arrival! A salmon-crested cockatoo arrives this day, and Frank gives me the honor of naming him. I decide to call him Michael after my oldest childhood friend.

The next few weeks I'm kept busy welcoming and naming new arrivals and learning the routine. I have to go capture some Koi fish that have been living in a pond under the Sky Tower and bring them to their new home. Then I get to head over to a local farm and assist our veterinarian in castrating a dozen goats. Ah, showbiz…

We get in two large Indigo snakes I name Arthur and Beatrice, after my parents, and a skunk I name Petunia. The skunk is supposed to have been de-scented, but after handling him for a few days it takes several showers before anyone can stand to be near me.

The snakes are more fun. We keep them close by the refrigerator so they'll be comfortably cool during the day, then I wrap one around my neck like an ice pack and head out into the compound to greet the guests (it is sometimes 105 degrees out there). I strike up a conversation with some nice old ladies and after a while I'll see their eyes drift down to my neck and suddenly realize what I'm wearing. I tell ya, some of those old people can really *move!!*

On the far side of the Children's Farm compound is an old shack that looks like it has been around forever. The illusion is spoiled only by the large air conditioning unit off to one side, put there to provide a breeze for Major. This is to be where he and I will spend our work days.

I ask my boss about the animal stories I'm supposed to be telling; is there a script or training manual? He knows nothing about that, so I figure that's something I get to contribute.

I let my hair and beard grow out to appear appropriately rustic and read up on Aesop's Fables, myths and African legends. I don't have anything scripted on opening day, but I figure I'll have my hands full just learning the ropes and dealing with the critters.

It doesn't matter. When the new area opens guests swarm in to pet the goats and sheep and llamas and admire our collection of exotic birds. Then they notice the shack and head our way... and freak out when they see a lion behind a picket fence. The chain strung loosely around his neck is hidden by his mane. The other end is fastened to a bolt in the floor boards, but he has enough free chain that he can stand and wander anywhere on the porch at will. The air conditioner blows a nice breeze across the shady porch, so we're pretty comfortable, even in the 100+ degree heat of midday Magic Mountain.

I spend my first days sitting in an old rocking chair next to Major with Michael on my shoulder, answering questions about the lion. Every so often someone will sneer, "Bet he hasn't got any teeth," and Major will yawn... and shut them right up. When some folks see he's real they get away fast. I never get a chance to tell stories, since all anyone wants to do is take pictures and ask questions.

It takes park management only a few days before they have a merchandise employee out there with a Polaroid camera. For $5 folks can step up on the porch and sit down next to Major for a picture. I must say he handles the traffic like a pro. He appears determined not to startle any of the small children; but if any grown-ups get pushy he'll stand up suddenly and just look at 'em.

Every so often someone asks, "Can my blind child come up and touch him?" I bring them up onto the porch and Major sits stock still – even while they feel his ears and paws (which are particularly sensitive). He'll even open his mouth so they can feel his teeth and he doesn't move. This is one wise lion.

Every morning, when the compound is relatively empty, I get to take Major for a walk out to our perch on the porch. Then, at the end of each day when the place is packed with people, it's my job to walk Major across the compound and back to his stall.

I unlock the end of his chain, get a firm grip and step out with him across the public area – through all the sheep and goats and tourists – roughly 75 yards to the barn. There are two or three attendants escorting us, clearing the way and opening the barn doors for us as we enter. Major never gives me a bit of trouble all summer; it's like walking Jacques.

Then comes the day the barn doors swing open and Monday is standing there.

Earlier that week we had our first birth at the farm; an adorable baby goat we named for the day she arrived. Monday has run of the barn, and our escorts have forgotten to put her safely back in her stall.

Major sees the three-day-old baby goat standing in the doorway and decides it's playtime. Suddenly this heavy thick chain is running through my determined fists like so much water. I try to hold him back... and land on my ass when the chain runs out.

Monday dashes into the nearest open stall with Major close behind; I've never seen him move so fast. Monday starts to circle the stall but Major cuts her off and scoops her up in his mouth. Guests are leaning in the open stall door, screaming. Major stops dead and starts waving his head up and down with Monday trapped inside. From my position on the ground I holler, "Major! Drop it!"

And he does. He opens his mouth and Monday hits the straw, not moving. We scoop her up and quickly realize she's fine – not a mark on her. She's in shock, though, and stays that way for two days.

Major hangs his head and won't move. I pick up his chain to lead him to his stall, but he seems rooted to that spot. It's another twenty minutes before I can get him to move at all. Even then he keeps his head down and won't look at anyone. I give him a hug and his dinner and leave him alone. This is the only time I ever see Major pick at his food.

Another favorite story concerns the time I'm bending over in front of Major and he bites me on the ass. I whirl around and glare at him. The guests are laughing hysterically but Major acts as if nothing has happened, "Who, me? No, Sir – must've been a fly… "

On my lunch break I tell Frank what Major did and he smiles. "That was a kiss. The next time you greet him, put your arm in his mouth."

Sure enough, when I return from lunch and press my forearm against his lips Major opens up and tenderly chomps on my arm. Needless to say, the watching guests are mighty impressed.

In June we take delivery of three baby lion cubs: Tasha, Sheila and Kia, each about six inches long and solid muscle. We set them up in their own straw-lined stall and I take a shift each afternoon sitting with them and playing. They have no teeth yet and love sucking on my finger and crawling up my back. I take to throwing them across the stall, a game they love; they come racing back every time, eager to go again.

But lion cubs grow remarkably fast! In no time at all they're a foot-and-a-half long and all teeth and claws. I can still play with them in the stall, but I only dare go in with one of them at a time.

Next to the barn is a small steam train ride that circles a low hill covered with trees and long grass. Some days I put one of the cubs on a very long leash and tie the other end to one of the trees. Then, just like a scene from *The Lion King*, we stalk each other through the tall grass. After a few minutes of moving slowly with our eyes locked on each other, I'll make a small, quick move toward Tasha and she'll leap up on my back and we tumble around playfully. The folks on the train get a good show – and I get dozens of small claw marks on my costume.

The cubs are the only exceptions I ever find to Major's policy of universal tolerance. Being an easy-going and primarily nocturnal fellow, he's usually happy to lay around most days and let us stupid humans carry on with our business; not so when I bring the cubs around to visit. He lays there glaring at me as they climb on his back or tumble around on the porch steps. And if one of them gets too near his mouth he snaps it up and tosses the little darling against a nearby wall. Unfortunately for him (and thanks to me), this is their favorite game!

Still, I learn never to forget and always to respect his strength. One afternoon when he's been napping on his side he wakes to find that he can't raise his head. A link in his chain has fallen between the boards of our porch and is stuck so he can't stand up.

Major panics! He plants his paws and pulls with all his strength, and when that doesn't work he starts to claw at the boards. I know better than to stick around. I jump off the porch and turn to watch as my old friend literally tears the front of that shack to bits. And when he is done he stops, looks around and goes back to his nap amid the rubble.

Finally the summer comes to an end and I move on again. But the following year I venture back to the Children's Farm where I find Major still in place, half asleep on the old front porch. I'm not in my red buckskin costume, and he hasn't seen me in at least eight months... but the moment I call out, "Hi, Maj!", he's up on his feet and searching the crowd with his eyes. I walk up and thrust my arm in the lion's mouth, again impressing the onlookers; I guess they've never seen two old friends kiss before. This would be our last visit together; a year later he was gone.

Working with Major was unforgettable – and not just because he was a lion. I could sense his 125 year perspective on life, his tolerance of our posing and poking him, his affection for the children and impatience with their parents.

I miss Major.

Chapter 5
1520 A.D. MEDIEVAL RESTAURANT (1972-73)

When summer 1972 ends, I'm sporting a magnificent mane of long hair and a beard which I don't want to lose: certainly not for the sake of getting a 'real job'. Against all hope, I scan the classifieds looking for something for an out-of-work hippie-type. Believe it or not, there's a tiny three-line ad in the LA. Times that very day: 'MAN wanted to play Henry VIII'.

I make the call and find myself in a huge, white building in the middle of Beverly Hills' famous Restaurant Row. I'm shown into a magnificent bar with large booths and a dance floor, like something out of a '40s Hollywood musical. Here I sit and wait with two other young actors, Richard Salem and Roger Reinhart. We're three large, cheerfully round-ish men who assume we are all in competition. Wrong. We are all hired that day for the very same role.

A bit of background...

A few days before disreputable British millionaire John Bloom is run out of the United Kingdom for shady business practices, he attends a themed dinner attraction called Shakespeare's Tavern. He enjoys the pleasant evening full of serving wenches, comic actors and variety acts... so much so that, after he lands on the west coast of the United States, he opens an identical show in Buena Park, California in the conveniently-themed Henry VIII Motel.

John's first attempt at recreating the show he saw in England is a tepid affair (he's no showman), but it catches the eye of two veteran period performers from the Renaissance Pleasure Faire circuit, Billy Scudder and J. Paul Moore. They convince Bloom to let them remake his dinner show into something more appealing to American tastes.

The resulting 1520 A.D. Medieval Restaurant is a wild, bawdy evening in the company of Henry VIII; full of double-entendre, naughty limericks, camp songs and manic audience participation. Diners leave elated and exhausted – and word of mouth takes off.

The show is such a success that Bloom buys the former Climax Nightclub in Beverly Hills and turns it into a restaurant complex with three – count 'em, three – showrooms. After passing through the plush lobby and the vivid red elevator decorated with a Devil's Head (more on that later), guests have their choice of two different showrooms on the ground floor: the two-story Red Room, ringed with a balcony and filled with immense wooden tables and benches, and sporting a large stage full of medieval heraldry and a throne... or the smaller Gold Room with similar benches and tables, the walls gleaming like something out of a French palace.

Twice a night, each room presents the same basic show that was still running in Buena Park. You read that right... Word of mouth is so good that John Bloom and company are presenting six performances of the 1520 A.D. show (most of them sold out, mind you) in the same building, seven nights a week.

Now you might think that Richard, Roger and I have been hired as replacement Kings for the Beverly Hills club. Not at all. Turns out that, at the time the ad is placed, the company is looking to expand yet again. Clubs are planned for San Diego, Toronto, Philadelphia, Dallas, Las Vegas and San Francisco. Richard, Roger and I are each instructed to go rent a medieval costume as we are now Kings-in-Training.

The *1520 A.D. Medieval Dinner Show* is an environmental experience on a level that folks in the '70s have never seen before. The serving wenches are each individual characters with their own attitude that makes interacting with them interesting to say the least. There are wandering fools, a fantastic magician and a trained bear (although I never saw a real bear I remember reading about that once; the only bear I ever worked with had a wench inside).

Arriving couples are stopped at the door and the women are informed that in the year 1520 they are considered chattel and therefore must enter the tavern walking three paces behind their 'Lord and Master'. There's no salt on the tables as it is very costly at this time; a bowl of salt is given to one lucky fellow who is designated 'Keeper of the Salt'. If a man desires salt for his meal he has to send his woman to beg for it on her knees. She then has to pay the salt tax – a kiss on the Keeper's cheek (either set… it's that kind of show). Applause is not permitted during the show; to 'clap' is frowned upon in these sexually-charged times. Instead, the crowd is directed to stomp loudly and bang their spoons on the table.

The evening's premise is that it is the King's birthday and his court and subjects have come to this tavern to throw him a surprise party. Master Will Sommers, Henry's jester, arrives and coaches everyone in the proper care and treatment of the temperamental monarch. We learn the King's Toast and response ('Drink Hail!' / 'Wassail!'), his favorite (bawdy) song and medieval manners. At last Henry VIII arrives and everyone knocks themselves out for the next 90 minutes to keep him amused.

And it ain't easy. Anyone caught not participating is thrown into the stocks; there, a suitable 'punishment' is carried out with the purpose of improving their mood. At one point each evening a man is so accused and held in the stocks while every woman in the place lines up and kisses him (and there are some gorgeous women who have been drinking heavily). There is a competition to see who can come up with the wildest limerick; the King always wins. Birthdays are celebrated, women objectified, fresh rolls thrown and childish songs sung with new and dirty lyrics.

As each evening progresses things can get pretty wild. If the audience gets too hyper, the King leads everyone in a 'Group Bang', whereby everyone blows off steam by rhythmically and powerfully banging their spoons on the table.

We Three Kings-in-Training watch the show a few times and are thrown into the mix to learn the royal ropes. We all play knights or lords and run from show to show to show (to show to show to show) doing the same bits, singing the same songs and telling the same jokes in all six shows in turn.

Then comes the inevitable night when I am thrown to the (drunken) lions; I'm informed that I will be playing King Henry VIII in the third room that night. Oh! I still haven't told you about the third room…

Remember that red elevator in the lobby? The one with the Devil's Head above the door? That elevator takes you down to the basement and into the third showroom: The Cave.

The way I heard it… Back before the building housed the Climax Nightclub, it was called The Millionaire's Club and the basement was a – er, 'place of business'. When the Millionaires moved out and the Climax moved in, guess who moved in with them? Oh… I don't know… could it have been… SATAN?! Yup, the Climax was happening upstairs while downstairs the members were worshiping the Anti-Christ. (Now, isn't that special?) That's when the room got its last make-over.

When I first see The Cave, it's a large room studded with realistic stalactites and stalagmites, a low ceiling and sculpted walls featuring hellish murals. When Bloom bought the building he added the long tables and benches and eventually removed the eight foot Devil's Head rigged for smoke, lighting and sound effects. And this is the room I inherit for my reign as King of England.

One more thing about The Cave. With the history that space has (not to mention the close quarters, poor sight lines and lousy access from the upstairs kitchen) the room is cursed. We seldom have a good show in The Cave. Guests are slow to laugh (or respond at all) and, at first, I think it's me. But I am assured (by folks who I desperately want to believe) that I'm fine. It's the room.

Then one night I come to work and Richard is gone; to the new Texas club as it turns out. Next, Roger is sent to open Las Vegas. And a week later I arrive at work to hear that I'll be leaving for San Diego the following day. I get my best friend Mike Schweitzer to come along as Master Squires the royal pianist, and we're off to amuse the peasants in San Diego!

There's long been a debate among Imagineers as to whether themed attractions can tell a story. Most of what we turn out – and all the landmark Disney Attractions – don't so much communicate a linear tale as create a mood, or generate a feeling in the guest.

This is why I love themed dinner shows. The guests are committed to investing two hours in your production. They are seated comfortably, kept well fed and lubricated, so you have their undivided attention. Here you can take your time and tell a story with a beginning, a middle and an end. You can cast the guests as characters in your environment, involve them more personally through the performing wait staff and theme the food and its presentation to your period setting.

You can (as we do at 1520 A.D.) create a repertoire of content that varies and reacts to your audience – to their response, their age, their interests. And you can put them onstage and involve them in the story; not just one of them, but a lot of them, creating video memories for the families to take home and help promote your attraction.

The other personal reason I love themed dinner shows is that I get to sleep in till after noon. I can mosey in to work around 4 or 5 p.m., do two shows and still make it home by 11:30 p.m.

1520 A.D. is my introduction to the form and I quickly learn to appreciate its challenges and potential…

Mike and I rent an apartment immediately behind the San Diego club and settle in for a long run. By this time, I've appeared in my share of theater and am quite comfortable onstage, but the 1520 A.D. show is a big change from anything I've done before. In our show, Henry is a rock star. I'm belting bawdy camp songs in white tights, a skirted tunic and a cape trimmed in faux fur, while everyone in the tavern makes outrageous claims about my virility. And we do this twice a night, six nights a week to the screaming, drunken approval of most of San Diego.

At the same time I can't help feeling a bit of an impostor; I certainly don't feel like the King of anything. I'm still awfully young and pretty much of an innocent. The rest of the cast have far more theatrical experience and knowledge than I, not to mention a more worldly outlook... something I'm reminded of each night after our second performance when we retire to a nearby pub for drinks (or the club parking lot to share some of the local herb). I tag along and 'supervise' – that is to say, I watch and envy their camaraderie.

Mike does what he can to initiate me into the rites of the '70s social scene, but I never acquire the taste for alcohol and I'm slow to appreciate the benefits of the 'heathen devil weed'.

My time in balmy San Diego is like a wonderful holiday that exposes me to a whole new type of themed performance, but soon I'm ready to take another step toward my goal of the Horseshoe stage. I need to mature, both as a person and a performer. So in the fall of 1973 I move back to Los Angeles and take up residence in the 'Windsor Home for the Theatrically Insane'.

Chapter 6
L.A.C.C.T.A. AND UNIVERSAL STUDIOS TOUR (1973-77)

In Hancock Park, Los Angeles' Old Money residential district, at the corner of 6th Avenue and Windsor, is a magnificent Tudor-style mansion. We, on the other hand, lived around back.

The 'Windsor Home for the Theatrically Insane' was founded by my college buddy Jacky DeHaviland and a small group of friends attending the Theatre Academy at Los Angeles City College. They're holed up in a suite of simple rooms around the back. At the time I join them, all the bedrooms are occupied so I get to sleep downstairs in one of the garages. It's cold but cozy.

I'm still picking up the odd show at 1520 A.D. in Beverly Hills but otherwise am unemployed and hanging around, while everyone else in the house is preparing to head back to L.A.C.C. for the start of the fall 1973 semester. One morning over breakfast Chris O'Meara asks, "Are you going to enroll at City this year?"

I'm ready to dismiss the thought out of hand... when I become aware that everyone in the room is now staring at me, silently waiting. As if my answer is going to be a big deal.

"Why are you all staring?"

Jacky speaks up, "Because we've all been dying to ask you but didn't know how!"

By this point I'd seen shows at L.A.C.C. and always been mightily impressed. In an instant I know it's the right thing to do. "Alright, I'm coming to City!" There are smiles all around and I am suddenly back in school.

As I say, I had seen shows at L.A.C.C.: *How to Succeed in Business Without Really Trying* starring Bruce Kimmel and Michael Lembeck, and a brilliant production of *You're a Good Man, Charlie Brown*. To my eye they seemed totally professional in every way – the kind of shows in the kind of setting I wanted to be part of.

It's my first day in the building. Classes are over, it's late afternoon and almost everyone has gone home; the place is relatively deserted. I decide I want to look at the big stage: the Camino Theater. I find the unlocked door to downstage left and step out on 'the boards' at L.A.C.C. for the first time. It has a broad cyclorama, a huge fly space for hanging drops, an immense sliding door connecting it with the scene shop...

I step onto the open playing area for the first time. The theater is nicely intimate with the seats not too far from the stage and a bank of windows across the top of the back wall, housing the tech booth and the office of Department Head, J.R. McCloskey. I look into the house and silently soak up the atmosphere of the room. I can't help wondering what's ahead for me in this place. All I know for certain is that – at the moment – I feel right at home.

I soon learn why I was so impressed with the shows I'd seen at L.A.C.C. The Acting Program is intense, a day-and-night commitment that demands total focus of a student's time to learning every aspect of the craft. I could almost forget my dream of that job at Disneyland, if it wasn't for my determination to someday apply everything I learn to live entertainment in the parks.

I'll remain at L.A.C.C. for three years as a student and one year on staff. In that time I get to participate in dozens of productions and learn much... including that an acting career is a constant drive to get the next job. The theme park life starts to look better and better; long-term employment, job security and a steady paycheck. Which would you choose: driving a cab between jobs, or a horse-drawn streetcar down Main Street, U.S.A.?

Two City College productions will have a big impact on my theme park career...

In 1975, I add Beginning Stage Direction to my class load, taught by the lovely Donna Tollefson, an accomplished teacher and director. For our final project we're to prepare a prompt book for a show we'd like to direct, an assignment to demonstrate that we are thinking like young directors.

I have long been a fan of the comedy ensemble The Firesign Theatre, 'Four or Five Crazee Guys' that came out of the L.A. radio scene. Their amazing records are dense with double-meanings, literary references, drug humor, social satire and multi-track flourishes that have made them the darling of the marijuana-addled youth of the day. One of their most popular recordings is a sci-fi comic adventure called *I Think We're All Bozos on This Bus*. Although *Bozos* is strictly an audio piece, I decide that my own stage adaptation will be the subject of my Beginning Direction prompt book.

A few weeks after submitting my project, the Theater Department announces that the senior class is invited to the west coast premiere of *A Chorus Line* at the Shubert Theater. We're seated, teachers and students alike, in the balcony waiting for the show to begin when the department head, J.R. McCloskey, leans forward to whisper, "By the way, Ron, we've scheduled your directing project as part of next season."

I'm thoroughly surprised. I had dreamed of doing the piece as a student-directed show in Bungalow X, but didn't think the school would let me get away with it, considering the subject matter. "In the bungalow?" I ask.

"No, on the main stage."

And so *A Chorus Line* starts and I hardly notice; my mind is too busy trying to imagine what I'm going to do with the challenge that has just been so casually dropped in my lap.

Thankfully, I have a few months to figure that out...

Hoping to pick up some money over the coming Christmas break, I drop by the school's October Job Fair and am delighted to find a booth of employment reps from Universal City Studios. My dad had taken us on the Studio Tram Tour in the distant past and I always envied the guide conducting the two-and-a-half hour tour who seemed to know everything about film history and the studio.

My enthusiasm (and performing background) strikes a chord with the recruiter; she tells me I can bypass the two follow-up interviews and hires me on the spot. I'll be one of the seasonal new hires for Christmas 1975, working full-time over the coming school break.

In the meantime, I start rehearsals at City for that grand old melodrama, *The Drunkard*. I'm pulling double duty on this show, playing the wealthy benefactor Arden Rencelaw and acting as emcee for the 'olios' (variety acts) afterwards. Hmmmm... Variety Acts...

An opportunity! I ask the director if I can put together an old-style medicine pitch, like the traveling salesman routine Wally Boag is performing daily at Disneyland. He agrees and I go out hunting for inspiration.

I visit the Hollywood Magic Shop, a great old operation on Hollywood Boulevard that caters to professional magicians; but when I get upstairs to the show room I find it closed. A bit of exploring leads down the hall to an open door where I find the owner of Hollywood Magic, Joe Berg, in his office.

I tell Joe I'm looking for material for a comic medicine pitch and he doesn't even pause – just reaches into the old roll-top desk in front of him and hands me two publications: one a pamphlet called, "This is It, Boys!" by Prof. Josephus Forrestus, the other an old issue of Genii Magazine for Magicians with several articles on pitchmen.

Joe asks for $8 and it's the best deal I'll ever make. The result works in the show so I keep that pitch routine in my repertoire, running through it from time to time for my own amusement. It makes me feel one step closer to my ultimate goal of the Golden Horseshoe stage.

Christmas break approaches and I report dutifully to Universal for training as a tour guide. The class is a week-long affair, riding through the immense backlot, listening to the more accomplished guides and studying a thick notebook of information on every artist, every set piece, every film and every film technique used in the history of Universal Studios.

The highlight for me is the day we trainees get to hop off the tram and walk the backlot on foot to see the historic sets and sights up close. It was a very different place back then, so much more was left of the old sets and stuff hadn't been moved and demolished to suit the tour. In the years since, it's become a sterilized recreation of the backlot we toured in the '70s.

Ultimately the job is to do two or three two-and-a-half hour tours every day. Beyond the basic history of the studio and the general facts about each stage of the tour, guides are free to present a tour that reflects their own interests and enthusiasms. And since every location on the backlot has been used for dozens of different productions, you can tailor your spiel to the genre of your choice or the particular point you want to make.

The backlot is not all city streets, or even paved roads. The last part of the tour ventures up into the hills on the south end of property. The 'GlamourTrams' are built to operate with three cars loaded with tourists. But with the recent addition of the special effect experiences ('The Ice Tunnel' and 'Jaws') management decides to increase capacity by adding a fourth car to each tram. This puts a real strain on the engines; breakdowns are common, giving me the chance to hop off the front car and walk along the tram, visiting with the guests and trying different comic bits and trivia while we wait for the studio mechanic.

Of course, we don't have complete creative freedom. Management has a strict policy (intermittently heeded) regarding jokes and ad-libs on the tour. Basically stated, we are to use no unapproved humor.

Here, for your enjoyment, is the only joke Universal Studios management has approved: "On the hill above us you can see the Bates Mansion, from Alfred Hitchcock's classic, *Psycho*. This is one set on our backlot that is rarely used since it's so easily recognized. Besides, it's difficult to get the lights and cameras up to the house since the only way to get there is to take the Psycho-path."

Everyone is careful about any additions or ad-libs. There is a constant reminder that management is watching; a dark, glowering presence that can be seen every morning on your way into work. This is The Black Tower <cue: foreboding music>, the corporate headquarters of MCA, owners of Universal City Studios (and therefore of us guides). Tales are told of The Black Tower and the personalities within. Not that anyone we know has ever been inside...

Between tours, though, is the real fun. The tour guides have a large break room full of vending machines and old couches, where we wait to be called out to our next tour. It's filled with a motley crew of Hollywood's finest – aspiring actors, writers and directors who joke around and network continuously. The behavior and personalities are so entertaining that Universal could knock out a wall, set up three cameras and some bleachers and they'd have a great sitcom.

One afternoon I overhear another tour guide reflecting on his experience as a Jungle Cruise skipper. I introduce myself and find a fellow spirit. Jeff Palmer had worked as a ride op, spieler, musician and driver at Disneyland for years. In fact, he had done every job at Disneyland that I had ever dreamed of doing, with the sole exception of comic at the Golden Horseshoe. We will remain lifelong buddies and collaborators.

· ·· ·*·
*

I Think We're All Bozos on This Bus is the story of a disgruntled computer programmer who goes back to his old place of employment to find out why he was mysteriously fired. Why did I pick it for my directing project? His former employer was an amusement park called The Future Fair.

The script is full of Disney-related satire: walk-around characters, singing holograms, oppressive regulation, robotized security, silly nomenclature, animatronic vegetables; in many ways *Bozos*, originally written in the early '70s, predicted much of what would be found a decade later in Disney's EPCOT Center.

I contact David Ossman of The Firesign Theatre to inquire after the performance rights for the piece. He takes me to lunch in his antiquated

Volkswagen Bug, an experience I relish as I pepper him with questions about the group and their inspirations for *Bozos*.

David explains that the group usually grants performance rights to any group who asks as long as they perform the works as written, but since this is to be a full-on adaptation of the album, performed in TFT's hometown, he feels some royalties are in order. We agree on a smaller-than-usual fee and then head back to campus.

Bozos gives me my first taste of what it must feel like to be an Imagineer. Motivated by my desire to give the audience a visceral experience of The Firesign Theatre's audio production, I keep asking for more sets and effects and props... Inspired by my enthusiasm, the people and resources of the Theater Department pitch in to make my vision a reality.

The record begins with the lead character taking a bus to The Future Fair, so my adaptation begins outside the theater with the audience waiting in line for the bus to arrive with our star. Fortunately the school has just received the donation of a 30' mobile home, which is painted up with circus colors for my show. It arrives at the theater entrance billowing CO_2, sporting a giant wind-up key on top, a red clown nose on the grill and covered in twinkling lights that spell out, 'Welcome to the Future'.

Inside, the theater is decked out like a Disney ride/show, equipped with 16mm film and slides and sets designed by Tad Anheier, who also created sets for "it's a small world" and Carousel of Progress. To capture the record's energy, the 70 minute show winds up requiring 120 light cues and 132 sound cues.

Before the bus arrives, the lead comic character, Barney, is going to make his entrance from across campus following a typically huge theme park map to the theater. But the show will run at night, so how will anyone see him? I tell my technical director, Gary Bell, that I would dearly love a spotlight to shine down on Barney – a light that seems to come from God. Gary asks, "How am I going to do that?"

I have to admit I have no idea. "Can you put a spotlight on the roof of the building?" He is skeptical but says he'll try.

Three days before opening and the show is just starting to come together. After a late rehearsal I'm heading home to my apartment across the street from L.A.C.C. I'm on the far side of the quad, about as far as one can get from the Theater Department when I suddenly realize I'm standing in a massive spotlight. I turn around to look back at the source and there's Gary on top of the theater standing by a huge Super Trouper spotlight, frantically waving his arms at me. I practically float home.

Two nights later is our final dress and technical rehearsal, and the show is a disaster. Cues are missing or late and it's a clusterf*ck backstage. I'm a nervous wreck. Finally I realize that my mood isn't helping any, so halfway through the tech run-through I quietly get up and sneak outside. I walk around the building once, twice, knowing that there's nothing I can contribute at this point. I decide to trust that everyone knows their job and how to fix what's wrong.

When I return, no one says a word – they never even noticed I was missing. The next night we open and the show is flawless; as it is for the rest of the run.

Thankfully we're a sold-out hit, with dozens of Firesign Theatre fans showing up to take the ride and chant the lines along with the actors. And best of all, the members of The Firesign Theatre all show up opening night and have so much fun they each return the following week with their families.

The following summer I'm back on the tram at Universal. Then I'm invited back for a fourth year at L.A.C.C. to work as an acting coach. As the summer of 1977 approaches I'm thinking of going back to Universal when –

Rehearsals are interrupted one afternoon by a summons to speak to the school's office manager, Karen Clark. She just received a call from the new atmosphere entertainment manager at Magic Mountain. He said he's looking for a number of variety performers for the coming summer season – including one Traveling Salesman/Medicine Pitchman. Karen told him, "You can stop looking. I have your man right here."

During my last day at L.A.C.C., I return to the deserted Camino Theater, through the same downstage left door... still unlocked. The stage is again deserted. Now though, everywhere I look there's a memory.

The time I played a suicidal actor jumping to his death off an L.A. apartment building and leaped into the orchestra pit to end the scene (my left knee has bothered me ever since)... loading the set for *The Threepenny*

Opera when the sling slipped and I got to watch an upright piano drop 10' to the stage (the sound it made hung in the air for what seemed like ten minutes)... The performance of *John Brown's Body* when the entire acting company launched into *The Night They Drove Old Dixie Down* off key so actress Liz Terry circled the stage, strumming her guitar and trying valiantly to guide us all back to the melody... and the year I hosted the weekly revue of scenes, a singular honor the faculty (unanimously!) awarded me with the proviso that I curb my famous sense of humor (and then April 1st fell on a show day and all hell broke loose)!

For four years this stage has been my home, just as surely as these people have been my family. I leave the Camino stage, very proud. And weeping.

Chapter 7
SPILLIKIN CORNERS AND POPPY'S STAR (1977-80)

This time I get to bypass the Magic Mountain hiring bungalow and go straight to a trailer by a construction site.

Ernie Guderjahn is a young, lanky, laid-back character with an idea for a new approach to Magic Mountain entertainment. It's his plan to create the 'Rainbow Circus': a team of jugglers, mimes, puppeteers, clowns and comics to entertain the 1977 summer crowd.

The other new development at the Mountain is a beautifully themed crafts village. Spillikin Corners is a rustic garden setting filled with artisans demonstrating glassblowing, candle making, blacksmithing, broom making, woodworking and other early American skills. New entertainment planned for the area includes live bluegrass music, a country-western revue, a rainmaking demonstration and a traveling salesman pitching 'Grandma Spillikin's Herbal Cure and Indian Elixir'.

Ernie and I step into the show area and he sits down on a bench, handing me the preliminary script for the Grandma Spillikin's Elixir medicine pitch. As I start to read it to myself I laugh out loud.

Ernie asks, "You like it?"

I say, "Oh yeah. I like it a lot." I don't want to tell him that it is almost word-for-word the same script I'd used at L.A.C.C. (having been lifted from the same source material). I start the audition; my familiarity with the material means I can rattle the dialogue off like an old pro. When a large construction truck rumbles by during my reading, I raise my voice so Ernie doesn't miss a thing. He tells me later that's what got me the job.

Ernie presents me with a black sample case bearing the legend, 'Prof. Samuel J. Spillikin'. Inside, I find a collection of props, gags and magic that he and his friend Bingo the Clown have prepared. I take the whole mess home to practice with, as excited as I've ever been in my life.

At last the day comes… The grand opening of Spillikin Corners Crafts Village. I ride the steam train around the park into the new Spillikin Corners Station, visions of Professor Harold Hill entering River City playing in my imagination.

I've made sure that no one can possibly mistake who I am or why I'm there: loud plaid pants, bright shirt with sleeve garters, green velvet vest and a string tie. A red kerchief hangs out my back pocket and a bamboo cane swings flamboyantly in my fist. My billboard/suitcase faces the mob as I step from the train and scan the crowd, obviously up to no good and looking for a chance to prove it. Out of the corner of my eye I see grown-ups look my way and smile; children regard me with suspicious wonder.

I head down the road where I know there's shade for my audience and a bench for me to use as a lectern. I get about ten steps into the village when some total stranger calls out, "Hey, Professor, sold any snake oil yet?" I smile and keep moving, even picking up the pace a bit. Apparently the look is working.

I drop my case on a bench and start calling to the passersby, inviting them to gather round… see the show… see a miracle… "I'm going to eat a bale of hay and drink a gallon of gasoline while singing *I Don't Want to Set the World on Fire!*"… I stop just short of yelling, "FREE BEER!" Nothing. No reaction. People give me a glance in passing — then walk on by.

But I notice the people on the other side of the road are watching, listening and laughing. On a hunch I yell at a kid standing nearby, "Hey, young fella – you want to see a magic trick?" He ambles over. I place him about 5' in front of me and say, just loud enough for him to hear, "If you watch what I do for five seconds without turning around, I'll make a crowd of people appear behind you." I drape my kerchief over my left hand, wave my right hand in the air and count slowly, "1... 2... 3... 4... FIVE!" When I whip the kerchief away, the kid turns around to find a crowd of strangers behind him and then looks back at me, amazed.

This is my first lesson in crowd psychology, something that will become a lifelong study. No one in that group would have stopped if they had been the first one to do so. Each person needed someone they could stand behind or next to; same reason most folks won't sit in the front row at a lecture. That first year at Spillikin Corners is a series of such lessons.

The medicine pitch started with the material I gathered in college, but it evolved – like Wally Boag's 'Pecos Bill' routine or any comic bit performed year after year. I add a small flea circus routine, different silly disguises and, in a tribute to Wally Boag, a comic take on balloon animals.

One large influence is the films of W.C. Fields. I find a lot of my 'professorial attitude' in his performances; especially his way with children like Baby LeRoy in *Tillie and Gus*, *The Old Fashioned Way* and *It's a Gift*. I wear a cloisonné pin of The Great W.C. on my vest in tribute.

I spend my days at Magic Mountain, but I'm looking for something to do with my nights, when I hear about a new restaurant opening in the Valley to be called 'Poppy's Star'. Neil 'Poppy' Morgan owns the 'Great American Food and Beverage Company' restaurants in Southern California. They specialize in great food served by performing folk singers and rock musicians; it's a wild atmosphere, very popular for special occasions and Hollywood parties.

Poppy's Star is his new project, serving the same kind of menu, but featuring variety performers of every type: mimes, magicians, musicians, jugglers, comics and one very large and loud medicine pitchman. My old boss from 1520 A.D., Billy Scudder, waits tables as Charlie Chaplin; his rendition of the character is so remarkable that he's soon hired by IBM to be their corporate spokesmute. I hook up with my friend Mitch Evans from Magic Mountain and we revive some great old vaudeville bits like 'Who's on First' and 'Slowly I Turned'.

The restaurant is located in a sprawling, old-style building with several large showrooms filled with big booths and easy access. Each room features an intimate performing space with a spotlight that's controlled by the performers. It's left to us to manage the balance of show and service in each room, so we're careful not to let the songs and comic bits get in the way of another's work.

The Poppy's Star operation caters to the restaurant staff, making our work as waiters and seating hosts as simple as possible so we have the time and freedom to perform spontaneously for the guests. Poppy himself is our benign leader and biggest fan, and working for him is as much of a party for us as the place he created is for the paying guests.

I start getting bookings around town for the professor character and get to travel up and down the coast doing corporate carnivals and events. Two performances in particular stand out:

I'm killing time before a show at the Century Plaza Hotel in Beverly Hills when I stop in the downstairs snack shop for a soda. The cheerful little bald guy behind the counter has been checking out my professor costume and comments, "That's a nice pin," pointing at W.C. Fields. I thank him and he adds, "I used to work with him."

I laugh, "You're not that old! You would have been a baby when he – Oh, my God!" The man smiles and it's the same crooked smile I remember from all those films I studied in my high school days. "You're Baby LeRoy!" He is, indeed, Ronald Le Roy Overacker.

According to legend, W.C, Fields put a couple of shots of gin in his formula one day on the set of their film, *Tillie and Gus*, to stop him from crying. I quickly ask him if that's true and the smile returns. "I remember it like it was yesterday." He shares stories of my hero until I have to leave to go onstage.

The other story takes place just after I am hired to perform at Magic Mountain. My maternal Grandmother, Yolanda Spiegel, was my all-time favorite relative and my biggest fan growing up; she always listened to my dreams of someday performing in the parks. She is very ill and in a private care facility when I get the job as Professor Spillikin, so my very first performance of the pitch is when I surprise her in her room one afternoon. As I say, she is in very poor shape, but one thing she can still do beautifully is laugh.

My Grandmother passes away a few short weeks thereafter, but it's long been a comfort that we shared that moment.

Every morning at Magic Mountain, all the members of the Rainbow Circus Troupe gather in the character trailer to get our props and any special instructions for the day. There usually isn't much, but it's great to spend time with such talent, especially since most of the time I'll be on my own back in the Crafts Village.

I'm especially impressed by the kids who portray the Magic Mountain Trolls. They work for minimum wage, wearing these giant fur-lined gumdrop outfits in 100+ degree heat... which means they love what they do (since they obviously aren't doing it for the money). They are as devoted to their work as anyone I'll ever meet.

Our walking puppet stages contain Mark Bryan Wilson and Terri Hardin, both of whom create the most wonderful puppet characters. They will go on to become accomplished puppeteers, sculptors and designers for movies and theme parks around the world. Frizzy the Fantastic (our juggler who *is* both frizzy and fantastic), Mary Lou the Mime, Bingo the Clown, Mitch Evans and the hysterical Don Lake make up a great utility group that, under Ernie's direction, serve up classic vaudeville-style entertainment all over Magic Mountain.

Back at Spillikin Corners, afternoon entertainment is provided by Handpicked, a three piece comic/bluegrass ensemble consisting of Mark McConnell, Bob Sofer and Phil Salazar. We are thrown together when the park opens and quickly set a pattern where I either seize the stage when their set ends or spontaneously introduce them at show-time.

Handpicked has come out of the music scene in Ventura County. Having just left a gig at Busch Gardens, they appear to have been manufactured by Disney specifically for the purpose of theme park entertainment. They are sweet, funny, quick, very talented and extremely professional.

Another Spillikin personality is young Larry Nikolai who runs 'Front

Page Press' and 'Memories on Tin'. We share a fascination with Disney, and when things are slow in the shop we talk about our dreams of a future working for the Company. Today, Larry is a Principal Concept and Show Designer at Walt Disney Imagineering; couldn't happen to a nicer guy.

When Handpicked leaves Magic Mountain, it's to take up residence on the streets of Frontierland in Anaheim. Our friendship endures and eventually Disney creates a nighttime show around the band, the *Yahoo Revue*, featuring Main Street Maniac Dick Hardwick alongside Nancy Osborne and Terri Robinson, who also fills in for the daytime show on Betty Taylor's days off.

The *Yahoo Revue* is performed five times a night in the Golden Horseshoe and is a charming blend of country comedy and excellent musicianship. My girlfriend and I become big fans; it's always great to hear Handpicked and the cast keep the show fast, fresh and funny.

The Jim Gibson Band, a more traditional country ensemble, takes over in Spillikin Corners and we become fast friends.

Through Ernie's efforts the Rainbow Circus talent has become an integral part of the Mountain and we are granted greater and greater creative freedom. We produce the end-of-summer employee talent show which Ernie turns into a comic spectacular in the 3,400 seat Showcase Theater. He asks me to host, and I get to perform the pitch for 2,000+ Magic Mountain employees at once – the largest crowd I've ever had.

My girlfriend and I are in Disneyland in March of 1979 celebrating her birthday. It's very hot in Anaheim and I'm waiting patiently for her outside the ladies room by the Plaza Inn when I look up to find Tigger standing in front of me, staring. I say, "Hi there." He waves. "Hot out here." Tigger points at his large fiberglass head. "Hot in there too, huh?"

Suddenly Tigger leans in close and I hear a small voice inside say, "You're that crazy Professor, aren't you?"

I reply, "I guess I am."

He says, "I'm a big fan of yours."

"Well, Tigger, I'm a big fan of yours, too."

Tigger tells me, "Don't go away," and slips through the employee backstage access. In a minute he's back with Eeyore and Chip, and I'm surrounded. Eeyore remarks, "I've never seen your work but I've heard a lot about you."

Hmmmm…

Chapter 8
APRIL, 1980

In December, 1979 my eldest sister Lisa is working in artist relations at Warner Records. Every day a copy of *Variety* crosses her desk and every day she delivers it unopened to her boss. On this day, however, she happens to open it.

The ad is in the lower corner of the page: "Disneyland looking to cast Dancers and Comics for the 25th anniversary season of the *Golden Horseshoe Revue*. Auditions to be held December 31st , 1979 in the Show Production Building at Disneyland. Dancers arrive prepared to move at 6 p.m. Comics arrive prepared to perform at 9 p.m." Lisa calls me immediately. I ask her to read the ad to me twice and hang up the phone in a daze.

There is a voice inside me shouting, "It's a miracle! This could be your break... You ought to be nervous!" But this audition has been my raison d'être for the previous ten years; and for the last three years I've done nothing but prepare.

So I ignore the inner voice and decide that I can afford to be merely excited. <u>Very</u> merely excited.

A few days before the audition I'm at the park and stop in to see the show. Wally, Fulton and Betty are in their typical top form and I keep grinning like an idiot at the thought that there's a chance, however small, that I could be a part of such a thing. As the show ends and the theater is clearing I head toward the stage. The floor is littered with dried baby lima beans, the 'teeth' that Wally spit out during the 'Pecos Bill' number. I pick one up and put it in my pocket. For luck.

December 31st , 1979

I arrive early at the Disneyland Show Production Building. There are dozens of beautiful women in leotards following a choreographer in the can-can, then leaping into the air only to land on the floor in a full split. All of us waiting comics sit at the back of the room, alternately grinning and wincing.

At the front table sit the auditors, the two men who are casting the show. There's Wally Boag in his jacket and cap, and the head of Disney Talent Booking, Walter "Sonny" Anderson. When the girls are finished Sonny and Wally turn around and greet us warmly, talking about the show and what they'll be looking for. From the crowd reaction, I'd be surprised if any of these guys around me have ever set foot in the Golden Horseshoe Saloon.

For a moment I wonder why a few of the comics are wearing identical white suits. Then it dawns on me – In 1979 Steve Martin is at the height of his popularity as a stand-up comedian. He has mentioned in interviews that as a youth he had worked in a Disneyland Magic Shop and was inspired by seeing Wally perform at the Golden Horseshoe. Knowing this, some comics have shown up wearing Martin's trademark white suit and carrying some of his typical props: bunny ears, a banjo, an arrow-thru-the-head.

I, on the other hand, am wearing my Magic Mountain professor suit and carrying my medicine bag and cane. I figure if they're looking for someone to understudy Wally, I might as well show them that I'm ready to fill the bill.

Each comic steps up in turn to show their stuff. Wally and Sonny are encouraging throughout, making notes and conferring with each other. Then my name is called. I grab my bag and step to the front of the room, swinging my cane just as I've been doing for 3+ years back at Spillikin Corners. And as I pass the front table I hear Sonny say to Wally, "This is the kid I told you about."

I start the pitch and everything is going well, the other comics are laughing and Sonny and Wally are smiling. At one point I smack the medicine bottle with the cane to emphasize a point but – as planned – the cane slips and I hit myself in the head. I stop for a moment, shake my head and spit out the single bean I'd picked up at the Horseshoe for luck. And Wally falls off his chair, laughing.

When everyone has performed we are thanked and informed they'll be making their selection in a week or two. And I go home to await the news. Three weeks pass during which I do my best not to think about the audition.

Then the letter comes. "Thank you for your audition. We're sorry but we have nothing for you at this time." When I read that a part of me wants to believe that I should sit and wait. Sure, it's a form letter... but maybe when they say 'at this time', what they might mean is, 'Not now, but soon'.

But another part of me says, 'Count your blessings'. The qualities that have made Prof. Spillikin such a hit – and a joy to play – would not fit in at Disneyland. First, I get to keep my long hair and beard, skirting the Magic Mountain grooming standards by virtue of my unique position. Then there's the Professor's character: he's greedy, dishonest, irascible and has absolutely no affection for kids.

Audiences love a rebel. My Professor treats them in a manner they don't expect in a family amusement park. By emphasizing my character's more unpleasant traits I've made him a hero to many... including, apparently, Tigger and the head of Disney Talent Booking. (The truly remarkable thing is the way kids react; they seem to sense my 'contempt' and enjoy playing along with it.)

Samuel J. Spillikin is custom made for me! I know I'll never find that in a Disney Park, so I decide to listen to the voice that says, 'count your blessings' and be happy where I am.

A few days later I'm making up some balloon animals after a show. I've developed a true-to-character approach that caters to the kids while adding an element of self-parody that the parents find amusing. I hand one kid a balloon puppy and smile, "There you go, kid. I think you know what you can do with that."

As I'm finishing my set a woman wearing too much lipstick comes over and says, "My husband works for MCA and he'd like to talk to you about a project. How can he get in touch with you?" After some convincing I decide to give her my right name and number, and think nothing more about it.

All this time I've been living next to L.A.C.C. and making the looong commute each morning to Magic Mountain. Then there is another looong commute to Poppy's Star in Encino to work the dinner crowd and then the late night haul back over the hill to L.A. At last I figure that, since my destiny is obviously tied to the Mountain, it's time to move there.

So on Tuesday morning I'm getting set to go apartment hunting around Newhall when I'm stopped by a phone call from Stuart Adelson, a lawyer for MCA Universal. He explains that the 'husband' who had caught my act in Spillikin Corners was in fact Jay Stein, the President of MCA Attractions and the boss of Universal City Studios. Mr. Stein wants to meet with me to discuss my participation in an upcoming project and would I be available to meet with Stuart the following Monday at Universal?

I'm moderately intrigued. Looking back on the incident with Mr. Stein's wife I half expect to be called to task for practically telling that kid to take the balloon puppy and shove it. On the other hand that could hardly be considered an 'upcoming project'...

The phone rings again. It is now 10:30 a.m. on April 15th, 1980. I pick it up and this is what I hear:

"Ron, this is Mike Davis at Disneyland Talent Booking. We'd like you to come to the park tomorrow and start training for the comic's role in the *Golden Horseshoe Revue*."

The first thing I do after I hang up the phone is shave off the beard.

Next morning I'm in the audience at the Golden Horseshoe. After the show, the house clears and Cast Members start preparing for the next audience. The Show Tech comes out to sweep up Wally's 'teeth', the service staff bus tables and straighten chairs and Wally Boag steps through the curtain to shake my hand and invite me backstage.

Behind the scenes I'm surprised to find it's deserted. No dancing girls, no actors, no one at all. I was to learn quickly that the cast has dressing rooms near the theater and when a show is over they are outta there!

True to form, Wally shoots straight through the building into a backstage area then out across Adventureland and through the Jungle Cruise exit. I just manage to keep up as he takes a hard left toward the end of the dock and steps straight off into the water. Only then do I notice the row of volcanic rocks that line the shore behind the Tahitian Terrace stage and lead into a narrow cave.

The cave leaves us behind Main Street by the kitchen for the Plaza Pavilion. Up a flight of stairs are some small offices and Wally's dressing room, a two room affair with an office, an upright piano and a media room with a day bed and a walk-in closet. It sounds more impressive than it is; everything backstage is in great shape but has obviously been there for decades.

Once we're settled in his apartment Wally asks, "What do you want to do?" Apparently it's up to me what the first part of my act, the traveling salesman, will contain. It takes me no time to reply: I want to do a blend of the best bits from my pitch with some of the classic lines of Wally's. It's important to me to carry on the traditions of the show.

Wally gives me a full-size six shooter and a bag of dried baby lima beans so I can practice twirling the gun and spitting out 'teeth' for the Pecos Bill routine. Once I get home I pack the beans in my coat pocket and take to the street to practice my tooth spitting, bouncing the beans off the windshields of passing cars.

For the gun business, Wally advises me to practice while standing next to a bed. I soon find out why; it cuts down on the number of times I have to bend over to fetch a dropped pistol.

The next few days are a loosely-organized whirlwind of hanging around backstage, watching the show, practicing the 'Pecos Bill' routine and getting oriented. I have a fitting for my costume with legendary Disneyland costumer Jack Muhs. I need a cowboy hat for the Pecos bit, so the show's costumer, Bernice, digs up a ten-gallon white affair that goes great with my size and personality.

Sitting backstage during the show is wonderful. The place runs like clockwork; everyone is totally focused but still so sweet to the new kid. I learn in time that this is a remnant of the way the whole park was once… in the Days of Walt.

The Golden Horseshoe Girls have their dressing room directly behind the backdrop onstage because they wear three different costumes over the course of the twenty-eight minute show. Betty Taylor also changes back there for her three outfits, though her regular dressing room is behind the theater on the second floor of Adventureland, next to Fulton Burley's.

On stage Fulton Burley is a high-energy, extremely friendly flirt who is constantly up for a joke or a song. Offstage, on the other hand – he's exactly the same. Vince Rossi is the piano player and show's musical director, R. Dale Olsen plays trumpet and trombone and young Chris Gibson is on drums and sound effects. Chris never seems to take his eye off the comic onstage so he can punctuate every move and moment with an appropriate effect; I often break up onstage at the stuff he adds.

Bernice is Mother Hen to the Golden Horseshoe Girls, managing their dressing room and wardrobe. Stage Tech Bobby Davis is a sweet little guy who looks exactly like Jiminy Cricket; he runs lights, sound and props. I find out early on that he is a bit of a wild man, but I have no idea until much later that he is also a leather biker who collects Nazi memorabilia!

Saturday comes and a clean-shaven Prof. Spillikin returns to Magic Mountain. Everyone in the Crafts Village is thrilled that my dream of working for Disney has come true and sad that I'll be moving on. I give my notice... For the next two weeks I'll be working weekdays at Disneyland and weekends at The Mountain.

And smiling almost constantly.

On Monday morning I report to the hill overlooking Universal Studios, passing the tram tour and guides' break room on my way to a construction trailer where Attorney Stuart Adelson tells me the following story:

For a long time Jay Stein, President of MCA Universal Attractions, has sat in his office in The Black Tower watching as the tour guests pour out of his Studio Tour and into Victoria Station, a British train-themed restaurant built just outside the exit. It's a magnificent building with a large dome, serving great food in authentic old railroad cars. What concerns Jay is this: MCA Universal doesn't own it.

So it's decided that MCA will build another restaurant across from Victoria Station with a larger profile that will capitalize on the current country-western craze. It will be themed to resemble an 1880s wagon factory and showroom, with a name pre-selected from a list of comically alliterative possibilities: Womphopper's Wagon Works.

Stein hires a writer to create a backstory about the wagon factory and its founder, C.L. Womphopper. They tie it into the history of the area, creating full page newspaper ads of the period and amusing nomenclature for the menu. The walls of the restaurant are to be decorated with the humorous ads, doctored photographs of C.L. and letters of complaint from people that Womphopper had ripped off. And the menu is to feature a full-length portrait of the scoundrel with a few stories painting him as the prototype of the shifty used car salesman.

Then one sunny day, Jay Stein takes his wife and son to Magic Mountain where he witnesses my Medicine Pitch. Afterwards, I make his son a balloon puppy and as I hand it to the kid I remark, "There you go, kid. I think you know what you can do with that."

Whereupon Jay turns to his wife and says, "This guy is C.L. Womphopper."

After the story, Stuart explains to me that he and I are now going to take a walk down the hill to talk with Mr. Stein. In his office. In The Black Tower <cue: foreboding music>.

Stepping off the elevator on a top floor of The Black Tower, I've never seen deep, white plush carpeting this deep and white and plush. One thing, though, is exactly as I imagined it would be: no one, not a single secretary nor any executive – junior or otherwise – is smiling. Stu escorts me into a corner office with a floor-to-ceiling view of the studio. There

I meet Jay Stein and a few cronies; men who seem bolted to the chairs that line the walls of Stein's office.

Jay is a thin, neat businesslike fellow with a curt demeanor and a reluctant smile. He tells me about the character of C.L. Womphopper and his plans for the restaurant. "I think you're the man to play C.L. We could have you greeting people in the lobby, introducing the band... "

My mind quickly flashes back to my experiences at 1520 A.D. and Poppy's Star. Off the top of my head, I offer, "If I am descended from the world's first used car salesman, I'm going to run the restaurant like a used car lot. Why don't we make all the waiters salesmen? And all the busboys mechanics? And all the seating hosts sales managers?"

Jay thinks about this a second and announces, "Okay. You're Creative Manager."

Next Jay shows me a mock-up of the menu. On the back cover is a large drawing of C.L. Womphopper, looking like the stereotypical melodramatic villain. I share my opinion that he looks a little too evil, that we might want to soften him up a little. When I say this I swear I could hear the sphincters of the men-in-chairs tighten around the room; my guess is that folks meeting Jay for the first time rarely offer creative criticism.

The decision is made that my image will grace the back of the menu. Later on I'll be photographed in my Womphopper costume for this purpose, but – while my hands and body are immortalized – my face will be replaced with that of the original villain's features.

At first I'm concerned about the timing of my two recent job offers. The Universal meeting is taking place in April, but Womphopper's doesn't open until October. The gig at the Golden Horseshoe is five nights a week through Disneyland's 25th anniversary summer, and then I'll just be on call to understudy Wally, leaving me free to manage Womphopper's. So I tell Jay I'll take the job.

Chapter 9
THE GOLDEN HORSESHOE AND WOMPHOPPER'S

After one more day of practice and observation, Wally tells me, "Your costume is up in my room. Tomorrow I'll do the first two shows, then you're going on while I go to the track."

In my beautiful blue custom-made period suit I race through the park and through the stage door of the Golden Horseshoe. As I listen from backstage, my first show starts. The ladies step offstage after their opening number and wish me luck. In the carpet bag I check my props; it's strange to see the gags from my Magic Mountain pitch in there.

The comic traditionally enters through the back of the house so I grab my bag and hat, strolling outside and around through Frontierland. Suddenly I'm back in Spillikin Corners, the town rascal-up-to-no-good… but I'm not at Magic Mountain. I'm in heaven.

I sneak in through the saloon doors and take my place at the back end of the bar, where Wally always waits to make his entrance. You can tell the regular Horseshoe fans, they'll turn and look at this spot to see who's doing the show that day. Today when they look there's Wally Boag in his street clothes standing next to me. Wally wishes me luck and I'm on.

My first show at the Golden Horseshoe is very comfortable. The only real adjustment comes right at the top when Fulton calls on me to introduce myself. Taking my cue from the rest of the cast, for the first-and-only time in my theme park career, I use my real name. "I'm Professor Ron Schneider and my father was an old injun fighter."

Fulton asks, "What was your mother?"

"An old injun."

I naturally settle into a more wholesome character than Prof. Spillikin, doing the same bits with more of a smile than usual (which isn't difficult – this is my dream-come-true). Bringing a kid up for some comedy magic comes easy; then I step offstage and Bobby's waiting to help me make the quick change into my Pecos Bill costume.

Off with the coat and derby, on with the chaps and ten-gallon hat. Tobacco pouch in the vest pocket, handful of beans in the mouth, Bobby steps up from behind with the double holster, guns preloaded with blanks... a quick walk to the center break in the curtain... wait a beat for my cue and I'm on.

Now I'm in strange territory. But not really – haven't I done this bit in my mind dozens of times over the years, listening to Wally on tape at home? The Pecos Bill number moves at a breakneck pace, but I've had just enough rehearsal that I can keep up. What strikes me is the few places where I break the rhythm of the classic bit to momentarily personalize what I'm doing, the rest of the cast – Fulton, Betty, the Band and especially the drummer – are right there with me, reacting to what I'm doing at each moment. I feel completely at home.

Only this is better than home. Home for four years was Spillikin Corners, where I was outside in the heat, battling to get a crowd, competing with roller coasters and beer vendors. Here I am surrounded by a talented team, in glorious air-conditioning and facing an audience of 310 Golden Horseshoe fans who have made a point of making reservations and waiting in line to see the show. They watch and listen attentively and they catch and laugh at everything I'm doing.

When the show is over Stage Tech Bobby Davis says, "That's the best first show I've ever seen". And I know Wally must have liked it because – after he watched my debut – he left for the track.

Nowadays Disney anniversaries seem to come at us with terrifying regularity, often accompanied by prize giveaways, copious amounts of commemorative merchandise and temporary architectural make-overs. But in 1980, Disneyland's 25th Birthday is a unique and heartfelt event.

There isn't much merchandising. There are t-shirts and hats to be sure, but the real collectibles are produced in truly limited quantities, as if management is afraid that no one would notice or care. This means that on the day of the actual anniversary, there aren't any collectibles left.

For two nights, Disneyland holds an exclusive open house for employees and their families, but with an incredible twist: every show and attraction is open for the guests to peek around backstage. There are tram tours of the support areas, walking tours of The Haunted Mansion, the chance to stand inside Space Mountain with the ride running (*and the lights on*), free food and entertainment and the Golden Horseshoe stage is open to the back wall with Wally Boag greeting guests in costume at center.

There is one special hard ticket public event, though. For the first time in its history, Disneyland will remain open overnight for a 25 hour party (actually the park stays open for 40 hours: from 9 a.m., July 16th to 1 a.m., July 18th).

On the night of July 16th I do my five shows at the Horseshoe, change out of my costume and head to Main Street for the countdown to Disneyland's 25th Birthday Party. The street is nicely filled, most people sitting on the ground with friends and relatives. At midnight there's a pre-recorded announcement and fireworks and the crowd heads off in all directions to enjoy the park.

The secret to enjoying a visit to a theme park, for me at least, is who you go with. On this night the park is nicely filled with People Who Love Disneyland and who wouldn't think of missing the party. Everywhere we go – in every line, at every table, on every ride – my girlfriend and I meet and bond with people like ourselves and share the most glorious times. We wind up at the River Belle Terrace in Frontierland, sharing breakfast as the sun comes up over Tom Sawyer Island; I recommend it.

The Golden Horseshoe runs ten shows a day all summer of 1980, but with the fall comes shorter hours and fewer late shows. I move out of my Anaheim apartment, find a place down the hill from Universal City Studios and report to the Womphopper's Wagon Works construction site.

With a little over six weeks till opening, I think I have a pretty good handle on what I have to do to get the place ready. I am to be responsible for casting the wait staff and crafting their guest interaction into something fun and different. General Manager Dick House and Day Manager Missy Moe will handle restaurant operations, leaving the atmosphere entertainment to me; I report directly to Jay Stein.

My (limited) experience in management has convinced me that the way to create the comic/service environment I envision is to hire responsible, funny people and work with them as a team leader and fan, rather than to take a dictatorial approach. I've seen it work at Poppy's Star, 1520 A.D. and the Golden Horseshoe. It is the atmosphere in which I have been happiest and have done my best work.

That, however, is not the Universal method. Jay Stein makes it clear from the beginning that no material is to be presented on the 'sales floor' that has not been personally okayed by him. If I am to give my people any creative input, it will have to be in selecting material from a pre-approved book. So I set about writing that book.

I break the Womphopper's experience down into a series of potential contact points then create five or six 'bits' for each one. I script routines for greeting the guests, taking them to their seats, collecting the menus, bringing food to the table, delivering the check… you get the idea. I deliver this novella to Jay who returns it with copious notes in the borders and various remarks indicating 'Approved' or 'No'.

Meanwhile I place newspaper ads for the seating hosts, waiters and bus staff. I make sure it's clear I'm looking for entertainers: 'Now Casting Characters to staff Universal Studios' new dining experience – Womphopper's Wagon Works'. Applicants are instructed to come to the restaurant to fill out an application, then based on their performing and work resumé I call some back as a group for a second interview.

When they arrive I gather everyone in a corner of the building and ask each one to get up and tell a joke to the entire crowd. We get to know each other, we laugh together and they come to know me as a friend and fan. I then tell everyone they've been hired and ask them to come back to our first meeting with a fictional character name for their name tag; something humorous and sales-related. Among the names they come up with are Hugh Ben Hadd, Hi Prices, Hugh J. Ripoff and Bux Upfront. Of course Jay has to approve all the names. (I am heartbroken to lose Selma Mother.)

Meanwhile the wagon factory is coming together to amazing effect. Universal spends close to $3 million on the place and it shows. The building is entirely covered with authentic barn wood. Real, full-sized wagons are suspended from the ceiling in the foyer and a mammoth mechanical fan turns slowly above the main seating area. There are numerous themed areas throughout, each reflecting a different aspect of the wagon business. There are elegant private (sales) booths for our Hollywood clientèle and a gilded VIP cage, representing Womphopper's former accounting department. The complex is so beautifully themed that a group of Disney Imagineers start coming in once a week for lunch!

I am especially pleased with the crew of Sales Managers/Seating Hosts I have working with me at the front desk. Sandy Silverthorne had been my idol back when I was conducting the Universal Studios Tour; his tour was the best, the warmest and the funniest of any of us. And Don Lake had been a clown at Magic Mountain and is simply the funniest guy I know. With these old friends and the rest of the talented crew, we have a perpetual blast at the front desk endlessly putting on each other and the guests.

Jay insists that there always be a C.L. Womphopper character at the front desk, so I have to pick two of my seating hosts to fill in on my days off. None of them resemble me in the slightest, so I pick the two who show the strongest knack for that kind of guest contact. And I'm very happy with my choices.

Womphopper's opens and folks like what they see. I convince Jay to bring the Jim Gibson ensemble over from Spillikin Corners for our house band, so we've got live music five nights a week and the country-western dance community shows up and proceeds to make us a hit. And it doesn't hurt that the food and drinks are spectacular (though we do win a prize for the region's worst potato skins)!

Besides greeting guests in character, I and my fellow seating hosts are responsible for running the front desk, managing our reservations and entertaining the waiting throngs. On Friday and Saturday nights guests sometimes have a two hour wait for a table, but the building, the music and the staff are so entertaining that folks stick it out. I have one other responsibility that I'm not wild about. I'm supposed to lurk and sneak and nose around and make sure everyone's doing only the approved material on the floor. With the challenge of a whole new operation, there's not a lot of 'performance' going on and that suits me fine; comedy is a luxury in such an environment and better to omit it than to bore the guests with forced or unfunny humor.

While Jay may have seen my material as something to be adhered to religiously, I never intended the stuff I'd written to be a bible. I only meant it as a guide to what's possible. I hired people whose experience and humor I admired so they could take those suggestions and create something I couldn't. It's a process I'd modeled on the life's work of Walt Disney. But this doesn't jive with the Universal 'style of management'. I have a few confrontations with the bosses about this, nothing major but as time passes I become aware of a growing dissatisfaction among the cast. Finally I'm ordered to fire one of my substitute C.L.'s and replace him with a cast member who I feel is totally wrong for the character.

I plead my case with General Manager Dick House, but he makes it clear that I have no say in the matter, this is the way Jay wants it. So I quit. I tell him I'll stay on as C.L. and run the front desk and keep a 40 hour week, but I resign as Creative Manager. I ask to be taken off salary and paid the same hourly wage as the other seating hosts. He agrees and the meeting ends amicably.

As a result, I don't have to spend any time ratting on my fellow employees. When I figure the time I'd spent in the restaurant each week while on salary versus the time I would work on an hourly rate, it comes to roughly the same amount per hour. The only change will be that I will lose my title, but it's my title that's keeping me – and everyone around me – from loving the work.

I'm not replaced in the Creative Manager's job – but I have served my purpose. I hired the right people, created and shared my vision of Womphopper's as an entertainment venue and played my part in character to set the tone.

The managers that are left are ill equipped to manage the actors and know nothing about theming or comedy. But they know when something is working – and as soon as the cast I assembled start to assert themselves, Womphopper's starts working like gangbusters!

That same atmosphere of benign neglect that I enjoyed at Poppy's Star, 1520 A.D. and the Golden Horseshoe settles over the Wagon Works and everyone blossoms. People come up with their own characters and bits and traditions that turn Womphopper's into the San Fernando Valley's Number One Party Place. And we – and the guests – have a ball!

Occasionally I'm at home on my night off and the phone rings and it's Wally Boag. "Can you work tomorrow? I'm going to the track."

I say sure and then I call Fulton who lives a few blocks away from me (on Fulton Avenue!) and ask for a lift in to work. He picks me up in the morning and I drive in with him. He shares kumquats he's grown in his home garden and regales me with stories of his career and Golden Horseshoe history.

The kumquats are slightly sour... but life is sweet.

Chapter 10
FROM DREAMER TO DREAMFINDER (1981-82)

Christmas of 1981, I book an acting gig at a Dickens themed party as Mr. Pickwick and hook up with an old friend, Sean Wright, president of the Non-Canonical Calabashes (an arm of the Baker Street Irregulars, the Sherlock Holmes fan society). We start brainstorming ideas for our own theme party company to be called 'The Play's the Thing'.

We create a grocery list of possible themes; *The Twilight Zone*, Robin Hood, Swiss Navy Reunion... I have hopes we can hook up with a local restaurant and do a semi-regular themed dinner show/attraction. In the meantime, we start booking one-of-a-kind Sherlock Holmes mystery parties for private functions.

Typically, we get a booking and meet with the host to scope out the location, then I write an original mystery where the guests get to solve the crime side-by-side with Sherlock. My favorite is a birthday party we create for a husband whose wife is a big Holmes fan. It's only the two of them and our cast of five actors in their home; we supply Beef Wellington, music hall entertainment and the theft of her birthday present by Professor Moriarty.

Womphopper's evolves, becoming more of an exact science. With the entire cast now contributing creatively, we discover great ways to handle our success and the crowds that grow as a result.

At peak times when the bar is jammed, guests cluster around our roll-top lobby desk, watching us hustle to get folks seated. As the guests stand around waiting to be called, we realize they form a captive audience. So we start improvising comic business and character relationships that appear to be accidental, but are designed to amuse our impatient mob.

Foremost among these is the way all the other hosts plot against and humiliate their boss, C.L. Womphopper. When I leave the lobby to seat a group, they'll set up some practical joke, up to and including death threats written in ketchup on a napkin, which will send me into a paranoid spasm. The guests love seeing the vain and pompous C.L. lose his cool.

Other times the desk phone will ring with a call from a real customer and I'll answer in character, "Womphopper's Wagon Works... Womphopper speaking!" Of course the waiting guests are listening in. "You want to make a reservation? You'll need to speak to the Reservation Lady; please hold!" I put the call on hold and take care of some other brief business before picking up and speaking in a silly falsetto, "This is the Reservation Lady! How can I help you? What? No... no, I'm a woman now!"

One more favorite routine of mine is reserved for late at night after the 'family crowd' is gone and we've stopped seating for dinner. The bar is still open and the dance floor is jumping and the seating staff are basically hanging around like employees at the company Christmas party. So, just like any other idiot boss after hours, C.L. Womphopper starts to drink.

I'm seen hanging around the lobby with a (non-alcoholic) libation, lording it over my 'subordinates'. When it comes time for me to step onstage and introduce the band, I forget their name or introduce some band that isn't there. Then, where I'd usually jump down off the stage, now I'm too afraid to jump the foot-and-a-half to the floor and I burst into tears. The hosts race to my rescue and carry me off the stage.

Finally, at closing time, I'm found lying on my back in the lobby, singing at the top of my lungs as the guests depart.

* ∵ *. . *. *.
*

And every week or two I pick up a shift at the Golden Horseshoe. One afternoon I'm sitting between shows in Wally's dressing room and the phone rings. I tell the caller Wally is out that day and offer to take a message. It's Bev Bergeron calling from his dressing room at Walt Disney World in Florida.

I just about fall over! Bev was Rebo the Clown on *The Magic Land of Allakazam*, the show that had inspired my interest in magic and performing when I was a kid. He's the star comic in the Magic Kingdom's *Diamond Horseshoe Revue*. We have a long, happy chat and I promise to look him up if I ever make it down to Orlando.

My old Spillikin Corners bluegrass friends Handpicked, who had preceded me to Disneyland, had long before been moved by the Company to play in shows and clubs at Walt Disney World. I pay them a visit in 1981 and Bev arranges for me to do a couple of shows in the *Diamond Horseshoe Revue.*

As a favor, Bev asks the head of the Entertainment Division to see one of these shows; it's that old friend from my high school days, Peter Bloustein. Peter was that Stage Manager at Disneyland, who'd let me watch him call the cues for *Show Me America* back in 1970.

When WDW opened in 1971, the Company moved Peter to Florida where he started out overseeing live entertainment for hotels and conventions. In 1981, I'm hoping he'll be able to catch my act at the Diamond Horseshoe, but it's not to be. The man is busy… with what, I'll soon find out.

On my final day in Florida, Phil Salazar of Handpicked asks me if I'd like to drive out and take a look at a big construction site on the other side of Disney property. We hop in his Volkswagen Beetle and take some unmarked construction roads out to where they're building the second theme park to grace Walt Disney World.

Phil drives up to the security gate… and doesn't even slow down. We barrel past the guard and proceed to tear around the perimeter of the

EPCOT Center construction site. We finally stop near the big ditch that will soon be World Showcase Lagoon so I can soak up the sight and size of this amazing project. The skeleton of Spaceship Earth is only half built; The Land Pavilion looks the most finished. (I can see it clearly because there's practically nothing standing in the spot reserved for the Imagination Pavilion.) EPCOT Center looks like it'll be something special.

The next day Bob Sofer asks me to drive his tiny Volkswagen Rabbit back to California so he can sell it on the west coast, so I head west on Interstate 10, back to my life of horseshoes and wagon wheels. Or so I think.

Things might have gone on like this for a while if it was anyone else but me. After 10+ years of keeping an eye on the horizon looking for the next step forward, I've gotten into the habit of moving on after a few years. Especially if my current situation isn't evolving.

Everything at Womphopper's has continued to grow and change for the better; everything, that is, but the MCA Universal management style. I begin to chafe at their way of handling the front-line staff, the folks who had made the place a success. In January of 1982 I let them know I'm moving on. It looks like 'The Play's the Thing' is going to pay off, and I still have the Golden Horseshoe going for me. That's a job I could do for ten to fifteen years at least…

But on my next visit to the Golden Horseshoe I find out that Wally has decided to retire. As sad as this news is to the fan in me, it also means that I could get two days a week steady employment covering the days Wally's Number One understudy isn't there.

Jim Adams has been Wally's alternate for years. Jim is a talented comic and ventriloquist and, more importantly, one of the sweetest guys you'd ever want to meet. I've enjoyed his work for years and think I'll be perfectly happy working under him.

Except that Jim is leaving with Wally. They are going off together to create shows and concepts for a new theme park being planned for Las Vegas. That's going to leave me and a comic musician from the Main

Street Maniacs, Dick Hardwick (who, you might remember, starred in the *Yahoo Revue* with Handpicked years before).

But when Wally leaves, I suddenly lose my voice. To this day I don't know why; it might have been nerves – but I'll never know. All I know is I can't do the show, so Dick Hardwick fills in for a couple of weeks and in that time falls in love with the job. By the time I finally return Dick has the full-time gig.

In spite of any full-time dreams I might have had, I have to admit and I believe to this day that Dick was the right guy for the job. He exudes that Disney brand of wholesome charm and he's funny and talented as anyone I've ever met. All the same, it is a bitter pill to swallow. A friend tries to console me with the old phrase, "When God closes a door, somewhere he opens a window." So I start looking around for a window.

Two benefits of working in Disneyland: 1) the opportunity to peek behind the curtain and see where and how the magic is created; and 2) the chance to network with the 'magicians'.

About this time the Disney University is hosts a seminar on careers at WED Enterprises, and the guest lecturer is Imagineer Tony Baxter. He shares stories of his early experiences in Anaheim, Orlando and Glendale and then turns to discuss his current project, a new pavilion for the upcoming EPCOT Center in Walt Disney World.

Walt used to delight in telling people about his next project, watching their reactions to each new detail as he described it, using their response to gauge the quality of each idea and to fire his own enthusiasm for the story being told. All Imagineers were like that once, in the days before we Disney Fans drove them underground as competition and legal concerns made secrecy a necessary priority

On this day, though, with this audience – Tony shares ideas and graphics from his latest effort, Kodak's Journey Into Imagination. He displays a series of concept sketches of the building and describes the ride system, then he shows us a sketch of the two host characters of the pavilion...

And once again, my life changes.

According to Tony, Dreamfinder and Figment represent the two halves of the human mind; Dreamfinder is the practical, experienced, educated left side of the brain, whereas Figment represents the impulsive, wild, childlike right side. Together they'll host a spectacular trip through the creative process... *and* they'll be the only Disney characters in EPCOT Center.

I'm suddenly seized with the same thought I'd experienced twelve years ago when I first saw Wally Boag at the Golden Horseshoe. I know what I want to do next with my life...

I want to be the Dreamfinder.

Immediately following Tony's presentation at Disney University, I head up to Wally's dressing room and call WED Enterprises. An old friend from my Magic Mountain days, Ken Lisi, is in charge of the WED Recording Studio. I ask Ken if he can get me a recording of the Dreamfinder's voice from the upcoming attraction. He is only too happy to help and invites me to come by to pick up a cassette of the attraction's opening scene the following afternoon.

The next day I arrive at WED Headquarters in Glendale, California. Ken meets me in the lobby with a cassette marked 'Imagination Turntable' and I'm ready to head home and start working on matching the voice on the tape. But before I can go, Ken leads me past the receptionist and back into the maze of Imagineering offices where he introduces me to Tony Baxter and his fellow Imagineer, Barry Braverman.

The three of them take me back to a staging area where I get my first look at the flying Dreamcatcher machine from Journey Into Imagination. It's set up on sawhorses in the middle of the huge room, connected by cables to a bank of computers. Tony explains that they have just finished programming the opening scene of the ride; and so saying he pushes a button and the Audio-Animatronic Dreamfinder and his airship spring to life.

The most amazing moment. To stand there and know I'm among the first to see this technological miracle, this brilliant piece of storytelling and to know that what I'm seeing could be the model for my next creative goal. Even as I stand there thoroughly enchanted, I am aware of the responsibility I'd be taking on – to bring this character and everything he represents into the real world. And as Dreamfinder creates Figment out of his component sparks, I feel like a single parent seeing his adopted child for the first time… charmed and challenged.

A large part of what makes the scene work is the voices of Dreamfinder and Figment. Originally performed by talented comic actor Chuck McCann, the voice of Dreamfinder is a nimble impression of film star Frank Morgan, who portrayed the title role in MGM's 1939 production of *The Wizard of Oz*. While people might not recognize the source, it is a voice they will have heard all their life, and it carries a strong emotional connection for anyone who grew up with that movie.

The Imagineers had a harder time finding just the right voice for Figment. Besides the popular voice actors of the day, they auditioned children, old women who smoke and lots of little people. They finally resorted to putting wanted posters around WED, featuring a sketch of the dragon with the caption, 'Have you seen my voice?'

It wasn't until veteran actor Billy Barty came in to read that everyone knew they'd found that wild, childlike sound they were looking for. With his vocal tracks sped up slightly, Billy Barty was Figment – and always will be. After I view the opening scene, Tony, Barry and I sit down for a long chat about the evolution of 'Imagination', the creative, inspirational agenda of EPCOT Center and their hopes for the new characters. As one desperate for direction I take their words to heart and start to plot my path toward inhabiting the being and world of Dreamfinder.

In no time at all I've memorized the opening scene of the Journey Into Imagination. I can recite all the dialogue; now I have to learn to recreate the Dreamfinder's voice.

My old friend from Universal, Jeff Palmer, is a talented director, working in media production at Chiat Day Advertising. We meet up in his Downtown L.A. recording studio where he coaches me into matching the sound and spirit originated by Chuck McCann. When I get home I can't wait to try out my new pipes, so I create an outgoing message for my phone machine in the Dreamfinder voice:

"Hello, there! So glad you called. Ron's off on a Flight of Fancy and won't be back for some time, so leave a message after the tone and he'll call you the moment he gets back!"

I head out for the evening and when I return my phone machine indicates that I have received ten calls. But when I try listening to the messages I find most of them are blank. Only the last caller left a message: it's my friend Ken from the WED Studio, telling me to call him first thing in the morning. I can't help imagining that all those other callers might have been Tony and Barry and other Imagineers calling to hear the voice of the Dreamfinder.

The next morning I call Ken at WED and he tells me I guessed right the night before. And can I come in that afternoon to record some pickup lines for the new attraction?

That afternoon I meet with Ken and X Atencio, the man who wrote Pirates of the Caribbean and The Haunted Mansion. They ask me to read a couple of lines of dialogue from the new attraction, then we go into the recording studio to lay down the tracks.

I'm thrilled to be in the recording booth at WED, filling in the bits of narration unrecorded by Chuck McCann: one of the couplets from the Realm of Science ("Skyrockets soar toward outer space/ Imagine yourself in an infinite place"), the dialogue for Dreamfinder on the camera crane ("Figment and I have certainly enjoyed our Journey Into Imagination with you..."), the instructions for the Electronic Philharmonic (this recording was never used) and the 'step out to your right' dialogue for the end of the ride.

A day or two later I'm back at Disneyland for another late shift. I show up early and head to the Entertainment Offices to meet with Sonny Anderson, who had recommended me to Wally Boag two years prior. I tell Sonny about my interest in playing Dreamfinder at EPCOT Center and my experience with Tony and X at WED. He picks up the phone and calls Florida as I'm sitting there. "Hello... Yes, I'd like to speak to Pete Bloustein, please."

I start giggling because I can't believe what's about to happen. "Peter? Sonny Anderson. Listen, are we still planning on having the strolling Dreamfinder at Imagination? I got a guy here who I think might be right for it... Ron Schneider... Why are you both laughing?" After a brief conversation (and after I tell Sonny to say hello to my old friend), Sonny hangs up and gives me the job.

I practically bounce out of Sonny's Office. His secretary asks why I'm so jubilant and I tell her about Dreamfinder and my new job. She asks to hear the voice of the new character. I lay a little of my new voice on her and am surprised to see her start weeping. I can see that I've lucked into something special, a role with such a great potential for affecting the public.

I'm scheduled to fly down to Orlando on Saturday, September 18th. Two weeks prior, early on the 4th, I'm still in bed when I get a call from Barry Braverman. "Ron, we need you in Florida."

Yawning, "I know, Barry. I'll be there in two weeks."

"No, today. We need you to fly down today."

Disney's contract with Kodak stipulates that at least one of the pavilion's three attractions must be operating on EPCOT Center's opening day, October 1st. But *Magic Journeys*, the 3D movie, is running behind schedule... the Imagination ride won't be open for another six months... and – because the technologies involved are so advanced – the interactive displays of the ImageWorks are deemed 'iffy'.

I'm needed to shoot a preview film for the pavilion to be run in the Magic Eye Theater in case *Magic Journeys* can't be delivered on time. That afternoon I fly in to Orlando and am whisked away to the EPCOT Center site.

Months before, Dreamfinder had made his public debut at the Imagination Pavilion's groundbreaking ceremony in the person of Joe Hudgins, a member of the Dapper Dans barbershop quartet. The day I arrive in Florida, EPCOT Center Costuming is piecing together a suit for me and the ladies of Cosmetology are re-styling Joe's wig, beard and mustache for me to wear. After a fitting, I'm driven over to the pavilion to take a look around as the sun sets; the plan is to shoot my scenes tomorrow morning.

Barry Braverman and I have dinner in the EPCOT Center construction cafeteria, which will later become Le Cellier in the Canada Pavilion. We hear they're running previews of *Impressions de France* so after dinner we walk over to catch a screening of the new film in the France Pavilion.

The following morning we shoot silent footage of the prototype Figment puppet and I strolling through the Rainbow Corridor in the Image Works and the Dreamport, the only section of the ride that looks finished at this point. Then it's back on a plane to L.A. for a three day shoot at WED Enterprises' production facility in Tujunga, California.

To Fantasy Film Fans of my generation, Mike Jittlov is a fascinating hero; a man of idiosyncratic vision and extraordinary skill. His experiments with living stop motion are legend, so when I arrive in Tujunga and find myself working with this talented young man I can hardly believe it. Mike has been hired by Disney (itself a cause for celebration) to create *Dream Finder Run*, a special effects sequence for the Imagination Preview Film.

Together we spend three nights in WED's Tujunga installation. In every shot the camera is undercranked – running at less than the standard twenty-four frames per second. I run full speed through the scene while WED Cast Members move around me, going about their business in slow motion. When the film is projected at normal speed, it looks like a pixilated Dreamfinder is racing through Imagineering at super speed, checking up on the progress of his new Florida home.

The best part of the whole experience is the long breaks between shots when I can go exploring through the deserted offices of WED Tujunga. Among other things, I find a book full of early developmental sketches of Dreamfinder, Figment and the Imagination ride. The worst part is all that running on WED's ultra-hard concrete floors; I'm in quite a lot of pain towards the end of the second day.

A week later I'm invited to Walt Disney Studios for a screening of the finished film. The staging and animation are brilliant but I can't get past the way I look. Instead of the fanciful Dreamfinder of my imagining, I look like A Guy in A Bad Beard. The talented young lady who had done my make-up had no doubt done the best she could with what she had, but – for me at least – the make-up doesn't work.

As it turns out, director Murray Lerner will finish *Magic Journeys* in time for EPCOT Center's opening, and *Dream Finder Run* won't be seen in its entirety for decades, when it will finally pop up online. I must admit I'm relieved that it will not be people's introduction to the characters.

Chapter 11
DREAMFINDING 101 (1982)

On September 8th, 1982, I perform for the last time in the *Golden Horseshoe Revue*, working with the great Jay Meyer and the lovely Terri Robinson. I wrap up the Traveling Salesman routine and step offstage. Jay comes on and announces, "Professor Ron Schneider, Ladies and Gentlemen!" while I come back for a fast bow before making my quick change into Pecos Bill.

But when I return, instead of the usual band play-off and thunderous applause, I hear nothing. Nada. No applause, no music. I look at the house, I look at the band and I look over at Jay who is grinning from ear to ear. Jay finally says, "Folks, let's send him to Florida in style!" The crowd cheers, Jay and Terry are laughing and I know I've been had.

Here's an absolute truth about opening any new theme park or attraction: you're never ready. It's always a scramble to get everything up and running for the guests and there's never enough time or money to have everything in place for the cast. Dining and break areas, maintenance and support systems are just a few of the things that may only come with time.

In the case of a new one-of-a-kind character like Dreamfinder, there can be only one advocate if the situation is to improve; it falls to me to step up and let people know what I need. I figure it will take one year before all the pieces come together to make things comfortable and consistent. It winds up taking two.

The prototype Figment is a crude puppet cast in very stiff rubber that is next-to-impossible to animate. He has been sculpted in such a way that if you hold your arm comfortably at your side, it looks like he's going to fall out of your grasp; to hold him upright, you have to hold your arm up with your elbow uncomfortably thrust forward. And his lower jaw is too small to accommodate my thumb, so I have to curl it under to fit inside.

The false arm that appears to support the dragon is a muslin tube full of cotton batting and is too long for the job. On set, it looks like my wrist has been broken in two places, so I spend my first eighteen months as Dreamfinder trying to keep my left side away from the guests – especially those with cameras

The wigs are fine, but we have no hand-netted beards or mustaches. The talented ladies from EPCOT Center Cosmetology have to cut them out of wigs, so they are thick and unwieldy and never sit right. I have to smile broadly when I glue the mustache on and if I dare to stop smiling it pops right off.

But by far my most pressing need is a break area. EPCOT Center is so large that a bus must carry me from wardrobe and cosmetology to the bus stop behind the Imagination Pavilion and even then it's a long walk to the building itself. There is a small break area for the attraction hosts, but the lack of privacy and preparation space makes it totally unsuitable for my needs. So I go exploring.

Upstairs in the ImageWorks, behind the Electronic Philharmonic, is a small access hall. There's a custodial closet, a couple of locked doors and a fire room: a bare concrete floor and four walls with a loud, continuously-running fan and oppressive fluorescent lighting. The room is meant to be used by handicapped guests in case of emergency if they can't get safely downstairs. The door has no lock, so I move in.

Three folding plastic chairs and a plank of wood make up the furnishings of my first dressing room in the pavilion. Ideal access to the ImageWorks – and a nearby staircase down to the Picture Taking Garden – are its only assets.

As soon as I was cast as Dreamfinder, I had started flailing around for some idea of what I would actually do on the job. I'd seen Disney characters pose for pictures all my life, but their only agenda was promotion and nostalgia. In their prime they provided a personal, spontaneous experience with the guest; with the advent of autograph books and managed crowd contact, this personal experience is often reduced to long lines and quick photo ops.

Dreamfinder, the Imagination Pavilion and all of EPCOT Center are about your place in the world and discovering your own creative potential. I'm determined to bring that to the experience of meeting the guest. If I'm going to last 5+ years in this new job (and not go stir crazy) I can't be just another notch-in-the-kids'-autograph-books.

First thing I do is study dragons. I find a book called, *The Flight of Dragons* (1979) by Peter Dickinson; he states that just because dragons are fictional creatures there is no reason they shouldn't be studied seriously. That really appeals to me.

My greatest early influence is Real Musgrave's 'Pocket Dragons', a massive line of collectible dragon figurines. In a store in Santa Monica I find a collection of greeting cards by Musgrave. They feature paintings of an elderly wizard with a long white beard who travels in an elegant hot air balloon with dozens of these little green dragons. The dragons are everywhere, get into everything, but the wizard takes it all in his stride. The paintings give me valuable insight into the relationship between Dreamfinder and Figment. I also find inspiration in *Creative Dramatics* (1958) by Geraldine Brain Siks, a textbook detailing a form of participatory improvisation with kids. I think this could be used in a storytelling show with the characters a couple of times a day. Beyond that I read up on topics Dreamfinder might be conversant in: creativity, science, nature… subjects that might make for interesting interaction.

What I don't know is… will any of this preparation prove useful when the rubber (dragon) meets the road?

For my first two weeks in Florida, the Company puts me up at the Holiday Inn and provides a rental car to help me get settled. I scout around for an apartment, shop for a car, attend fittings and learn my way around backstage. The park isn't open yet, but there's lots to see and do.

One night I return to my room to find a thick manila envelope on the bed. Inside is a script for the *EPCOT Center Grand Opening TV Special*. My name and 'Dreamfinder' have been written on the cover.

Excited, I open the script and check to see what I get to do in the show. At last I find my scene. I'm to appear as if by magic in front of the Imagination Pavilion, to explain the new attraction to young Drew Barrymore, fresh from her success in *E.T., The Extra-Terrestrial*, and to the host of the show – Danny Kaye.

Danny freakin' Kaye! I have a scene in a network TV show with Danny "The-pellet-with-the-poison's-in-the-vessel-with-the-pestle" Kaye!! I can't help thinking, 'It's good to be the Dreamfinder'.

On the day of the TV shoot, EPCOT Center is completely mobbed with media. There are TV and film crews and radio hosts everywhere, broadcasting live from every landscaped area and pre-recording segments in every nook and cranny.

Meanwhile, it's my very first day in character in the park. I don't know what I'm about to face, all I know is that whatever mistakes I make will be recorded on tape, broadcast live across America and will probably haunt me for the rest of my life.

Before heading over to Imagination for my scene in the TV Special, I report to the Italy Pavilion with Figment to be interviewed live on NBC for *The Today Show*. Bryant Gumbel interviews Barry Braverman and I about Imagination. The interview goes pretty well, although when I see the tape later I hate the way I look and sound. The wig and beard are all wrong and I'm pushing too hard… like a new employee on his first day. Not surprising, I guess.

Arriving in Future World, I find the video crew on the walkway between Imagination and The Land. Drew is waiting to start and we have a great time; she's charmed by Figment in spite of my primitive animation skills.

There's a fourth performer in our scene... and when I arrive for the shoot, I'm greeted by a robot named Seco. I've never seen a character like him, and while I figure there has to be someone nearby voicing and operating him I never manage to spot him.

At last here comes Mr. Kaye followed closely by his umbrella handler. I watch as a family of guests approach him for an autograph. Danny begs off (not at all politely) before hurrying over to where we're waiting. He's very brusque with Drew, but she seems to expect the treatment. I quietly put away any illusions I have of connecting with My Hero, or of telling him what his work has meant to me.

We wrap the scene pretty fast. The script is simple and a lot of what I do will be heard as a voice-over in the broadcast while viewers watch clips from the Mike Jittlov-directed preview film. When we're done I bid a fond farewell to Miss Barrymore; and I get a warmer goodbye from Seco than I do from Mr. Kaye.

Before I can duck backstage and finally peel off the beard and mustache, I head over to the sound man to have my body mic removed. He opens the front of my vest and shirt and is fishing around for my mic pack when a Disney photographer comes over with Danny. "I'd like to get a few pictures of Mr. Kaye with the Dreamfinder!"

At this point we're outside surrounded by guests and I'm only half dressed (and remember, this whole time I'm still animating the dragon, trying to 'keep him alive' for the on-lookers)! "Please give us a second while I button back up... "

But Danny won't wait. "We don't have that much time." He grabs my shirt and vest and holds them closed under my chin... and Danny, Figment and I smile for the camera.

Somewhere in a file drawer under the Magic Kingdom there are pictures I've never seen of me and my childhood hero, where it looks like he's about to punch me in my broadly-smiling mouth. What they don't show is that inside I feel like I've swallowed the pellet with the poison.

A few days later Figment and I step out for our first regular day on the job – and all anyone wants is to have their picture taken with us and to get my autograph. And I pose and I sign and I pose and I sign... and the whole time I'm thinking: Is this it? Have I come all this way just to pose for pictures?

How can I get these people to engage with me creatively? How can I get them to play like they did back in Spillikin Corners? And most importantly: How can I make our interaction an extension of the themes and ideas presented in the ride?

Then one day – a miracle. I spontaneously react to a small child as if I've never seen one before. His parents laugh and the child himself grows very serious and explains to me what he is (a boy named Michael) and where he comes from (Orlando). I act fascinated... his parents are amused... and he is suddenly thinking about himself and his life in a new and objective way.

I have inadvertently stumbled on the perfect premise for my guest interaction. By turning the spotlight on the child as a unique and wonderful being   , I am in essence echoing the opening scene of the Journey Into Imagination; but the sparks I'm collecting now are the guests that I meet.

I had been letting the guests' priorities dictate my actions. But now I am playing the Dreamfinder's game and making them play along. Figment becomes an interested onlooker; by playing down his importance their fascination draws them in even deeper. And finally, by taking control of the crowd I'm able to turn each guest interaction into a show that reinforces the Pavilion's themes while entertaining those waiting to play.

The guests' desire for a picture and an autograph is my 'operational reality'. By choosing to deal with it creatively, I'm able to turn what could be a burden into a positive asset (and my job into an absolute joy).

My day of Dreamfinding begins at EPCOT Center Entertainment Costume Issue where I pick up my suit and my co-star. Then I head over to EPCOT Center Cosmetology to get my wig, beard and mustache.

Finally I catch the bus over to the Imagination Pavilion and my dressing room. The park is just opening so I rarely run into guests on my way upstairs.

As soon as I'm settled in I head down to the garden area, which is also deserted. Guests are just starting to pass overhead on the monorail, checking out the pavilions as they ride by. They're especially excited because for most of them this is their first look at the new park, and they'll be packed in, standing room only, with their eyes glued to what's happening on the ground.

I'll stand close by the building with my back to the monorail beam, chatting with Figment about some architectural feature. As the monorail comes by Figment looks back over my shoulder, sees the people on board and gets excited. He gets me to turn and I spot the guests a moment after they see me. I can practically hear them... and I clearly see them, pointing and waving at us as they sail past.

Another favorite morning bit is to walk up behind a kid in the ImageWorks who is intently filling in a drawing of Figment and I on the Magic Palette. We silently watch a while, then I softly remark to Figment, "He's very good." The look on the child's face when they turn and see us is a great way to start my day.

I especially like to pose in pictures I'm not supposed to be in; nowadays this is called a 'photobomb'. If I see someone at a distance looking toward me but focusing on something close to them, I'll smile and wave to their camera; I like to imagine them examining their pictures at home and being surprised to find Dreamfinder and Figment waving at them in the background.

In these early days I am constantly surprised the guests seem to know who we are, in spite of the ride not being open. Still we stroll the gardens, up into the pyramid and through the ImageWorks playing with the crowds and trying our new wings.

Every day I use one of the breaks between my 30 minute sets to venture into the ride to see how everything is progressing. The first time I do this I take Figment with me and we play at discovering everything together. This, as you might imagine, causes quite a stir. It's a big building and a lot has been finished, but suddenly I'll hit a pocket of activity and everyone reacts to seeing the Dreamfinder walking around under his own power.

Strolling through the Dreamport one day I hear a call from above, "Hi, Ron!" I look up and there on a scaffold is Gary Bell, technical director of my L.A.C.C. production of *I Think We're All Bozos on This Bus*. He stands up there waving at me, just as he did that night on the theater building when he surprised me with the spotlight. He's been freelancing with WED Enterprises and is assisting on the installation.

Another time I discover Tony Baxter sitting at the entrance to the ride's Realm of Image Technology. He's cutting plexiglass rods, fashioning a directional sign to replace a projection that has failed to materialize.

My constant, casual walking tours of the ride reveal many wonderful details in the sets. The toilet bowl float and gelatin mold used as dressing on the Dreamcatcher... the Mickey Mouse-shaped island on the globe in the Realm of Science... the revolving panel in the Performance section that shows an applauding white glove – with four fingers and two thumbs!

It seems I'm always discovering something new in the ride. And even when I'm convinced I've seen and learned it all, it can still surprise me. A year or two later I ride through completely shocked to find the place filled with the most beautiful low-lying fog! This gives the entire experience the feeling of floating along on a cloud. In the Realms of Art and Literature you cannot imagine the effect this has and I'm thrilled to think this is a new, permanent addition to the ride.

Alas I'm wrong on both counts. It's not new... the 30+ fog machines that are supplying this glorious haze have been there, built into the sets, since the opening. And it's not permanent; it can't be; the long-term effect on the ride would be disastrous. The way it was explained to me, it's a water-based fog and the sets were painted with water-based paints.

Ah, well... Like so much of life, it was great while it lasted.

Being the only Disney characters in EPCOT Center, it falls to us to make the rounds of press and public events before, during and even after opening. We're usually accompanied by a Kodak Representative, but when it becomes time to do a parade, photo shoot or broadcast, we're left to my own devices.

The unique nature of the character means that I can discuss the reality of Walt Disney, EPCOT Center and the creative process without having to limit myself to the backstory of Imagination, a distinct advantage over the regular stable of Disney fantasy folk. Before each interview I take a moment to explain the difference to my host, inviting him or her to ask me anything (except about the real me).

I do, however, warn the various cameramen to avoid shooting my left side since – when seen from that angle – my phony arm looks particularly fake. On a Miami phone-in program where the cameraman chose to ignore my warning, we only receive one call: "That arm that's holding the dragon; that's not your real arm, is it?"

I am momentarily nonplussed. All the preparation I've done, trying to imagine every possible question or circumstance, and I'm caught short on this first call. I don't know where it came from, but without thinking I shoot back, "Can you keep a secret?"

The caller says, "Yes."

"So can I." Crisis averted.

Chapter 12
MORE THAN I
IMAGINED (1983-87)

Finally, in April of 1983, all of Kodak's Journey Into Imagination pavilion is ready for its official debut. The Entertainment Division creates an opening spectacle featuring the Kids of the Kingdom in turn-of-the-century costumes and daytime fireworks and a wonderful arrangement of *Flash, Bang, Wallop!*, the song about old time photography from the musical *Half a Sixpence*. The plan is that halfway through I will roll in with Figment aboard one of the electric coaches from Main Street, U.S.A. to introduce myself and my little purple creation to the world.

This event will use the same music track as the Pavilion's groundbreaking did many months before. On that occasion, Joe Hudgins of the Dapper Dans had portrayed Dreamfinder and sang *One Little Spark* for the very first time. Joe carried the prototype Figment puppet, voiced on the music track by Billy Barty himself, and the two characters sang the verse and chorus together – simultaneously – in perfect counterpoint.

Now the Dreamfinder script has been updated for the ride dedication. I will introduce myself and sing the verse about creating Figment. Then the pre-recorded voice of Figment will interrupt me and we will chat, while I animate the dragon to Billy's dialogue. The tough part comes after our scene together, when I will sing the chorus of *One Little Spark* while Figment sings the verse; I'll have to perform one set of lyrics while manipulating my co-star to sing something entirely different.

After much practice I learn to move my left hand in the rhythmic pattern of the verse while singing the chorus – and the whole thing looks seamless. Now I just have to do it in front of the world press and the Board of Directors of both Eastman Kodak and Walt Disney Productions.

I check in at the pavilion at four in the morning, ready to run through everything. Scores of seats have been set up in front of a small stage by the pavilion marquee. The first run-through goes well, I rattle off my lines and lyrics flawlessly and Figment's voice comes in right on cue, interrupting me as planned. Our duet is fine and I even get a few compliments on my puppetry. We run it two more times and then everyone scatters to grab some food before the big show.

When we return, the seats are filled with all the Disney and Kodak executives. I take my place in my electric car up in the garden behind the temporary stage and wait for my cue.

When we drive up to the stage, I'm juggling a bulky microphone in my right hand and the dragon in my left, but manage to hop off the car without incident. I start the dialogue and launch into the verse about, "two tiny wings, eyes big and yellow," and I can see children in the crowd utterly charmed by what they're watching. A little more dialogue and now it's time for Figment to interrupt.

I open the puppet's mouth to catch Figment's first line of dialogue... and there's no sound. The background music is still playing under the scene, so I know the system is working, and everything I've sung up till now has been in perfect synch with the music, so I know it's cued up properly.

My mind is racing. After what feels like an eternity I deliver my next line to Figment, but nothing comes back. At first.

Finally Billy Barty's voice blasts forth smack in the middle of his second line of dialogue. It's right where it should be, so I know for certain what just happened. Up in the sound booth, whoever is running things had the volume turned down on Figment's track. When he saw the situation he had to scramble to turn it up quickly.

The rest of the show goes perfectly; I match Figment's movements on the duet and we finally invite everyone to join me in taking the inaugural ride on the Journey Into Imagination.

The audience rises and follows me onto the ride. Figment and I are in the first car of the first train, joined by a couple of dozen other lucky travelers. I'm working Figment all the way through, playing his amazement at what we're seeing... and then we get to the introductory moment, where Dreamfinder is discovered flying in the Dreamcatcher; the same scene that so amazed me when I first saw it at WED.

But this time – about thirty seconds into the scene – the sound cuts out. The Audio-Animatronic Dreamfinder is just getting to the point of creating his imaginary friend and all we can hear are the clicks and hiss of the show effects and animation.

Without missing a beat, I start delivering the Dreamfinder's dialogue, synching my performance to that of my mechanical doppelganger. After a minute, the sound returns and I'm rewarded with a round of applause from the rest of my tour group.

When the ride ends we all gather in the garden area for a reception and I have my picture taken with Dick Nunis, Tony Baxter and the CEO of Kodak, before going upstairs to collapse in my dressing room. Thank God – we're finally open.

Oh, and in spite of my best efforts I never do find out who the sound technician was that screwed up Figment's cue.

Soon I'm sharing my dressing room with other actors as a new operating schedule is implemented. Each day finds two of us working, both covering an a.m. and p.m. shift to provide around-the-clock Dreamfinders for visitors to Imagination.

By this time we have a real dressing room behind the Electronic Philharmonic with real furniture and a make-up table. I bring up some milk crates for book shelves and fill them with the reference materials I used for the characters: books on the creative process, Disney history, Walt's life, the evolution of EPCOT Center and improvisational storytelling.

I try to share my own research and teach each one what I've learned since I started. They're just not interested, so after a while I take the books back home for safe-keeping.

I'm disappointed that I can't pass anything on to the other actors, but the fact is that, while I've been given the responsibility of training them, I have not been given the authority. So each man develops his own approach to the character, his own take on the voice and his own way with Figment.

There are very few 'average' days for my imaginary friend and I.

An attractions host comes back one day to tell me there's a family upstairs from Give Kids The World, so I hurry out to meet a sweet twelve year old blind girl in a wheelchair. She asks me if I'd like to take an imaginary trip with her, so I ask, "Where shall we go?"

She tells me, "To the moon." Then she takes my hand and leads me on this wonderful Adventure in Space. Here I am – the 'spirit of imagination' – totally left in the dust by this wonderful, creative child.

Another time I'm kneeling to talk to a young man in the garden and out of the corner of my eye I see Mark Wilson, star of *The Magic Land of Allakazam*, watching me work and laughing with his son. He doesn't notice me notice him, so when Figment sees him first and then lets me know he's watching, my reaction really busts him up.

I get to meet a lot of famous people by hanging with Figment… comic legend Red Skelton, writer Ray Bradbury, rocker Eddie Van Halen, ventriloquist Jimmy Nelson and ubiquitous TV host Regis Philbin.

I get a call one afternoon that Michael Jackson is downstairs in the garden and asking to see us, so down we go. The entire garden is roped off and he's out by himself watching the Leap Frog Fountains. *Thriller* had debuted the night before on MTV, so I mention that Figment and I had watched it together. Michael gets a big kick out of this.

Some time later I'm told that, while visiting the park, M.J. would use our Dreamfinder dressing room as a place to take a break from the crowds, so I and the other Dreamfinders redecorate. We put up a Captain EO poster, but we cut out Michael's face and replace it with a giant picture of Howard the Duck.

In an effort to draw more guests over to the national pavilions in the afternoon, Creative Entertainment dreams up *Skyleidoscope*, a weekend air and water spectacular for the World Showcase Lagoon. This is to be a battle between giant dragons and the World Showcase Navy, under the command of the Dreamfinder – in his flying machine!

So they build these giant dragon boats, buy dozens of jet skis and some ultralight aircraft and start choreographing daytime fireworks and writing a script and an original score to be recorded by the London Symphony Orchestra. I'm called in to Studio D, the recording studio located under the Magic Kingdom, where I lay down the dialogue. I even get to do three different voices: the Show Announcer, a British Commander and the flying Dreamfinder.

And they build a real flying replica of the Dreamcatcher to be piloted by a live actor (no, not me) in a Dreamfinder costume. One little bitty problem… In order to lawfully fly the Dreamcatcher over the public as intended, the pilot has to have one hundred hours of training in the machine under the tutelage of a pilot who has had one hundred hours of training in the machine. That means, kids, that 200 hours of training had to go on and – the Florida weather being what it is –that isn't feasible.

So when *Skyleidoscope* premiers, instead of a flying Dreamfinder 80' in the air, the guests see me – riding in a speed boat around the perimeter of the lagoon. I then mount a 20⊠ Genie lift on a barge and 'direct' the action while my voice blasts from speakers all around me and jet skis and fireworks do battle with giant dragons.

Skyleidoscope is spectacular; there can be no doubt about that… it also makes very little sense. I speak to a large number of folks who are thoroughly puzzled by *Skyleidoscope*, which is dubbed by some, 'The Mistake on The Lake'. Somewhere between the original concept and the execution we lost the guests. I think there's a lesson here somewhere.

It's fascinating, when opening a new park or attraction, to watch it evolve as all the dreams and plans collide with operational reality. And no park has gone through more dramatic changes than EPCOT Center. The corporate shifts of the past twenty years have virtually re-purposed the park, changing its core message substantially. This is especially true of Future World.

But back in the '80s Future World isn't just about the future; it's about your future. The shows and experiences of EPCOT Center are meant to resonate after your visit. This is deeply felt by the WED team that created it and, because of the Disney corporate culture of the time, they are free to let that purpose drive every creative decision.

That's why there is no Mickey Mouse in 1982 EPCOT Center.

A decision like excluding the Disney Characters from the new billion-dollar park could only have been approved by an executive board that was 100% behind the Imagineers' Grand Vision. They had to know what it would cost them in potential revenue to keep the Mouseka-Merchandise out of the Centorium and other merchandise locations. One unfortunate side effect of this decision is the rumor that 'EPCOT Center is boring'; folks who actually visit the park find it isn't true, but to a lot of people the idea of a Disney park without Mice is unthinkable.

When we open, Figment is a financial bonanza waiting to happen... and will have to keep on waiting-to-happen, since the Company has little faith in his marketability. That changes with time, though. (I'll never forget Figment's reaction the first time he and I run into a kid wearing a 'Figment Head' hat!)

When the time comes for a regime change, EPCOT Center is an established success. In the time since opening, more pavilions have come along, new technologies have been introduced and the philosophy is working. EPCOT Center is moving forward as the Imagineers had planned. It might not be making as much money as its sister Kingdom, but it is successfully fulfilling its higher purpose.

Then along comes a new management team; one with a different way of measuring success. They perceive, and rightly so, that the Disney franchise is worth a lot more than it's taking in. And it should be said that most of their ideas are pretty good... especially that first ten years of expansion.

How did The Mouse move in on our territory? The way I heard the story is that the new owners were taking their first stroll through EPCOT Center with their families when one precious offspring expressed a desire for Mouse Attire. When their guide informed them there is no Mickey Mouse in EPCOT Center, the New Leader announced, "There is now."

And the Merchandising Gods smiled.

Figment is no longer the only game in town. There is *some* satisfaction, though: I'm told that in every shop where both are offered, The Dragon outsells The Mouse.

Back in the '80s, the Company would throw an annual Christmas Party for Cast Members in the Magic Kingdom. The park closes early to guests and we have run of the place, including free cookies and hot chocolate, a free color portrait and a special performance of *Fantasy on Parade*.

One year as I'm watching the parade, it strikes me that there are thousands of EPCOT Center Cast Members in attendance, but nothing at the party that represents their home park. Thus begins my campaign to bring Figment to the Magic Kingdom for Christmas.

After two years of nudging, the powers-that-be decide the dragon and I will ride the Teddy Bear Chair in the next Christmas Parade for Cast Members. This is a special seat that swings out on a boom from the front of the Toy Factory Float. It can move up and down and from one side of the street to the other, controlled by a joystick on the left side of the chair. (Well, normally it can move up and down... Apparently Figment weighs a LOT more than the Teddy Bear, so we just swing side-to-side.)

At the appointed time, we report to the parade staging area behind Main Street's City Hall and ride the fork lift up to our perch on the float. We're up there for a few minutes, waiting to start, when it starts drizzling. Under my top hat it doesn't bother me much, but the next thing I know there's an umbrella being pushed up at me. I look down to see who my angel of mercy is...

I should have guessed. Snow White.

When we finally roll onto Main Street the cries of "Dreamfinder! Figment!" are thrilling. Everyone is surprised to see us (especially since I told no one of my little campaign). We make the loop of Town Square and turn toward the castle when it occurs to me that my Li'l Purple Buddy has never been in the Magic Kingdom before!

Suddenly I'm back in high school, guiding a first time visitor through the park. I start pointing out the landmarks to Figment who's wide-eyed with excitement (as opposed to his normal state of just being wide-eyed).

Soon the park discontinues the private Christmas Party for Cast Members, but I'll always be thankful we had that night to celebrate and show-off. And that Snow White is one thoughtful kid.

If you've ever visited Central Florida in the summer months, you may be wondering how I could stand to perform all day in that heat. The answer is I really didn't have to; I had an entire pavilion to play in.

The cold, hard facts are these – guests are less likely to play if they're uncomfortably hot, cold, sweaty or soaked... if it's too windy my hair gets completely wild... and at certain times of year we get inundated with swarms of 'lovebugs' (and not the Disney kind) which love to nest and procreate in my whiskers. So when I decide it's advisable, I move indoors under the pyramids or play in the ImageWorks.

Management frequently 'suggests' that I remain outside in the Picture Taking Garden; however, those who make that suggestion never have the last word. I make a point of finishing every such conversation with this: "I'll absolutely be outside... unless it's too hot, too cold, too windy, too rainy, too muggy or too buggy."

It's quite an adjustment going from performing at the Golden Horseshoe to Dreamfinding for a living. At the one you've got 310 happy people who have made reservations and stood in line to see you and who laugh and applaud your act; at the other you're competing with rides and restrooms, performing anonymously, seeking your reward in the look in a child's eyes or a spontaneous moment with a family of skeptics.

One day I'm working upstairs, surrounded by guests and having a swell time, when I notice a young man with a clipboard and a hand clicker standing on the far side of the room, watching me and clicking away madly. Once I've worked my way through the waiting guests I amble over and ask what it is he's doing.

"I'm counting the number of people you're affecting. Not just the ones who interact with you, but the number that stop and smile or stay and watch for any length of time. You're averaging about 600 people every thirty minutes." Roughly double what I was doing at the Horseshoe! That's good to know.

The role of Dreamfinder offers its own special frustrations. The custom made beards and mustaches are fragile things that will look good for only so long, growing threadbare over time. And the talented Disney cosmetologists might not have the time to make the most of what's there. The result is that I never know until I walk into the costume shop each morning how I am going to look that day. This uncertainty begins to rankle; after all, we've had five years to get this right, right?

Then one especially broiling summer day, I leave costuming in full regalia and board the shuttle to the Imagination Pavilion; a long, slow trip on a packed bus that delivers Cast Members to all the World Showcase pavilions before finally arriving on the far side of Future World.

It's standing room only on this day and I'm jammed in right by the front door. The air conditioning on the old bus isn't working, and the only window that opens is – you've guessed it – the one by the driver, so she's the only person on the bus who enjoying the hot breeze from outside. I ask about the air conditioning, but her reply is, "I just drive the bus." Obviously, a serious deficit of Pixie Dust.

Even for a crowded bus on a hot day it seems ridiculously hot on board. In desperation I scan the panel of switches at the driver's elbow and notice that the switch marked 'HEATER' is in the 'on' position. "Excuse me, I hate to bother you, I know you're very busy... but you've got the heat on in the bus and we're all dying back here. Could you please just reach over and at least turn the heater off?"

"I just drive the bus."

This is the moment I decide that – if I can help it – I'm not going to be Dreamfinding much longer.

A young lady online asked me once, "I've always dreamed of working in the parks, but I've heard it's a grind and not as much fun as I think. Tell me the truth… If it really is unpleasant, why do the Cast Members seem so happy?"

And in case you've ever wondered the same thing, here's my answer:

The Disney Company makes it possible for its employees to create magic every day, but they can't always make it easy… and it seems to get harder every year.

When someone is hired at Walt Disney World they go through an extensive training program where they learn about Walt, the Company history and the operating philosophy. Back in the day, this was referred to as 'Getting a Dose of Pixie Dust', and the result would stay with you, inspiring and motivating you for months.

The Company still supplies new hires with that first Dose of Dust; but now it comes with a healthy serving of legal warnings and security issues and your work day often has more to do with handling a mob that delighting a child.

Think of it this way: you still get doused with Pixie Dust, but the Dust is now cut with milk sugar and chalk; it doesn't stick like the old stuff. Whatever magic it still provides flakes off quickly, leaving you to deal with the realities of a hot summer day, long lines and guests who resent paying $14 to park.

But since you're still dreaming of creating Disney Magic, I'll tell you a secret: you have to make your own Pixie Dust. You must decide every day that reality is not going to get in your way; instead you embrace it and use your knowledge of the system to your advantage.

You look in the eyes of every happy child and mine the gold that lies there. You learn to endure the operational ironies and focus instead on meeting and exceeding guests' expectations, because the joy in their faces makes it worth the extra effort. You take to heart the words and legacy of Walt and invest yourself in keeping them alive for the child in every adult.

And sometimes it's worth it…

One day I'm wrapping up my last set and heading back to my dressing room to pack up the dragon and go home. I'm moving quickly through the crowd and almost to the door offstage when I break through the crowd and find myself face-to-face with an adorable five-year-old boy.

He's by himself, gazing up at us with a look of total wonder. Assessing the situation I determine I'm safe stopping for a minute to chat so I kneel down and introduce him to Figment. I ask him if he's having fun, how he liked my ride, where's he from – but can get nothing from him except an astounded look. Finally I stand up and tell him, "Well I gotta go now... Goodbye!"

That's when he finds his tongue. "Bye-bye, Jesus."

If moments like that are enough to make you happy, you're going to love working in the parks.

It's just possible that the opening of EPCOT Center called for the largest hiring of performing talent ever undertaken for a new theme park. With all of Future World and nine World Showcase pavilions to populate, a lot of talent is put under contract simultaneously. There are storytellers, candy sculptors, mimes, puppeteers and musicians, singers and dancers of many nations... the list goes on and on.

One highly successful discovery is SAK Theater, a troupe of improvisational storytellers that are discovered performing at local Renaissance Faires. Their unique street shows tell classic stories with only two or three actors by using the audience members to play all the characters. They are fast, funny and perfect for EPCOT Center's World Showcase.

Time for another basic truth about the business: no one works in a theme park because they want to sell Lemon Skweez or put people through a turnstile. Everyone wants to be the guy who dreams up the multi-million dollar projects.

So most of the people in this immense group of talent start thinking up ideas for shows and projects and sending them upstairs to the managers and directors in the hope of making a name for themselves as the next great Imagineer. (Yes, this was going on long before there were Internet Disney Fans.)

The greatest success in this unofficial competition has to be the directors of SAK Theater, who are quickly snapped up by Creative Entertainment and Imagineering to create everything from convention shows to grand openings. The SAK formula of broad characters, improv games and storytelling is applied everywhere and group founder Craig Wilson is eventually installed at WED Enterprises as Imagineering's live performance guru.

I have one good friend who wants to work more hours, so he decides to submit an idea for a new character for the Magic Kingdom. His only problem is that he has no such idea. So, being aware of my background, he asks for my input. I sit down and create a premise, an original character for my friend to play and outline several comic bits. I type all this up and put both our names at the top; mine because I wrote it and his because I want him to get the job.

He distributes the treatment with his name at the top only. One night over dinner I ask him why he took my name off the project. He answers, "I want to have a reputation for creative ideas." Since the fellow is a good friend I decide to chalk it up as 'A Lesson Learned' and let it go… but I swear to myself that I won't make that mistake again.

Not long after that I'm walking through the entertainment offices when a supervisor asks me if I'm Ron Schneider. "I hear you know about medicine shows," he says. He and a fellow supervisor are another pair trying to build a 'creative reputation'. They have an idea for a medicine show for Disney Conventions and ask for my help.

Now here are two members of middle management; people who, supposedly, have the connections to get my work seen by those in power. I write a treatment… and then a full show script and put my name on it next to theirs; by the time it's distributed my new friends are listed as the writers and I'm credited for 'Additional Dialogue'.

I'm furious… and swear to myself that I won't make that mistake again – *again*.

Then I have an idea for a live Dreamfinder show to go up in CommuniCore: a simple storytelling adventure with me, Figment and a large group of young guests. I mention this idea to a friend in video production at EPCOT Center who thinks it will make a great TV series for the new Disney Channel. Again, he's in the position to get the ear of the Disney Brass, so I throw in with him.

He pulls together a committee with a writer, animators and a puppeteer and we start building a massive show proposal with artwork and storyboards and a model of the set and there's a cast of puppets now and a cartoon series and a cast of kid regulars and we spend thousands of dollars on a presentation for all the top executives. The whole time this is happening, I'm torn between the exhilaration of the process and the certainty that we've lost the charm and originality of my original idea. Sure enough, we make our presentation to Michael Eisner who remarks, "It's too big."

Soon I'll be recognized (and paid) for my writing skills. But before I can get to that point, I have to go through what I'm going through. I have to cast my bread upon the water, as everyone does who wants to be promoted from within. Especially in the competitive atmosphere of Disney or Universal, the only way to convince people to hire you as a writer is to be seen writing. This opens you up to being ripped off and rewritten, but it can't be helped.

By the way, that medicine show I wrote for conventions is read and remembered by my pal Peter Bloustein who recognizes my work. In a little while, he's going to leave Disney and take that script with him; and me along with it.

Chapter 13
FORT LIBERTY WILD WEST DINNER SHOW (1987)

During five years at Journey Into Imagination, I've made inroads in voice-overs and commercial work and can count on a Santa gig or two when 'tis the season... but I'd love a new creative challenge.

Meanwhile, Director of EPCOT Center Entertainment Peter Bloustein leaves Disney to go to work creating dinner shows for British entrepreneur Robert Earl, including *King Henry's Feast* and *Mardi Gras*. In fact, it was one of Robert's dinner shows in Britain that gave John Bloom the idea for 1520 A.D. Medieval Restaurant when Bloom ate there just before being evicted from England in the '70s.

When Peter leaves EPCOT Center, he takes with him my script for the medicine show; and when Robert Earl decides to open a western-themed attraction in nearby Kissimmee, Peter gives me a call. So in May of 1987 I hang up the dragon and go to work for Peter and Robert to create, direct and star in the *Fort Liberty Wild West Dinner Show*.

Because I've seen *King Henry's Feast*, I'm wary of working for Robert at first; the food is okay but I find the show to be rather dull. Where 1520 A.D. had been childish, bawdy and fun, I feel *King Henry's Feast* is too authentic and stuffy for the tourist trade. If I'm going to create a show from scratch, I want it to strike a note somewhere between the two: exciting and funny, but with a real plot and audience participation integral to the story.

Any misgivings I have vanish when I meet Robert Earl. He's a small man with a great smile and a warm British charm that belies his tremendous drive and knowledge of the restaurant business; I'll come to think of him as the 'fiscal pixie'. When Peter introduces me, Robert shakes my hand and says, "Ronald, I need you to understand one thing about me. I charge people $28 for a meal that costs me $1.50; I put on a show so they won't complain about the food."

I can feel all my concerns about show quality leaping to the front of my mind. I quickly ask him, "Do you mind if the show's good?"

He replies, "Not at all."

I smile, "Then we'll get along fine."

One thing Robert Earl's dinner shows have down perfectly is the timing: the four courses of dinner are integrated brilliantly into each show. So my first assignment is to time each segment of *King Henry's Feast* and see to it that their timing is perfectly matched at Fort Liberty. Again I have to 'Deal Creatively with Operational Reality', but over the years I've found that such constraints almost always make outlining a new show much simpler.

The script I'd created while at Disney had been a simple traveling medicine show starring Professor Gladstone (me) and his daughter, Kate. Peter hands me a list of new show elements to integrate: the new setting will be a U.S. Cavalry Fort... live musical accompaniment will be provided by a guitar and piano... and the show will include a selection of variety acts and feature the Big Mountain Family of performing American Indians. It's up to me to make this new combination work.

I start reading everything I can find about the U.S. Cavalry. The troops were such a motley bunch that I know I've found the perfect roles for my wait staff and the band.

I decide to cast the guests as folks from the surrounding frontier who are attending a 'territorial gathering'. The Indians will be a local tribe, friendly to the Fort but suspicious of the Professor, and the variety acts will be part of the Professor's Traveling Medicine Show. For a 'B' plot, I have the commanding officer of Fort Liberty, Capt. Charles Hancock, fall in love with the Professor's daughter.

While I'm pulling the script together, I'm also getting an education watching Peter and Robert produce the restaurant end of things – taste testing food, selecting table service suitable to the period, building the venue and dressing it with period décor and fittings. We hire my buddies Handpicked to help with the music and Peter introduces me to a wonderful actress named Ellie Potts, who has years of experience dancing and choreographing for the Disney parks. I promptly cast her as my daughter, Kate.

Our new Manager is a former Marine Drill Sergeant; we'll call him Sgt. Moron. At first I think he's too much of a hard ass for the collaborative atmosphere I want to create, but he does come in handy for getting our wait staff/soldiers to march and respond in a military manner for the top of the show – so we get along fine for now. To play Kate on Ellie's nights off, I hire a wonderfully funny former stripper, Wendy Clay, who contributes some great comic material to the show. And for the Fort's commanding officer I'm delighted to get Norm Riggins, former Ringmaster at Circus World. Jacob Witkin comes over from ruling England at *King Henry's Feast* to fill in for me and Norm twice a week.

For the finishing touch, I head out to the costumer's to pick up my new Professor suit. My hero, W.C. Fields, used to wear the most outrageous costumes; I called these 'parade coats', because they seemed designed for making a big impression from a distance. I had told the costumer to make me a suit as garish and colorful as possible. She succeeds admirably. The Professor Gladstone parade costume is the ugliest and most comfortable costume I will ever wear. I decide I want to be buried in that suit.

After an encouraging run-through, I'm giving notes to the cast: "Aside from a few particulars, I'm very happy with what I saw tonight. Everyone's enthusiasm, energy, characterizations… I feel we're ready to open and we're going to have a fabulous show.

"With that said, a word of warning: we are at the beginning of a <u>very</u> long run. We'll be doing this show twice a night from now until forever, getting lots of laughs and some very healthy tips, but… this thing you did so enthusiastically tonight is going to get old. And we can't let it.

"It'll be exciting for a long time, especially since we'll spend the first few months finding new things to play and sharpening each moment till the whole thing shines. But that will pass, and the show will become set. And after it becomes set, it will become routine… and after it becomes routine, it can become boring.

"Not boring for the guests – because they'll be seeing it for the first time. But we'll be singing these songs and telling these same jokes twice a night for the foreseeable future. And that's the job. To convince the guests that all this has never happened before.

"Creating this 'Miracle of the First Time' is a central discipline of any live performance. The only way this thing works is if you show up every night ready to play… ready to pretend you've never sung these songs and never heard these jokes. The moment you don't play along, the moment you decide it's more important to amuse yourself or another cast member, the guests will pick up on it. Believe me, they will be taken out of the moment and the laughs will grow less, the applause will fade and – believe it or not – this will affect your tips. The guests pay their money to take the ride and anyone here dragging their feet can kill the goose that lays the golden egg."

A few days later the show opens and we're a hit. The food is actually great, the variety acts are impressive, the musicians kick ass, the jokes land and the medleys work. And the waiters! The Men of E Troop (I like the idea of being immediate neighbors of TV's *F Troop*) turn into an hysterical bunch of wild characters, thoroughly believable as Cavalrymen desperate for a night of R&R after their daily grind. Everyone in the building is smiling each night, looking forward to what the next show will bring. Even Robert Earl steps over to tell me he feels it's the best dinner show he's ever produced.

Then, eighteen-or-so months into the run of Fort Liberty, the musicians start speeding up.

During the carefully-timed main course medley (during which the troops serve the main meal and everyone has a chance to dig in) I notice the band has upped the tempo a bit. This medley is my favorite because it's composed of western TV and movie music, and we get to sing the seldom-heard lyrics to the themes from *Bonanza*, *The Adventures of Rin Tin Tin*, *Branded* and (of course) *F Troop*.

But now the stand-by guitarist (he sits in two nights a week) is playing the tunes too fast for the lyrics to be understood. And why? He's bored, of course. So I ask him to slow down. He says he will. Then he doesn't.

Eventually our stand-by guitarist becomes our full-time guitarist and the tempos continue to speed up. I take this up with Sgt. Moron who he informs me there's nothing he will do about the situation; apparently, he's bored as well.

Then one night I'm onstage doing the medicine pitch and I look down to see a waiter standing in front of me lip-synching my dialogue to the audience. Why? Bored. Sgt. Moron thinks this is funny and again says there's nothing he will do about it.

Finally, I'm about to start the opening number with my 'daughter' one night. The music begins just as Sgt. Moron steps over to tell me she hasn't arrived yet, so I'll have to do the opening song-and-dance duet alone. He didn't think this information was important enough to tell me any earlier.

The next day, I go to corporate headquarters to bring these communication problems to the attention of management. And I'm fired. Apparently, the only person Sgt. Moron is willing to do anything about is me.

For me, Fort Liberty was a grand experiment. I'd set out to prove that a dinner show could be smart, funny and entertaining for all ages... that the production could be fulfilling for the cast as well as profitable for the company... and that a management philosophy that respects the talent, seeks their input and gives them their creative head can survive and thrive.

That it worked was a tribute to Peter Bloustein, the cast and, most especially, Robert Earl, who had the guts to stand back and let us shine. I had been able to create and manage (for a time) the kind of atmosphere I long suspected would enable great things to come forth – from the performers and for the guests. After this taste of what can be, it'll be tough to go back now; to put myself back under the heel of the corporate 'creative' mindset.

Unless, of course, the right position comes along...

Chapter 14
FREELANCING 1 (1987-90)

With Fort Liberty as my nighttime gig, my days are free for freelance consulting jobs that give me some good times and fascinating insights.

Steve Hansen started at EPCOT Center as The Puppet Man, doing his strolling show in the Germany Pavilion, but he's soon put to work developing puppet- and character- related projects all over property. In 1987, someone at Disney Creative has the brilliant notion to put him in charge of the entertainment for Mickey Mouse's 60th birthday celebration.

Since the Magic Kingdom hasn't had a big new draw in some time, it's decided to create a whole new land for the event – Mickey's Birthdayland. The setting is Duckburg and will include Mickey's Country House, a petting zoo and a new stop on the WDW Railroad line. Two giant circus tents are set up behind the house for a great new live show (and the inevitable merchandising).

To promote this new land (and to help guests find it, located as it will be in the farthest reaches of the Kingdom) it's decided to re-theme the Railroad as Mickey's Birthdayland Express. Main Street Station and the locomotives themselves will be covered in balloons and banners and

– for the first time ever – a pre-recorded spiel will be created for the Florida trains to set the mood for the party.

Steve starts looking for someone to handle this added responsibility since he'll be creating and producing the new stage show from scratch. Through our prior work together, he knows of my love-for-and-knowledge-of Disneyland and its assorted ride narrations, so he asks me to create the new train show and to perform the pre-recorded spiel.

Off I go with pad, pencil and stopwatch to ride the rails, carefully noting the timing between landmarks so I can create the illusion that my 'conductor' is performing live, describing what's there as he travels along with the guests.

Steve has an idea to place scenes along the track of characters heading to Mickey's party and we brainstorm these simple placards and cutouts. Donald and his nephews will be seen on the river on a raft and in a canoe. The Mad Hatter's Tea Party will be deserted, the tea pots still spouting steam and happy music; a sign is posted: 'Gone to Mickey's Party'.

I have an idea for an amusing scene utilizing the Disney Villains. Up ahead, we'd hear a clanging bell and then come upon a railroad crossing with an active wig-wag sign. Cruella de Vil's sedan is at the crossing; she's stooped over the wheel, glaring at us as we speed past, and packed into the back of the car are all the other Disney Villains – Captain Hook, Maleficent, the Queen of Hearts, etc. The demon Chernabog from *Fantasia* is crammed in the back of the car, his giant bat wings folded over uncomfortably.

Later I'll be disappointed to learn that a Disney executive shot the idea down, claiming "The Disney Villains would never do that." Shortly thereafter *Who Framed Roger Rabbit* is released, revealing that the 'Disney Villains' – like all toons – are just actors; I like to think they'd have appreciated the joke.

Remembering Goofy and his busted jalopy from Disneyland's *Fantasy on Parade*, I suggest we see Goofy with his car broken down by the tracks. Steve asks, "Do you mean a live character in the woods?"

I tell him, "Of course not, that would be impractical. I mean a life-size cutout of him, perhaps standing by a real jalopy that's got steam coming from the engine." Then I reconsider. "Though it would be great to have the real Goofy out there, running after the train… maybe having to run back to get his present. It would be a thrill for the guests."

I script a routine where a napping Goofy is roused by the train, jumps up to try to get on board and *almost* makes it, but the voice of the conductor sends him back to his car for Mickey's present and he just misses us. Amazingly, Disney puts the character out there in the woods for a few hours every day; and all that time, wherever I am and whatever I'm doing, I keep wondering:

If Goofy trips and falls in the woods, and there are no guests there to hear it, does he still go, "AAAH-hoohoohoohooweeeee..."?

Shortly thereafter, I get a call from Disney Imagineering. Craig Wilson is working on the development of Disney-MGM Studios' Streetmosphere program. He asks me to dream up original material for their new cast of characters.

The characters have all been named and outlined; they want me to write backstories, sketches and solo character comedy for the cast, as well as audience participation scripts for the Hollywood Boulevard Screen Test Experience. I create a thick notebook of character history and performance material...

...which is promptly ignored. Craig, a strong proponent of improvisation in the parks, hires folks with improv experience for his Streetmosphere program. I have no way of knowing, but in hindsight I suspect that my writing assignment was not dissimilar to all the writing I did for Jay Stein back at Womphopper's; a way of placating a nervous management team until the actors hit the streets.

I spent some time those first weeks observing the Streetmosphere cast. They were greeting people and improvising a lot, but not doing any organized bits. Instead they were relying on the charm and personality of the talent, which was considerable. But the guests, at least at first, didn't know what to make of these people; if they were meant as entertainment or set dressing.

Today the improvisation of the Streetmosphere performers has become a regular sight on Disney Studios' Hollywood Boulevard and the Magic Kingdom's Main Street, U.S.A. And they still rely on hiring charming, talented people, dressing them exquisitely and turning them loose on the public. It's a formula that has worked for many, many years.

From time-to-time I get a call from Studio D to come in for a recording session for one project or another. Talented folks I met and worked with as Dreamfinder will think of me for a job and arrange drive-on clearance through the north gate. The great thing about this is it allows me to park directly behind Fantasyland... right at the entrance to the Utilidors, the underground complex that allows Cast Member access to all areas of the Magic Kingdom.

I find the mood in Studio D always playful because of the man who runs the place, Gary Baldassari. Gary is a rascal who does splendid work even though he harbors a twisted sense of humor about Mickey and the Company. He loves to share comic soundtracks he's found, especially if they're Disney-themed.

In every session I seize the opportunity to improvise around the material, showing off to Gary and whoever is supervising from Creative Entertainment. In this way I let people see my range... which leads to more varied work than just being Dreamfinder. I especially profit from my ability to capture the "Ladies and Gentlemen, Boys and Girls" warmth of Jack Wagner, the 'Voice of Disneyland'.

My work on Mickey's Birthdayland Express leads to me recording the narration for the Magic Kingdom's Liberty Belle Steamboat. I start doing park-wide and preshow announcements for EPCOT Center along with the occasional character voice for attractions and show proposals.

In 1989 I'm asked to announce the grand opening events for the new Disney-MGM Studios. There'll be two shows: a nighttime event for the press, VIPs and celebrities, and a morning show for the public. Most of the announcements are pre-recorded, introducing the guest speakers and executives.

The morning event, however, will feature a roster of guest stars from movies and TV. Since there is a chance that this line-up may change right up to the last minute, I have to be there in person, in the tech booth at a live mic to call out the celebrity names as they step onstage.

I'm in the booth at five in the morning on show day with a long list of names that might change anytime, but I'm ready to roll with the punches. After a couple of perfect run-throughs, the cast and crew are set to take a break. In a little while they'll open the gates, letting the first paying guests into the studio and it'll be showtime!

As we're wrapping up the rehearsal, I turn to the Stage Manager – the man who will be calling the technical cues for the show – and say to him, "I have one little concern... " I proceed to share my experience at the dedication of the Journey Into Imagination attraction six years prior, when the volume was turned down on Figment's vocal track. "I just want to make sure that, when it comes time for me to start reading this list, my mic is going to be live."

The Stage Manager turns to the sound man and tells him of my concern. They both reassure me that everything will be fine, that the mic will be turned on well in advance and they show me the little dial indicating the volume level for my mic. I thank them both and put it out of my mind.

Showtime comes and I'm in the booth with virtually nothing to do, since most of the announcements were recorded days ago. At last it comes time for me to step up and introduce the visiting stars. "Ladies and Gentlemen, please welcome, Rose Marie... Morey Amsterdam... Stan Freberg... Red Buttons... Don Knotts... "

I'm totally focused on the list in front of me, glancing up between names to check the timing of each star's entrance and walk across the stage. They're moving along at a pretty good clip – but a part of me notices that my voice doesn't seem to be reverberating like those pre-recorded announcements did.

There's a sudden quick movement on my left and I become aware of the sound tech fiddling with some knobs. The Stage Manager says, "Where's his mic?" I keep reading until the sound tech says, "Okay, start over."

I start over, reading a little faster, aware that the people I'm introducing have already left the stage. "Rose Marie, Morey Amsterdam, Stan Freberg, Red Buttons... "But now I can tell I'm talking into a dead mic. There are more desperate adjustments being made around me and the Show Director dashes into the booth to declare, "I'm not hearing him!" and someone else says, "Start again!"

"Rose Marie! Morey Amsterdam!" and in the middle of the word,

'Amsterdam!' the mic goes live and a-little-too-loud, startling everybody. I finish running through the names in double-time, trying to get through them all before the parade of stars stops.

The show finally ends and everyone is very complimentary. But for the rest of my life I'll have trouble trusting a sound tech to activate my mic on cue.

One gig I *almost* get really breaks my heart. Most, if not all, of the star's voices in the Great Movie Ride were done by impressionists (for example, character actor Robert Ridgely contributed his excellent impression of John Wayne). The last scene of the ride shows Dorothy Gale and friends standing on the Yellow Brick Road admiring the distant Emerald City… but that wasn't the original plan.

Instead we were supposed to see Dorothy and friends in the Wizard's chamber facing the Great and Powerful Oz. As we pass out of that scene, our ride vehicle would turn a corner to reveal Prof. Marvel, 'the man behind the curtain'. I'm called in to Studio D to audition for the voice of Frank Morgan, who played the Wizard for MGM and inspired the voice of Dreamfinder. Gary and I have fun trying to recreate the booming echo of the full-blown Wizard and then a quick transition into the humble tones of Prof. Marvel. I later learn that I got the job… but a lack of funds – or sufficient performance rights – meant the scene is cut. Pshaw.

I'm in Studio D with Steve Hansen and Gary Baldassari recording the narration for Mickey's Birthdayland Express. I find the trick is to picture myself sitting among the guests on the train; this helps to keep my tone light and informal. In playback it gives the impression that I'm standing over their shoulder, pointing out the landmarks as if to a friend.

When I write the first draft of a script, I always picture the person who's going to be reading it that first time, and I'll occasionally put in a gag or remark just for them; something I know won't be in the final show but is intended to get a laugh from the client. I had done this in my first draft of the train narration, picturing my pal Steve reading to himself: 'There across the river is Liberty Square – home of the inspiring Haunted Mansion, and the spooky *Hall of Presidents*.'

When we get to this line in the script, Steve and Gary both tell me, "Do it."

I say, "We can't put that on the train."

"Do it."

So I do it. And we don't record an alternate take. Later, when management rides the train to check the narration, the gag sails right over their heads. My pre-recorded conductor will continue to point out the 'spooky *Hall of Presidents*' for years; and attentive visitors to the Magic Kingdom will hike to City Hall on Main Street almost daily to point out his mistake.

When I finally get to ride the finished train experience, it comes off better than I could've imagined. Disney composer Steve Skorija has composed the perfect musical theme, *Rollin' on the Mickey's Birthdayland Express*. When my conductor asks the guests to shout hello to Gator Joe, an animatronic sitting by the river, they all actually shout, "Hello, Joe!" And the kids react enthusiastically to seeing Goofy run after the train.

In the years that follow – as things evolve in the Magic Kingdom – I'll get a call now and then to record some new lines for the train. Finally, when Mickey's Birthdayland becomes Mickey's Starland, a staff writer takes all the attitude out of the script, making it a straight Disney-style narration. I miss the character, but keep the gig.

More years pass and I check in from time to time to see if I'm still on the train. Finally in 2000 I hop aboard and listen and think, 'Yes! I'm still talking!' Until we get to the Frontierland Station, when I hear a couple of jokes that are so bad that I know I'd never have read them. It isn't my voice – it's a guy doing an impression of me! I have to laugh…

When I finally leave Fort Liberty, I'm out looking for steady work in Orlando for the first time since I moved to Florida. For close to seven years I've had steady employment… but now I'm on the open market and so start making the rounds.

One of my first stops is *Medieval Times Dinner & Tournament*. I no sooner walk in the door than a very large Spaniard cries, "It's you!" Turns out he's the show director for the chain and had seen Fort Liberty seven times; he claims he wants to hire me for a new show they're opening in another state. In the meantime, they need someone this very night to portray the Duke (owner of the castle). He asks if I'm available and loans me his personal costume.

The Duke's first responsibility is to welcome the guests to his castle and pose for a souvenir photo with every group and every single individual – which includes kneeling down next to all the small children. After an hour of kneeling and rising to pose with hundreds of guests, I now have two exhausted rubber bands where my legs used to be.

I then have to make my entrance walking majestically the length of the arena in very deep, soft sand and scale a set of thirty steps without a hand rail. Later, when I stand to bless the horses, I'm so weak that I collapse on the floor and have to haul myself up to my throne.

During a break in the show, while the guests are eating, I turn to the very young lady seated next to me – playing Duchess to my Duke – and ask her how long she's been with the company. "Oh, I just moved here today from Tallahassee. I came in to apply to be a waitress and they asked me to do this tonight."

After the show, I have to sit in the bar and banter in character with the guests for another hour. For all this work and injury, I'm paid the princely sum of $15.

Early next morning the phone rings, but I'm far too sore and exhausted to get out of bed and answer so I let it go to voice mail. The message is an invitation to come back and do it all over again that night. After a long, painful crawl to the phone, I return the call to beg off with apologies.

One good thing does come out of my relationship with Medieval Times (after I regain the use of my legs). Months later they open an authentic Medieval Crafts Village next to the attraction. I offer my services, as a tour guide and writer, to create an educational program for visiting groups. I portray the village architect and each tour begins with a visit to my workshop where I explain the evolution of the town and its technologies; then I lead the groups through each of the exhibits and interact with the various artisans and townspeople.

The installation is very well done and I enjoy bringing the press and VIPs through during our opening week.

But after that, things get very slow indeed. I find myself sitting alone in my primitive architect's space with nothing to amuse myself for eight hours a day, waiting for someone to come by. None of the hoped for school groups show up; it seems the only folks who visit are those who have come by to book seats for the dinner show.

Finally, I'm let go for being financially undesirable; I had refused to work for $5 an hour and the extra $3 an hour they had agreed to pay me is, apparently, breaking the company.

Moving on...

My luck improves when royalty comes to the 33rd Street Hotel. *King's Manor* is a silly yet successful themed dinner show in Chicago which is looking to expand into the Orlando market. They run on weekends in a convention room at a relatively small hotel and have lucked into a very talented group of performers to put their show across (not surprising, since Orlando has all that local talent living nearby because of the parks).

The show has been up and running for some time when I am hired as understudy to the King, a role I only get to play a few times. But I make many good friends before the operation folds, most especially the jester, Danny Burzlaff, and our head wench/show director, Sharon Miller. More on them later...

I have a great deal of success with one particular consulting job – writing scripts for the chain of Chuck E. Cheese's Pizza Showrooms. Every few months they change out the video-and-robot shows and I work with Jeff Palmer and others creating new themes, scripts and lyrics for over a year.

I get called in one day and invited to participate in a redesign project that will radically rethink the CEC showroom concept. With this bug in my ear I go home and put together a two-page treatment laying out what I would do with the Chuck E. shows... basically eliminating all the other characters except Chuck (so as to repurpose the robotic budget to upgrade his animation) and using the video elements more prominently, turning the showroom into an imaginary vehicle (not unlike the old Mission to Mars at Disneyland).

Next day I walk into the Project Manager's office and present him with my treatment for the new Chuck E. Cheese Showroom. He reads it over and tells me, "You can't show that to them, Ron. We've scheduled a three day retreat in a Vacation Villa, we're bringing in mechanical and design consultants; the whole thing has been planned out and paid for."

After three days of debating and brainstorming, the group (which includes the Disney supervisor who had tried to take credit for my medicine show script) comes up with the same idea I had in an hour at home working alone.

One of my ideas is to add something to the show videos that could be promoted... that would make each new set of shows its own, unique event: A Guest Star.

My first suggestion is to do a series of shows built around the theme of 'A Day in School' and to hire as our guest star Cheech Marin. Cheech has released an award-winning children's album called, *My Name is Cheech, The School Bus Driver*. I suggest we do one segment where he does a number from the album, then he could play the school principal, a gym coach, a science teacher and finally a home economics instructor (in drag).

The Chuck E. Cheese people are enthusiastic about the idea and a phone meeting is set up with me, Cheech and the CEC creative director. Cheech is delighted with my ideas and eager to participate.

But then someone at CEC Headquarters finds out that Cheech Marin used to be part of a comedy duo call Cheech & Chong, that was famous for doing <shudder> drug humor. I'm informed that Cheech is out, and when I protest that this was years ago and remind them of his album's success with the children's market, they tell me, "Disney would never hire such a person!"

I quickly point out that Cheech had a featured role Disney's *Oliver & Company*, but to no avail. Cheech is out, and with him any possibility of booking name talent to act as a draw for future CEC Entertainment.

Moving on…

When I moved to Florida in 1982, I found an apartment in a relatively undeveloped area of South Orlando midway between downtown and Walt Disney World. There were only one or two other apartment complexes and a golf course nearby, and no street lights.

All that changes, though, when Norman Bates and his mother move in next door.

The Bates Mansion is built on a hill in an undistinguished vacant lot a few blocks from my place. This is how I find out I'm living next door to the future home of Universal Studios Florida (USF). Construction stops shortly thereafter, while the company searches for someone to help them pay for the thing. Soon Disney announces plans to build *their* studio tour and the media starts raving about Orlando's future as the film-making capitol of the east coast. I have a bumper sticker made for my car: 'Hollywood East – Live the Myth'.

A little research leads me to the temporary offices of Universal Studios East and an interview with the head of Operations for Universal, who informs me that he will also be in charge of entertainment since the new studio attraction will have no entertainment department. I think, 'What a novel concept for a theme park.'

Construction resumes at Universal, and the day comes that they hold auditions for tour guides and actors for the new studio. They set up at the high school across the street and the turn-out is massive. I prepare my one minute monologue and show up, along with hundreds of others.

In a town that has grown accustomed to the Disney way of conducting auditions, Universal is a revelation. There is no warm welcome, no encouraging greeter and when I finally get called before the auditors I'm lined up with a group of nine others onstage. We are asked to step forward and say our names one at a time. I and some others are then instructed to step through the door on our right, and we are surprised to find ourselves back outside in the parking lot.

As you can imagine, by this time I'm feeling pretty frustrated. Two new Hollywood-themed parks are opening in my town and I'm not a part of either project. I've been shut out of Universal without so much as a second look and, what's worse, I've been paid to contribute to Disney-MGM but am unable to participate.

Finally I call the head of Disney Talent Booking, Ronnie Rodriguez. Remember I mentioned the warm welcome you'd always get at Disney Auditions? That was Ronnie. When Ronnie had you in to audition he always went out of his way to make you feel welcome and encouraged. Before they started calling folks in to audition, he'd personally address the waiting talent, thanking you for showing up and telling everyone what he was looking for and what the jobs entailed. While you performed, he'd sit there watching and willing you to give the best performance you could. For those of us who invested our time and effort in these cattle calls, it meant a lot.

I should mention here that Ronnie learned these valuable lessons from the former head of Disney Talent, Sonny Anderson... the man who had hired me for the Golden Horseshoe and cast me as Dreamfinder. Plus, Ronnie was a good friend and supporter of mine throughout my years of dreamfinding; this is why I feel comfortable calling him now to ask for work. Ronnie asks me to meet with him after-hours in his office.

He expresses surprise that I'm not already on board as a member of the Streetmosphere cast and dials the phone. When he's connected to the supervisor in charge of atmosphere entertainment at Disney-MGM, Ronnie pushes a button – putting the call on speaker phone. He looks at me, raises a finger to his lips and winks. I sit there, obediently silent.

"Have we got a role in Streetmo that would fit Ron Schneider?" Ronnie asks.

From the speaker: "Ron would be perfect for Streetmo. There are a few roles he could fill. Besides with Ron you're getting an actor, a director and a writer as well."

"Why hasn't he been cast?"

"In my opinion? Politics. Some people were reluctant to have Ron on board because he is a good writer and director."

Ronnie smiles at me. "Well, I'd like to bring him in next week. Can we do that?"

"No problem, I'll set it up." What a relief! I thank Ronnie profusely and head home with my spirits lifted.

Granted I won't be on my own, creatively speaking – as I was at Magic Mountain and Fort Liberty – but I like the new park and I'm sure there will be lots I can learn from the folks I'll be working with.

I'm out of the woods at last!

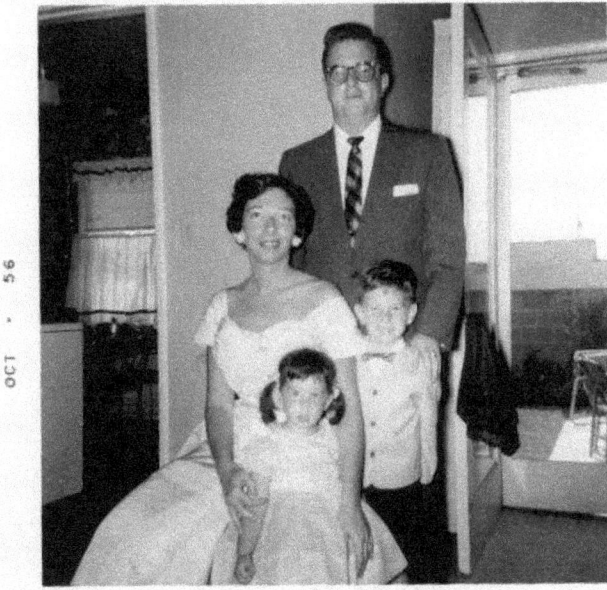

The Schneider Family – 1956:
(Top to bottom) Arthur, Beatrice, Ronnie & Lisa

With my first partner, Jerry Mahoney – 1962

With Michael at Magic Mountain
Animal Farm – 1972

(Left to right) My pal Major with Petunia, Bill Kiker
& Michael – 1972

Henry VIII & His Court – 1973:
(Left to right, back row) Grandmother Yolande &
Mother Bea;
(Front row) Sister Lisa, Me, Sisters Suzy & Lauren

As Professor Samuel J. Spillikin, B.S. – 1977

My Disney Dream Comes True...
'Professor' Ron Schneider at the Golden Horseshoe – 1980

As Pecos Bill in the Golden Horseshoe Revue – 1980
(Golden Horseshoe pictures by Larry Nikolai)

Womphopper's Wagon Works Restaurant – 1980

As C.L. Womphopper – 1980

(Left to right)
Gregory, Dreamfinder
& Figment – 1982
(Photo Courtesy of Greg
Dlouhy)

29 years later...
Together again for
D23 – May, 2011
(Photo by Josh Young)

As Prof. Gladstone at the Fort Liberty Dinner Show – 1987
(Photo by Michael Barry Schweitzer)

Universal Studios Florida's Jake (Dan Meisner) & Elwood
Blues (Keith Kobee) with their #1 Fan, Dan Aykroyd – 1992

What I miss most...
(Photo by Mark Bryan Wilson)

Chapter 15
UNIVERSAL STUDIOS FLORIDA
(1990)

Two days before my meeting with Ronnie Rodriguez at Disney Talent Booking, I got a call from Danny Burzlaff, former jester at *King's Manor*. He and Sharon Miller have been put in charge of the animated characters that will be populating Universal Studios Florida. He asks me to come in for a meeting in the new administration building at USF.

Danny tells me that the new park will also feature a cast of celebrity look-alikes – live performers who will portray classic Hollywood stars: Charlie Chaplin, Laurel and Hardy, The Marx Brothers, W.C. Fields, The Blues Brothers, Marilyn Monroe and the like. From our time together working at *King's Manor*, he knows I'm a devoted and knowledgeable fan of old Hollywood and classic comedy, and asks if I can help him with a little freelance project.

Danny wants me to write a short treatment for the Universal Look-Alikes, describing what they might do in the park to entertain guests. The 'Celebs' at Universal Hollywood only ever pose for pictures and sign autographs; he thinks they should do more in Orlando and asks me to put together some suggestions, along with a 'creative philosophy' for the performers. I happily accept the challenge and say I'll see him in a few days.

Look-Alikes. I have no experience with that part of the business, but I certainly know enough about most of the characters involved that I can come up with material for W.C. Fields, The Marxes and Stan and Ollie. The question is: does Universal want recreations of their classic bits of business, or new material that will be true to the characters?

I decide that, since they've asked me for a 'creative philosophy', they've left that up to me. I work up a couple of pages where I argue for letting the characters keep their classic idiosyncrasies while living in the moment with our guests. I advise against trying to recreate the past, suggesting an approach whereby the past can live again.

I deliver my proposal to Danny at Universal the day after my meeting with Ronnie at Disney. Danny skims the page and seems happy with what I've written... until I mention that I will soon be going over to work at Disney-MGM in the Streetmosphere program. Suddenly he gets very serious and leaves the room; I sit there waiting for his return for ten minutes.

When he finally comes back Danny seems less-than-pleased. "Ron, we want you here full-time to direct and supervise the Celebrities. The problem is: the funding for the position has not been approved yet, so I can't offer you the job. I can tell you I'm sure it'll happen, but that's not a guarantee."

I thank Danny and head home, my head spinning. Once again, both Disney and Universal have offered me long-term employment within hours of each other. But this time I can't accept both.

There's really no question, though, which offer I should take. One is a step backward into performing, the other a chance to explore a new horizon – and to do it in my own style. That night I write out a note to Ronnie and drop it by his office at Walt Disney World Entertainment:

'Ronnie – Thanks for your help with the job and for being such a good friend, but I've been offered a creative position with Universal Studios Entertainment. And after all... It's better to reign in hell than to serve in heaven. Ron Schneider'

When the budget for my position is approved, I discover there is, in fact, a very healthy entertainment department at Universal Studios Florida; one that seems to have blossomed under the same atmosphere of benign neglect that proved the saving grace at Magic Mountain, Poppy's Star and – yes – even Womphopper's Wagon Works!

Since top management's focus is on the rides and attractions, and the animated and look-alike characters are considered no big deal, our efforts float neatly beneath the radar… kept buoyant by some fortuitous casting on the front-lines and behind the scenes.

First there's the Director of Entertainment, Neil Miller, whose combination of imagination and experience, along with a healthy suspicion of corporate management, makes him an instant hero to some of us, myself included. Neil delights in playing at 'executive', a tongue-in-cheek attitude which makes it a pleasure to play his 'adoring toady'. Besides, unaccustomed as I am to functioning at this level of management, he constantly helps me step up to the task.

Danny Burzlaff is the calm center of my world – a man of infinite patience and exquisite taste. He seems to have limitless faith in my ability to run the Celebs (eventually, if not immediately). Sharon Miller works as his second-in-command and, along with 'aging hippie' Terry Wines, runs the animated costume character program.

This team has been at it for months before I come on board, promoting the park and shaking things up in Orlando. I remember reading about a visit to the EPCOT Center parking lot which the Universal characters had made months before, not-so-innocently trying to 'pay a call on the neighbors'. Knowing the way Jay Stein felt about competition, I could easily believe he'd approve such an insolent, nervy move from them.

The press is filled with bitter sniping from Universal management about how Eisner ripped off the idea of a studio tour in Orlando. I know a movie-themed pavilion had been planned for EPCOT Center, but comparing the early plans for Disney-MGM and Universal Florida it's easy to believe that there was some kind of hanky-panky going on. And now, as I settle in at Universal, I come across the studio's dossier on Disney-MGM; they'd obviously done quite a bit of 'research' themselves.

My first job is to scout rental prices and availability of lights, cameras, generators and equipment for a phony film crew to inhabit the streets of our New York City backlot. Since I know absolutely nothing about film shoots and since this is far from the kind of creative work I've been hired for, I am immediately resentful. This is the first test of Neil Miller's patience with me; he passes with flying colors.

I can't believe that we are going to waste manpower and money setting up a phony film shoot. Surely no intelligent human being is going to stand in the Florida heat and watch a bunch of technicians killing time waiting for a shoot that will never happen. (I don't know that, five miles south of us, Disney is pulling the same dirty trick on their guests.) But every time I raise the issue with Neil, he smiles, listens patiently, and sends me out to another rental firm.

Months later, I'm racing to a meeting in the entertainment offices when I spot a small mob of guests gathered on Brownstone Street. I swing over to see what they're watching; it's a collection of our park techs sitting and sipping cokes in the shade, surrounded by a lot of rented camera equipment, pretending they're waiting for filming to resume.

Livin' the myth.

USF is my first experience with the 'electric leash' – the hand-held shortwave radio – and I enjoy the prestige for a while. It can also be a source of unintentional amusement.

In the weeks before opening, E.T. Adventure is the first attraction to start test runs; it is a popular practice for studio management to hop aboard, if only to get out of the heat. Problems arise, though, with folks who keep their radio in their hip pocket. Sitting on the bicycle/ride vehicle, their backside would key the radio, so everyone in the park has to listen to the entire soundtrack until they disembark. (I don't mind as much as most, as I had provided dialogue for one of the cops: "They've got E.T.!")

One day as storm clouds gather, Security sends out a call that we will be experiencing a 'Code 10-13'. My limited knowledge of radio codes leaves me scratching my head, and I'm just naïve enough to call back for all to hear, "What's a 'Code 10-13'?"

With his typical blend of patient amusement and exasperation Neil's voice comes back: "Ron, it's a musical starring Gene Kelly and Donald O'Connor." So enlightened, I hasten back to the office just ahead of the rain… singin' all the way.

There are already a handful of talented look-alikes working freelance for the company. Keith 'Satchmo' Kobee – our multi-talented Elwood Blues (we were still looking for a 'Jake')… B.T. Pruyn – a grand Mae West… Billy Scadlock – a passionate and talented Charlie Chaplin… Fred Franco – an uncanny double for the classic Groucho… Joe Wesson – a great clown who made an exemplary Harpo… Michael Andrew – a charming Stan Laurel (in desperate need of an Oliver Hardy)… Lisa Barr and Cynthia Haeffner – our sweet Marilyn Monroes…, and Bob Bouchard – a fair match for W.C. Fields.

My first practical lesson in managing celebrity look-alikes comes quickly; physical resemblance is not the most important quality in casting. Keith (Elwood) bears no resemblance to Dan Aykroyd except in height and Joe (Harpo) has the black eyebrows from hell… but each generates in an audience the same emotional response as the original. Keith can exude a comically cool apathy and Joe's angelic innocence is tinged with the malicious energy that is often missed in recreations of Harpo. Bob Bouchard, on the other hand, is the spitting image of Fields – but I always sense his mind is elsewhere (usually on the ladies).

One lucky bit of casting happens almost immediately, when a former choir director from Hawaii shows up to audition. His church-bred manners and roly-poly physique put me in mind of our missing Oliver Hardy; upon closer examination all he needs is the black patch on his upper lip to complete the character. So impressed am I with Jamie McKenna's manners and confidence, I simply ask him to mimic a bit of Oliver's characteristic hand flourishes and hire him on the spot. He will turn out to be, not only one of the world's leading Oliver Hardy impersonators, but a brilliant asset to the operation as he can fashion almost any comic prop that I can describe.

On the other hand, Joe Wesson can't come on board full-time. What am I going to do for a new Harpo Marx? And – more troubling – where am I going to find someone to tackle the more elusive characteristics of his brother, Chico?

A few months earlier I had joined a stand-up comedy workshop conducted by stand-up agent and teacher Vicki Roussman. I learn a lot from Vicki about presentation and writing comedy that will help me in the years to come. I also meet a lot of talented, funny people.

There's a short, chunky Jewish comic in the class who shares my love of classic comedians. When Lou Burnstein hears I'm casting celebrities for Universal Studios, he starts campaigning to get hired as Groucho. I explain to him that I already have a great Groucho Marx, but with his knowledge of the Marxes and his quick wit and energy he could make a pretty good Chico. I know he's not happy having to settle, but he'll be a fine fall-back Groucho and I'm delighted to have him as part of the team.

There's another guy in the workshop with a kind of pixie/angel look, ideal for Harpo. He even has a knack for physical comedy. Banks Helfrich's only drawback as a stand-up comic is that I don't think he's nearly as funny when he talks… Perfect!

As someone who's done very little traveling in his lifetime, I'm thrilled to quickly find myself on the road with Danny, Sharon and character lead (and all-around terrific guy) Joe Lamere going state-to-state as part of a promotion for our new park. We're conducting a search for celebrity look-alikes in several major cities. This has been going on for a while; when I join the group they have yet to visit St. Louis, Milwaukee, Miami and Indianapolis.

The turnout is gratifying: a lot of people who love the characters, a lot of people just looking for work. Not a lot of folks who know how to do an impression of who they're supposed to be, but a few real look-alikes (One cab driver who is a double for Peter Lorre, and a ranch owner who is the spitting image of John Wayne). We pick one winner in each town and they are flown to Orlando to compete for a job with the new studio.

Out of twelve semi-finalists we finally select Howard (not his real name), because he has two things going for him: we desperately need someone to play Jake Blues and Howard looks exactly like John Belushi.

So I've been handed this amazing collection of talent and this glorious opportunity and all this creative freedom… and now all I have to do is – everything. Where to start?

I decide to write each character a new 'classic' bit. But the administration offices at Universal are mighty packed these days; I'm sharing a desk with Joe, Terry and Sharon and it's not the best conditions for writing comedy. So I put on my company-issued hardhat and head into the studio to find an alternate (hopefully temporary) office.

Once again I'm walking the construction site of a new park — still the greatest feeling in the world. There's lots of mud and not a lot of privacy. I stumble through the new home of the *Horror Make-Up Show* on Hollywood Boulevard. The exit hall is carpeted, quiet, deserted and heavily sloped which makes it easy to sit and write. The old movie posters lend the room a touch of nostalgia, and the size and central location will be helpful when I need to start using it as a rehearsal space.

I start crafting new routines for the cast based on sites within the studio they might use as performance locations. There's a lovely recreation of Central Park that brings to mind Joe Papp's productions of 'Shakespeare in the Park', and the classic nature of the Marxes seem a perfect fit. I mash together the story lines of *Hamlet* and *Macbeth*, casting Groucho as a King, Harpo as a Queen and Chico as Everyone Else. I'm hoping that working with this new story will help wean my cast off the habit of quoting the classic material and encourage them to live creatively in the moment.

Brownstone Street suggests door-to-door sales, perfect for Oliver

Hardy (especially if he has Stan Laurel along to 'help'). And since there is nothing on Hollywood Boulevard but facades, W.C. Fields becomes Honorary Mayor and tour guide, making up a totally bogus backstory for each location.

Finally I call everyone in to the park for our first cast meeting. Before distributing the new routines I've written, I share with them a few thoughts about the job before us:

"The main thing I want to impress upon you is this. You are, each of you, taking on a great responsibility. You have inherited the character, the reputation and the legacy of a great artist. Our guests will be looking to you to make your celebrity live for them. Not merely to recreate a classic routine but to share a new, spontaneous moment that includes them.

"We are remarkably lucky, in that the characters we have assembled are definitely not wholesome, innocent characters. Because this is Universal we can afford to be rebels, non-conformists, anarchists. If the Blues Brothers behave like good little Theme Park Cast Members, or The Marx Brothers aren't a disrupting, unpredictable influence, or if W.C. Fields greets a small child with anything less than contempt we're doing something wrong.

"I will be working with each of you to discover the independent creative sparks that will make that happen... but my goal is to bring you to a point where I'm simply a fan; where you surprise and entertain me and our guests in the same way. When you can experience that ownership of your character – that's when the fun will really begin and we can make this thing about more than a pack of look-alikes. Then you'll be Stars."

Things start slowly, with lots of photography shoots and on-site promotions. Our first big challenge comes in early May, when Universal will hook up with the local symphony orchestra for a concert in the park. The program will consist of music from film scores of classic Universal Studios pictures and, in a meeting with Neil and the entertainment staff, we decide to use the look-alikes to introduce each selection.

Laurel and Hardy will come out in fishing gear to introduce the theme from *Jaws*. The Blues Brothers will drive up in the Bluesmobile to introduce *The Peter Gunn Theme*. The cast of our *Ghostbusters* show come over from USF Operations to present the theme from their movie.

The question comes up, how should we introduce the music from the notorious shower scene in *Psycho*? At this point in the meeting I must've lost my head because I dredged up my vocal impression of Alfred Hitchcock, learned from watching his old commercials for the Studio Tour in Hollywood. Neil gleefully announces, "You're going to do Hitchcock."

I try to beg off, pointing out that, while my vocal impression may be good, I don't look anything like The Master of Suspense. My discomfort only doubles Neil's sadistic resolve. Come show day, I have to spend four hours having a bald pate and make-up applied, only to have most of it peel off in the humidity of a hot Orlando night. Still it is fun... My introduction ran thusly:

"Good evening. Our beloved conductor asked me if there is a particular piece of music I'd like to include in this evening's celebration. And I said, "With Mother's Day just around the corner, what could be more appropriate than a musical tribute to a boy's love for his mother?"

(At this point I reached into my suit pocket and produced a shower cap, slipping it on over my bald head.)

"So now let's all settle back and enjoy Bernard Herrmann's Love Theme from *Psycho*."

One disturbing development... When we start doing promotional gigs, Howard – our new Jake Blues – starts not showing up. After this happens a few times the rest of the cast, looking out for one of their own, step up as watch dogs and try to keep him out of trouble. The night before the concert the entire look-alike company venture out to party together, with everyone directed to make sure that Howard gets safely back to his hotel room. But the next day he's nowhere to be found, and Elwood has to drive the Bluesmobile onstage for the concert and handle the introduction bit alone.

Rumors start to circulate among the cast about Howard's recreational habits. It's noted that when he does show up on time for work he seems tired, weak and distracted.

When Howard's late one morning I have to go fetch him and on the drive back to the studio he's busy making excuses; I'm trying hard as I can not to laugh and failing miserably. He asks what's so funny and I explain, "Here I am in the car listening to the spitting image of Jake Blues make excuses. It's like a scene out of the movie... And this is my job!"

It's not too long until Sharon and I get a call from a local sheriff's station to come pick Howard up at 4 a.m. and we drive him out to rehab. Turns out he really is exactly like John Belushi. I'll never see Howard again.

Chapter 16

USF CELEBRITY LOOK-ALIKES
(1990-91)

It's the final push before opening day and I'm walking through the studio when I spot a USF marketing rep escorting some reporters through the site, accompanied by a familiar-looking robot. As they draw alongside of me, the robot suddenly turns his giant head in my direction and says, "Hello, Dreamfinder!"

I instantly remember Seco from the *EPCOT Center Grand Opening TV Special*. I snap back, "Hi, Seco!" and whirl around, determined that this time I'm going to spot the guy controlling him.

No such luck.

The Silver Stars Restaurant is Universal's attempt at a high-end sit down dining experience: upscale menu, wine list and waiters with white shirts and black bow ties. To give the crew a chance to practice serving the public, management passes out tickets for a free meal at Silver Stars to folks in the front office. I secure five of these comps: one each for me and a friend, and one each for Groucho, Harpo and Chico. I tell the boys they are to arrive in costume and in character. (Ain't I a stinker?)

I and my date arrive early and secure a booth on the far side of the room. Shortly thereafter The Marx Brothers enter, all proper manners. They present their invitations and are escorted to a booth by the door. Orders are taken and drinks are delivered… and then, as they wait for their food, the boys strike.

Harpo makes himself at home eating the condiments at an adjoining table. Chico picks two attractive-looking diners to charm and Groucho starts to tango between tables with an agreeable female guest. The other employees are watching this with smiles and laughs all around. Everyone is enjoying this first glimpse of what my characters can bring to the park.

Everyone that is, except the Assistant Manager. He watches for a moment, then stalks backstage; a moment later he returns with the Manager who is doing his best impression of Franklin Pangborn, the stereotypical stick-in-the-mud. I tell my friend, "I'm about to get a call on the radio."

A minute later: "Entertainment 4, the Marxes have to leave Silver Stars immediately." I respond in the affirmative then raise my voice to be heard over the laughter. "Oh, boys!"

As if in a film buff's dream, The Marx Brothers drop what they're doing and race across the room to line up in front of my table. Chico says, "Yeah, Boss?

Putting on my best managerial airs, I tell them, "Gentlemen, we have been invited to leave. However I think it would be terribly rude if you were to go without shaking hands with every person in the building."

Groucho, Harpo and Chico spontaneously salute and scatter, warmly shaking the hand of every guest at every table. Then they duck into the kitchen to shake hands with the kitchen staff and hug the manager before dashing out the front door.

At our next gathering, I let my people know that they are all to steer clear of Silver Stars in the future. Eventually they are welcomed into every other Universal eatery. They can get free fries anytime they come to play in Mel's Drive-In, and the Blues Brothers are invited to crash the gate and feed each other free shrimp when they drop by Lombard's Landing. But no one goes in or near Silver Stars Restaurant.

Roughly a year later at a park-wide manager's meeting, people are remarking on the success of our look-alike program. The manager of Silver Stars asks why the Celebs don't come into his location. I think it is Danny who gets to tell him, "Because you told them to leave."

Coming out of a writing session in my Hollywood Boulevard hallway/office, I stumble onto a spontaneous party just outside of Mel's Drive-In. Folks are gathered to bid farewell to Richard Crane who has built much of USF (and all of Womphopper's); as Richard is a friend I invite myself to join in. That's where I am reunited with my old Womphopper's Boss, Jay Stein.

To say that Jay is surprised to see me pop up on the east coast would be a gross understatement. I explain that I've been hired to oversee the celebrity look-alikes, and that I'm available for any writing chores. "Uh-huh" Jay says skeptically. "So if I ask you to write me a f*cking speech...?"

I'd forgotten what it was like working with Jay. He says what he means and pulls no punches; he doesn't have to. And I always believed that the reason he liked – or at least tolerated – me, was that I always treated him with the same attitude of irreverent disrespect he showed everyone else.

And that's why I reply, "I'll write you a f*cking speech."

And Jay says, "Well, okay."

The night before Universal Studios Florida opens everything seems quiet and peaceful. Since all the attractions are either indoors or behind the scenes, whatever desperation is going on (and there is plenty) is hidden from view.

Terry Wines and I have finally been given our own office in a small trailer near the park entrance; the same trailer that houses all the character costumes, dressing rooms and break area. The Celebrities and Animateds are slammed together for the time being, but everyone seems to be handling the situation.

I cannot remember ever feeling so excited or so fulfilled. I'm living a dream beyond my dreams. Whatever goals I may have had for performing, I'm now directing and creating through others, passing on what I've learned and watching as people I love take what I share to the next level.

That night I manage to acquire a Pargo electric golf cart from operations and decide to take a celebratory ride through the studio. I've never had the use of a vehicle inside any park, and I'm beaming as I speed through the night for no good reason at all.

As anyone who was around that day will recall, Universal Studios Florida opens with more than a few technical setbacks. As in: the major rides – Jaws, Kongfrontation, Earthquake: The Big One – don't work. My fondest memory of opening is a series of video clips of a friend from publicity touting our rides before opening, then trying to put a good face on all the technical glitches as the day wears on. Even with decades of performing experience, I couldn't have handled that role nearly as well as he did.

One TV station airs footage of Park President Tom Williams bravely confronting angry guests outside Earthquake; another shows the growing mob waiting to register complaints at the Guest Relations Office. Free passes are issued to everyone in the park that day so they might return in a few weeks when (we hope) everything will be up and running as intended.

My celebrities, on the other hand, are definitely up and running. For this I will take very little credit; the main thing I do right is tell them to let the characters drive their behavior. Rather than trying to control what they do and where and when they do it, I turn them loose – so they really have a chance to shine. The highlight comes for me at the VIP-only nighttime dedication. The stage on Hollywood Boulevard is filled with stars and Universal Big Wigs about to cut the ribbon and I spot The Marx Brothers standing on a nearby roof, silently looking down on the whole affair. The mist around them gives their presence a supernatural impact: classic Hollywood watching the start of a new era.

Once we're over the operational hurdles of opening day, I and my celebrities settle in to scrounging up the new bits and props that will put them on the map.

I'd seen Belushi and Aykroyd in their concert at the Universal Amphitheater back when Womphopper's opened, and I adored the movie, but I still have a lot to learn if I'm going to create new material for these guys.

Fortunately, Keith Kobee is a walking encyclopedia of their music. An accomplished guitar, harmonica and keyboard player, he has the set-up and talent to produce whatever music tracks we might need for any future shows. Keith also works as a musician for hire, plays in clubs and tears it up at dueling piano bars – but he's totally devoted to and serious about his day job representing Elwood Blues.

Shortly after Howard departs, I find Dan Meisner, an accomplished comic actor who is not an exact duplicate of John Belushi (Saints be praised!), but who slips into the physical and emotional make-up of Jake with surprising speed and accuracy. Like John, he's not a singer or a dancer (and it will be a while before he can turn a convincing cartwheel), but he really steps up and matches Keith perfectly. With the two of them together, we've got the makings of a world-class Blues Brothers act.

Danny locates a car for the boys... not an exact match of the real thing, but close enough for The Blues, and the studio prop shop paints her up and fashions a giant air raid speaker for the roof. She still looks too good, though, so Danny and I take a tire iron to the body and give her that 'driven through a shopping mall' look.

I haven't written anything for the Blues yet; it's always been in the back of my mind that they'd eventually perform somewhere in the studio. One night I grab a video camera and just follow them as they prowl the park. They fall naturally into troublemaker mode. The guests love seeing this (shades of Spillikin Corners), but the cast members, new to their jobs, are legitimately suspicious.

We slip into Schwab's Pharmacy and Ice Cream Parlor on Hollywood Boulevard. A group of teenage girls are in a booth enjoying their sundaes when The Blues slide in next to them and flash their wallets. "Good evening, ladies. I'm Jake; this is my brother, Elwood. We're quality inspectors for the Schwab's Organization, charged with making sure your ice cream measures up to our high standards." Staring intently at the frozen treats and licking his lips, Jake asks, "Is it, uh – flavorful?"

After several minutes of hints and flirting, Jake leaves the girls to Elwood and sneaks over to the souvenir stand to intently examine the postcards and assorted knick-knacks, handling everything in a highly suspicious manner. To her credit, the young lady behind the counter never takes her eyes off him.

All this time, I'm watching the guests watching The Blues; they are charmed, finding themselves suddenly cast as extras in a scene straight out of *The Blues Brothers*. Because the guests are familiar with the characters' universe, they step easily into the roles of amused bystanders – unselfconsciously investing the scene with their reactions and participation. I become determined to find a way to capitalize on this phenomenon.

Over the next few months, my people manage to surprise me and delight our guests with their creative growth and initiative. Everybody steps up and, as I had originally asked, I become a simple fan of their work...

I had no idea when I hired Jamie McKenna what a tremendous asset he would be to the program. He proves himself an expert scrounger and prop maker. Jamie locates a Model A Ford of the type used in the old Hal Roach films. He wires the car for sound, and finds recordings of the background music from the Laurel and Hardy short films, so when The Boys drive by the guests hear the appropriate tunes coming out of the car.

Jamie and Michael Andrew find some overalls and buckets of white wash and spend hours in the Amity Harbor area, painting an old rowboat that had been set there as decoration. Guests wandering by see Laurel and Hardy eating lunch when they aren't covering the boat – and each other – in the messy white paint.

Finally, Jamie constructs a piano crate so as to recreate Laurel and Hardy's Academy Award winning routine from *The Music Box*. The crate has tiny casters set into the bottom so they can push it along the street. It weighs practically nothing so it can fall on Jamie without killing him and the interior features a brilliant construct of bungee cords and metal pipes, so when the crate falls over it sounds like the piano inside has been utterly destroyed.

We hire a tiny marching band under the leadership of Tony Aleguas. We don't have band costumes, so we dress them in leftover lab coats from the (as yet unopened) Back to the Future: The Ride. Since there are only eight or nine players, I suggest they don't try to march in formation but rather travel in a swarm that can move freely in and out of the crowds. And how do they repay me for this stroke of genius? Every time they spot me lumbering through the park, whatever song they're playing immediately segues into *Baby Elephant Walk*. Thanks, Tony.

Anyone playing Marilyn Monroe has a hard time with the male guests (especially those on leave from the nearby Central Florida Naval Base); and the fact that the park sells wine and beer doesn't help. We wind up pulling a male escort out of the Animated Character ranks, dressing him as a chauffeur, and putting the two of them in a silver convertible which drives around the studio (and away from any uncomfortable situations).

Since our Marilyns are so talented, I create a show around the character to play on Brownstone Street. Our Universal Band drives up to her apartment in the convertible to pick Marilyn up for a group date, which leads into a medley of her signature songs. The finish features Marilyn sitting on the back of the car as they drive away playing *Diamonds Are A Girl's Best Friend*. For something so hastily thrown together, the show is a surprising hit.

Walking toward the front gate one morning, I see a crowd gathered around a table at the cafe. I break through the mob to find two beautiful ladies in the middle of a game of cards with The Marx Brothers. It's like a scene straight out of *Animal Crackers*, except that the material is original and it's happening spontaneously to our guests.

Another time I'm walking down Hollywood Boulevard after hours reading the star's names in the sidewalk. Tucked between John Forsythe and Janet Leigh there's a blank square – that isn't blank anymore. A big star has been drawn in chalk and inside that, in a childish scrawl, it reads

'Jake & Elwood'.

The next morning when Keith and Dan report for work I call them into my office. "Gentlemen, that stunt with the star on the sidewalk is brilliant. Go wash it off."

Dan is puzzled. "Why?"

"Because you have to do it again. It isn't funny if it's already written, it's only funny if guests see you sneak up and write it."

Two side effects of my job: 1) I find myself looking at everyone I meet and trying to figure out who they look like; and 2) folks are always auditioning for me, trying to get into the look-alike program.

Two great guys, Dave Jackson and Michael Rafferty, carry on an enthusiastic campaign to be cast as Kramden and Norton from *The Honeymooners*. I love their work and think they'd fit beautifully in our New York area, possibly alternating days with Laurel and Hardy. Trouble is Universal doesn't have the rights to the characters so my efforts to get them hired go nowhere.

We do, however, have the rights to Lucy Ricardo. We cast Melissa Radley, from the Entertainment Department, to play Lucy and I start casting about for a good Ethel Mertz. It seems obvious to me that if I can get Lucy and Ethel on the street, there's a lot we can do to sweep the guests up in their shenanigans.

But it's not to be. While this is going on, I try a new barber shop around the corner from the studio... where the fellow cutting my hair, a Cuban named Adrian Israel, is the spitting image of a young Desi Arnaz. So Lucy gets her Ricky and Ethel is forever out of the picture.

When I'm conducting auditions, I try to make the experience as positive and as much fun as possible. I pattern my auditions after Disney's format, making the whole thing more of a look-alike workshop than a typical audition. Finding the perfect performer for this kind of job is rare, so I work with people to see whether they can be trained; or at least show them what work they might do so they're better prepared for the next round of auditions.

Instead of isolating the auditioners I keep the group together in the room, so everyone has a chance to watch the process, act as an audience and encourage each other.

Folks often show up with an (often misguided) idea of who they can portray. I start by giving them a realistic assessment of whether they're physically right for the part while emphasizing that resemblance is only part of the job. I then share what insight I have into the celebrity they've chosen and the challenges it presents to the performer. If it's a character we have the rights to, I encourage them to keep working and to try again another time.

With this approach I have remarkable success creating a fun atmosphere and building goodwill for both Universal and the look-alike program.

Chapter 17
THE WRITE STUFF (1991-92)

As I experience it, Universal Studios Florida starts as 'The Park with No Entertainment Department' as a cost-cutting measure. As a result there is a strange division of effort, with live performance across property being divided between 'Operations' and 'Animated Characters & Celebrities'.

'Operations' is responsible for casting, directing and managing the tram tour and live attractions created by the show designers (*Ghostbusters*, *Hitchcock*, *Post-Production*, *Horror Make-Up* and *Earthquake*), while 'Animated Characters & Celebrities' create, cast and manage atmosphere entertainment and special events. Many of my old friends from Disney are working in attractions, but they might as well be in another world. There is no communication between their managers and ours… and more than a little competition.

Just like at EPCOT Center, everyone is soon jockeying to be recognized as a creative resource for the company, and nowhere is this more evident than USF's backlot.

Shortly after opening, the Operations team puts the Ghostbusters on the street in the Ectomobile, roaming the studio to promote their attraction. They start using audio clips from the movie to set up scenes where the Ghostbusters come out of a facade as if they've just exterminated ghosts within. Not so much a show itself, it's more like the end of a radio play and gives the actors a chance to repeat some bits of dialogue from the movie.

Then we get the rights to use Beetlejuice as a strolling character. Our first 'Juice' is none other than my boss, the multi-talented Danny Burzlaff. The character fits right in with the anarchic mood of our park; in fact I create a special hat for him – a pair of WDW mouse ears with a vicious bite taken out of one of them.

I write a proposal for a simple stage show in which the Ghostbusters from the attraction meet Beetlejuice and I circulate it throughout the Administration Offices. Next thing I hear my idea is being rehearsed over in front of the New York Public Library facade by the folks in Operations. I finally manage to get a letter from management recognizing my contribution, but it still stings to be back where I was at Disney: casting my bread upon the water, watching as others take credit for my work.

Ah well, I remind myself, this is the process one has to go through to be recognized. And Lord knows I have my own creative resources and opportunities right where I am.

Of all the characters we have roaming the studio streets, none generate excitement like the Blues Brothers. They quickly become the focus of every situation for two reasons:

First, because of *The Blues Brothers* movie, people always expect something inappropriate from them, some subtle-but-outrageous behavior. This means that people light up when they drive around the corner or walk into a shop; and they watch them... they watch very closely to see if they can catch what they're up to.

And second, we have been blessed with two actors who have not only captured Jake and Elwood physically, but that have come to inhabit their personalities completely.

When these facts are combined with the musical prowess of our

Elwood (Keith) and the tightly-wound energy of our Jake (Dan), it's soon obvious that these two deserve a musical outlet for these characters...

We need a Blues Brothers show!

Our first mini-concert is pulled straight from the trunk of the Bluesmobile; two stand-up mics hooked up to speakers on the car roof, with a music track coming from the cassette player in the dashboard. Nothing but a few songs at first, but Dan and Keith invest it with as much personality as possible and the guests eat it up.

After a couple of weeks of that, I start looking around for a real venue; something that is <u>not</u> a 'theme park stage', but a setting that will fit these rough characters.

In the backlot's New York area there is an abandoned construction platform right next to the front stoop of a brownstone apartment. The stairs, the sight lines, the elevation... it all seems ideal!

I'm determined that this time, instead of a collection of songs, the Blues Brothers will have a complete show – with a storyline and characters to play with. The script I create is loaded with original dialogue and comic byplay; too much, in fact.

The day before the show is slated to debut, everyone's working very hard to pull this thing together, but it's still too long. I know the script needs cutting but I sense I'm not the one to do it. So I tell my boss, Danny, that I won't be attending the final rehearsal; and ask that he cut and polish the show himself.

The result is that the first time I see the finished show is when it premieres in front of guests and USF executives, where it's an immediate hit. I don't even miss what's been cut; and a version of the show that debuts that day has been running in Universal Studios parks ever since.

Mind you, it's been rewritten and 'fixed' by every team of Creative Managers that have come to power since, but no one has managed to do anything to improve on our first Blues Brothers Show.

*   *   *   * *
      *   * *
  *

Having just opened the previous summer, the company doesn't plan much that's special for the Christmas season, but in our own little way our division steps up to put a jolly shine on our efforts. Little Christmas-y additions to the character costumes, for instance... candy canes, holly and bows. And since my biggest and most recent success has been *The Blues Brothers Show* (and since ideas are cheap), I decide to create *The Blues Brothers Christmas Show*:

Jake and Elwood Blues
(sung to the tune of Winter Wonderland*)*

City sings, are you listenin'?
On the street somethin's glistenin';
A beautiful night, we're feelin' alright,
Drivin' through a Winter Wonderland.
Blown away is the new bird,
Here to stay is the Blues Bird,
He sings us a song as we roll along,
Drivin' through a Winter Wonderland.
In the alley we'll be singin' 'Soul Man',
Jammin' with the brothers through the night,
Wailin' till the neighbors holler, "Whoa, man!"
Singin' till we see them flashin' lights!
Then the cops come a-callin', while the snow is a-fallin',
They take us away, looks like we may
Spend the rest of Christmas in the slam;
They haul us away for songs that we played
Drivin' through a Winter Wonderland!

Jake produces a small artificial tree and decorates it with toilet-paper/garland, packs of cigarettes and an empty-beer-can/angel on top, then there's a touching scene where the boys exchange gifts; each one presenting the other with a new pair of sunglasses.

The effect is surprisingly emotional, building on the guests' affection for the characters. And it has the added benefit of costing next-to-nothing to produce: just the cost of a few props, the time to produce the music tracks and two days rehearsal.

(Only last night I watched a Youtube video of the 2011 edition of USF's The Blues Brothers Christmas Show. *All the gags are the same, but they're presented without the careful pacing and emotion that made them funny*

originally. The result is that the guests aren't laughing, and we don't get any special 'Christmas' feeling from the show. Seeing the show in this state makes me appreciate all the more the talent and skill of the team we had back in the '90s.)

For one weekend in 1991, Universal Studios Florida is the best-armed theme park in the world. Kicked off with a tribute from none other than U.S. Secretary of Defense Dick Cheney, USF fills the park for Armed Forces Day with tanks, missiles and military vehicles of every description for a massive parade and ceremony on New York Street with guest speakers and live bands.

Aware of the part '40s Hollywood played in the war effort, it seems like a natural opportunity for my Celebs to do what they did back in the day: put on a show supporting the troops. I sit down with each member of the team and figure what we might do that will be historically accurate, respectful and fun.

I manage to sell management on the idea of the celebrities putting on a small pre-parade, and everyone steps up – Laurel and Hardy and Charlie Chaplin wear recreations of period military uniforms from their films and our new W.C. Fields, my buddy Bob Joles, makes a (rather cynical) Uncle Sam.

It's another victory for our team, showing off what we can do given a small budget and a little time. And it doesn't hurt my reputation that our little idea makes the company look good and a lot of people – waiting around for an afternoon of military pomp and circumstance – laugh.

Every time Publicity or Marketing calls for our look-alikes to make an appearance, they arrive prepared with original, character-appropriate material. Even our 'Wolfman Jack', Chip Foreman, stationed behind the mic in Mel's Drive-In, displays a genius for extemporizing original rants in the style of his namesake.

One day I get a call from the Operations side of the company. In a few days USF is going to debut their new *Wild Wild Wild Wild West Stunt Show*, and they have been given the task of scripting a dedication event for the press. They've lined up a bevy of real western stars to make an appearance, but can't think of what they might do or say as part of the event. At their request, I race over to see if I can help.

The list of stars is truly impressive, including Denver Pyle, Harry Carey, Jr., Hal Needham and The Rifleman, Chuck Connors. I suggest the best approach would be to ask each one to share their best story of the good old days of making westerns... and where do cowboys share stories? Let's put them around a campfire! The camaraderie of these old hands would be a joy to watch (and would no doubt inspire some great ad-libs) and we'll finish by having Park President Tom Williams join them to introduce the Stunt Show.

I get my pals Handpicked to come over to supply some live background music and we pull this thing together. I put an old coffee pot on the fire and direct every star to sample the coffee when they first sit down, then spit it out and comment on how bad it is. Finally, when Tom comes in, I tell him to try the coffee and act like he loves it; this gets a big laugh.

The preshow is a smash. Everyone loves the chance to see these classic stars spontaneously playing and sharing the moment. The Stunt Show itself is swell; a great piece brought over and much improved from the version at Universal Studios Hollywood.

After the event I stand and watch as everyone in the company congratulates the Operations team on the success of the show. I'm standing right there and neither the person who called me asking for help nor anyone else ever thinks to say 'Ron helped' or 'Nice job'.

Moving on...

Just as I discovered at Womphopper's, there something about the atmosphere of MCA that drives good people out the door. The first to go is Sarah Whitten from Operations, a sweet lady loved by everyone in the company (she had been transferred from the Universal Studios Hollywood tour guide ranks for the opening of USF). A huge farewell party is planned, with everyone providing some kind of tribute.

Since I know that everyone in upper management is going to be there, I immediately recognize this as a chance to show off what I can do with special material. I write a half-dozen song parodies in tribute to the departing Guest of Honor, teach some of the songs to her friends and print up lyric sheets (with a big 'Written by' credit on top) so everyone can sing along.

I feel a little slimy pulling the stunt, but I genuinely like Sarah so it's easy to write the stuff and it certainly didn't hurt anyone. Anyway, the songs are a hit.

Shortly thereafter Danny Burzlaff leaves. This time there is no company-wide farewell party, but I wear a mourner's black armband for days.

While I love the job of Creative Supervisor, I must confess I'm having more success with the Creative part of the job than I am with the Supervisor part. Terry Wines has an assistant to help him with the animated characters' schedules and payroll, but it's decided that I have to learn to do these things for myself. And while I did learn eventually, it never came easy. When it becomes obvious where my shortcomings lay I am finally given an assistant, so things lighten up a bit; but I long to live in the creative world and let the rest of the job go hang.

Thanks to Neil I'm given that chance when I'm pulled out of Celebs and put on full-time to help create Universal Studios Fright Nights.

USF's first Halloween project will be dwarfed by its efforts in the years that follow, but there is a raw excitement in its creation which will never be equaled. This is a team effort spear-headed by the team of Neil Miller and Tim Sepielli. Tim is our tech guy, a character in a cowboy duster and hat who loves tackling a big project, getting in over his head just for the chance of surprising everyone when he comes out on top.

Tim designs and executes our first-ever haunted house, built in the long-unused queue line for Jaws. I contribute a few ideas, nothing fancy… it really is a showcase for Tim's skill at making something out of next-to-nothing. The house ends with the guests making a circuit around a large cage filled with strobe lights, loud rock music and a collection of classic Universal Studios Monsters wandering around inside, threatening the guests. This is where I make my big contribution to the house – a lost little girl trapped with the monsters, sweetly asking the way out while clutching a map of the Magic Kingdom.

There is a huge rally on Hollywood Boulevard featuring a lot of our attraction actors pulling double duty; this is notable for the random guests who are put to death in each performance. Otherwise, I have a hand in just about every other element of Fright Nights, but two stand out for me… two shows you'd never find at Disney.

In laying out his ideas for our first Halloween event, Jay Stein doesn't have much to offer in the way of specifics; but he does say, "I want a chainsaw massacre in New York." So it falls to me to script a 'massacre'.

I know immediately what I *don't* want, and I know that it is most probably the very thing Jay is thinking of. So my task becomes trying to make us both happy. I know Jay will want at least one beheading, at least one real "Ewwww!" moment, at least one chainsaw-wielding hockey-masked maniac and some blood.

I, on the other hand, want a story – one with a beginning, a middle and an end. It has to happen spontaneously and unexpectedly, has to directly involve the guests to some extent and it has to be funny (preferably sick/funny):

NAZARMAN'S CHAINSAW MASSACRE
Final Draft Show Script

Stan and Mitzi are an attractive married couple visiting USF for halloween. They are strolling through new york, carrying on a mild argument that heats up as they approach Nazarman's pawn shop.

STAN
I don't understand why you're so hard on everyone…

MITZI

I'm not 'hard on everyone'... You're a wimp! When
someone charges you forty-five dollars for dinner,
you have the right to complain if the food is cold!
But you sit like a wart on a dog hoping they'll read
your mind and heat up your meal...

STAN

That kid had a dozen other tables, he couldn't...

MITZI

Couldn't what? Do his job? Show some backbone!

STAN

Sweetheart, people are staring...

MITZI

Let 'em stare! It's Halloween, isn't it? They've come
to see a freak show; you should feel right at home...
Step right up, folks! See the half-man, half-wimp!

She's shouting at the other guests, humiliating Stan. a hockey-masked
chainsaw maniac walks up, toting his weapon. He tries walking by the
couple, but Mitzi lays into him, too.

MITZI

Where do you think <u>you're</u> going, 'Masked Man'?

The maniac stops abruptly and turns slowly toward Mitzi.

STAN

Sweetheart, I don't think you should talk to the
nice man like that.

MITZI

Oh, I'm terrified! What's hockey-puss going to
do? Knock the puck outta me?

The maniac fires up his chainsaw. Stan freezes, but Mitzi is simply disgusted. The maniac swings his blade at Stan who quickly takes off his watch and holds it out to him. Mitzi grabs the watch out of Stan's hand as Stan goes for his wallet, offering that to the maniac as well. Mitzi takes the wallet from Stan and hands him back his watch. Stan keeps trying to give the maniac one thing as Mitzi keeps trying to stop him. The maniac swings at Mitzi.

MITZI

Oh, big man! Picking on a defenseless woman!
Well...

He 'cuts her off' with a roar and a lunge. Mitzi screams and runs for the fire escape. She throws herself against the barred gate and pulls on it violently; the maniac walks slowly into the street. he spots Mitzi at the gate and advances toward her. Her efforts grow more frenzied. Just before he cuts her in two, she throws the gate open and scrambles up the stairs. He follows slowly, deliberately. Just as he rounds the corner out of sight, she appears in a second story window, screaming.

MITZI

Stan! Call nine-one-one!

STAN

I can't! You've got my wallet!

She throws him the wallet just before she is dragged screaming back into the room and out of sight. Stan fishes out a bill and waves it at the crowd.

STAN

Anyone got change for a ten? All I need's a quarter...

Screams and unintelligible shouts again drag our attention upstairs; then a quantity of blood is splattered against a closed window. The chainsaw stops. Stan moves under the window, shouting.

STAN
Mitzi! Mitzi!! Are you all right?! <u>Say something</u>!!

Something comes flying out the window toward Stan. Reflexively he catches it, but shouts in terror when he realizes he's holding... the maniac's head. It drips blood on his suit; Stan tosses the head into a nearby trash can and slams the lid on. A second later, Mitzi descends the staircase carrying the chainsaw. Her outfit is a bloody mess.

MITZI
Alright... Who's next?

STAN
Mitzi, he could've killed you! Why didn't you let him take the damn wallet?!

MITZI
Oh, and I suppose <u>I</u> should pay for dessert?!

STAN
What?!

MITZI
(Glancing at her reflection in a shop window.)
Look at my hair! I'm a mess! Find me a bathroom! And a gas station (waving the chainsaw) - this thing's empty...

They move off into the crowd.

Another request from Jay is for a small show for the spot behind the Bates Motel, adjacent to the Hard Rock Cafe; a tour of a specially-built 'Graveyard of Rock Stars' to be hosted by Beetlejuice.

This will indeed have to be a small show. The space is only about 20' by 30' and there is no place for seating, it's just a patch of grass next to a sidewalk. The one thing I like about the location is that it's directly behind the Motel and under the looming Bates Mansion. It occurs to me that a black cable run from Mother Bates' bedroom to the back of the crowd would be invisible at night, so I ask around to see if we could finish the show with 'Mom' flying out of the second story window and over the guests' heads. Jay likes that. Everyone likes that. They encourage me to keep thinking like that and to see what else I can add to the show.

I start writing a tour narration and some gag headstones. When I get to thinking about specific tributes I have a brainstorm: what if a partially-decomposed Elvis climbs out of the ground and sings a commercial for the Bates Motel?

Dead Elvis
(sung to the tune of Heartbreak Hotel)
Well, since my life has ended – I found a new place to dwell,
It's under the stairs with Mama Bates at The Bates Motel;
I tell you, you'll love the décor, baby, you'll dig the plumbing,
The tub's so comfy you could die!
Now if the joint is crowded, you never need to shout,
Cuz ev'rytime a pretty girl checks in she soon checks out;
I know that Norm and his Mama, baby, they'll make you welcome,
That's why the Bates is where I lie!

Can I get a tunnel dug from inside the motel so Elvis can actually climb out of a grave? Jay likes that. Everyone likes that. And so it goes. It's when I suggest adding the Blues Brothers that I am given permission to use the entire motel set, including the parking lot and the Bates Mansion.

Ten large bleachers are set up surrounding the property… a large graveyard is built covering the entire parking lot with tunnel access from the motel for Elvis, Beetlejuice and explosive effects… and lights and sound units are installed in the mansion and motel facades. Actor Paul Sanders makes a very convincing Norman (and his Mother) and I even get to do my Alfred Hitchcock vocal impression for the preshow and record a rant as Mother Bates.

The shows are very well received and performances are added to accommodate the crowds. Afterwards, Jay demands that next year everything is to be bigger and better; the only thing from 1991 that he definitely wants to repeat unchanged is *Beetlejuice Graveyard Tours*.

One more change results from Fright Nights; I am moved out of the Celebs trailer and into the Entertainment trailer. I will no longer write exclusively for the Celebrity Look-Alikes. From now on my job title is Creative Writer for Universal Studios Florida.

Chapter 18
GLORY DAYS AND THE NEW GUYS (1992-93)

It isn't too long after Fright Nights that I have to dust off my black armband and go back into mourning when Neil Miller leaves Universal. Everyone who had worked under Neil feels they are losing a friend and mentor; no one more than I.

Mitzi Maxwell has been running the tour guides and actors in Operations since Sarah left and she steps in to oversee the Animateds and Celebrities. I don't know Mitzi at all; to me she has simply been one of 'those other guys'. It isn't long before she becomes as much of a patient supporter and cheerleader for me as anyone has ever been... and USF finally has a truly cohesive Entertainment Division, overseeing all aspects of live performance in the park. Along with actor supervisor Bryce Ward and secretary Amy Henry (and without anyone ever saying 'you guys handle this'), Mitzi and I form a loose creative coalition that takes on whatever needs doing.

For my part, I write complete audio descriptions of the rides and shows to comply with the Americans with Disabilities Act... research and compose 'stall material' to cover delays and breakdowns... write scripts for touring promotions and marketing efforts... create dedication and press events for additions to the studio... and continue to consult and advise the Celebs on new hires and routines.

⁂

Each year the March of Dimes holds a huge fundraiser in Orlando called the Gourmet Gala. Top chefs associated with major hotels and attractions compete to create imaginative dishes and desserts around a central theme. This year the theme is comic books, and Universal chooses to base its entry on my favorite cartoon character, Popeye.

Part of the judging criteria for each entry is 'presentation', and it falls to me to create a live skit to present our entry, Wimpy's Gourmet Spinach Burgers. I create a scene with Popeye and Olive Oyl escorting Mr. and Mrs. Wimpy; and since our head of Food and Beverage bears more than a passing resemblance to Wimpy, I cast him and his wife in the supporting roles. Bluto shows up and faces off against the one-eyed sailor as our dish is served to the judges; everything is resolved with a quick food fight and the *Popeye* theme.

Our prop shop is busy creating Popeye's boat and Wimpy's truck – beautifully themed electric vehicles – and costuming is pulling together the outfits, when we get a further invite from the March of Dimes. As part of the evening's entertainment, Orlando's three major attractions are each invited to provide ten minutes of live entertainment to promote themselves and their latest offerings. Disney has already agreed to send over a large part of their Party Gras Parade, and SeaWorld is preparing a live video hook-up featuring Shamu on his home turf. Would Universal like to provide a ten minute production of some kind?

Not being exactly set up for such a situation, the message is sent back, "Thanks, but no thanks!" But, when word gets back to MCA corporate headquarters, our answer changes. Their thinking is: if Disney gets to show off we had damn well better show off, too. I'm called in to Mitzi's Office and told to create something impressive and fast.

I've seen Disney's Party Gras, an exquisitely-produced triumph of costuming and characters featuring happy music and giant balloons imported from Disneyland's 35th anniversary parade. In other words, Disney will be stepping up with their strengths. We have to do the same for Universal.

Our newest addition to the studio is a small character show based on Universal's new animated release *An American Tail: Fievel Goes West*, featuring Fievel and his family, a few supporting characters, some 'dance hall girl' mice and some great music. That will make for a cute opener, but where do I go from there?

Our strongest advantage over the other parks is our family of characters, because they're so unlike anything else in the industry. I start making a list of all our live performers: celebrities, stunt people, monsters, ride operators, animateds, classic TV characters – including some from Universal Studios Hollywood that we've never had in Florida. Mitzi then confides to me that USF has just out-negotiated Disney for the exclusive theme park rights to two of the funniest and most beloved characters in all of TV animation history… and I can debut them at this event.

This gives me an idea.

The Gourmet Gala is held in a massive ballroom at one of Orlando's mega-convention hotels. The judges are seated onstage while the guests are at huge tables flanking an enormous hardwood dance floor under a thirty foot ceiling.

The evening begins with the food competition; each company is doing its creative best with the comic book theme while delivering their dish to the judges for tasting. After all the entries have been tasted and judged, SeaWorld does their video presentation. And then Disney takes over. The room easily accommodates a huge chunk of Disney's Party Gras Parade and a couple of lit-up ladybugs from the Electrical Parade. Dick Nunis, Chairman of Walt Disney Attractions sits at a ring-side table leading the applause. Across from him sits Tom Williams, President of Universal Studios Florida, visibly nervous that our little show will pale by comparison. The stage is set.

House lights dim and strains of Fievel's Theme, *Somewhere Out There* are heard as Fievel and family wander into the room pulling a hay wagon onto the dance floor, looking lonely and lost. A voice-over describes their new film adventure, then says, "Join us as the cast of Universal Studios

Florida welcomes the stars of *Fievel Goes West* – There's a new mouse in town!"

The rousing song *Way out West* starts up and EVERY UNIVERSAL CHARACTER IN THE WORLD pours onto the dance floor: stuntmen, tour guides, Marx Brothers, classic monsters, the Munsters, the Ghostbusters, Laurel and Hardy, Beetlejuice and Lydia Deetz, the Blues Brothers and their dates, the Ricardos, Doc Brown, Woody Woodpecker and all the Walter Lantz characters, the Flintstones and all the Hanna-Barbera characters and Popeye and company. The place is suddenly swarming, overrun with characters – and unlike the gorgeously-costumed Disney dancers, these are all individuals, people we recognize – blocked and directed in character.

They're all dashing around, greeting each other and the Mousekewitz clan. Suddenly everyone sits down, the music mellows and Beetlejuice steps up to the mic in a cowboy hat and carrying a guitar to sing:

Beetlejuice
(sung to the tune of Streets of Laredo*)*
Life in a theme park ain't no bed of roses,
You can't drink and smoke and you can't pick up dames;
But I stick it out 'cuz I don't know another
Place where a dead guy can earn a good wage!

The Blues Brothers and their whip-wielding hot dates step onstage and perform the *Theme from Rawhide*, then Groucho takes center stage and starts calling bizarre square dance directions as everyone gets back up to dance. Chico takes over, but instead of a square dance he starts calling football plays straight out of the Marxes' movie *Horse Feathers*. Footballs suddenly appear on the dance floor and the mob starts tossing the pigskin as the music builds. (The goal post at one end of the floor is Frankenstein's monster; at the other end, Herman Munster.)

A western sheriff rides onto the dance floor ON A REAL HORSE, shouting for everyone to be quiet a minute. Since no one's listening he pulls his gun and fires into the air. A LIVE STUNT MAN FALLS OUT OF THE CEILING and lands in the hay wagon, sending feathers flying out over the crowd and spoiling Dick Nunis' and Tom Williams' dinners. (I'm standing behind the tech console; at this point

I look over at the Disney segment director in time to see his jaw drop.) The characters all shut up; we have to wait for the guests to do the same.

The Sheriff asks Chico Marx about a rumor he'd heard that there is a 'new moose in town'. Chico corrects him, "No, boss… You mean a *mouse*!" But the Sheriff insists he's heard talk of a *moose*. And from the back of the crowd enters Bullwinkle J. Moose and his pal Rocky the Flying Squirrel.

This is the premiere of these costumes and has a great effect on the crowd. The stars make their way over to the frustrated Sheriff to find out what he wants; fortunately, it's only an autograph.

Way Out West starts up again, everybody dancing informally until the music segues into the classic can-can. The dancing girls/mice step up to show off, but they are met at center stage by an equal number of REAL DISNEY CAN-CAN GIRLS complete with name tags. (We hired former Horseshoe dancers, they brought their own dresses and we mocked up the name tags).

A dance-off ensues, each team challenging the other until the 'Disney' dancers give up the ghost and storm off defeated. The music builds one last time, with all the characters now dancing in perfect formation, but with each putting their own idiosyncratic twist on their moves. As the number concludes fireworks shower the stage, then everyone breaks ranks to shake hands with the guests before exiting.

This was a team effort unlike anything I'd ever seen. As I was creating the script, I couldn't believe it would happen, but everyone – property-wide – stepped up at the last minute to do this… and the effect was magical.

Mitzi produced and choreographed with the help of Ray Hatch and Elaine Hansen, while Tim Sepielli oversaw the technical end of things. Our cowboy in the rafters had arrived hours before the show and sat there throughout the evening, waiting for that hay wagon to roll into place under him.

Backstage afterward, and for days at the studio, the cast is on cloud nine. We had gone toe-to-toe with the best in the business on their turf, and with nothing but passion and imagination, our little USF Entertainment Team kicked Mickey's ass.

Our next big event is New Year's Eve 1991, and Tim jumps into this with both feet. He plans a truly unique countdown, starting fifteen minutes before midnight. It's a rock & roll blast through the past, featuring music from the '50s, '60s, '70s and '80s, leading us through the years to the big moment.

There will be fireworks on the lagoon, choreographed to coincide with each decade. I suggest using Doc Brown from *Back to the Future* as a narrator, as he is our studio's 'Authority on Time'... then Tim has a brainstorm! We'll build a water-going DeLorean which will speed through the lagoon to trigger the final big blast of fireworks.

The time machine is built; a speed boat decked out with touches to make it look like the car from the movies. Flame exhausts are added to the back of the boat, and speakers are placed along the side of the lagoon. The plan is that Doc Brown will enter from the boathouse and circle the lagoon before the show, finally docking his time-traveling vessel at the south end. Just before midnight he'll fire that sucker up, and zoom through the lagoon with flames shooting out the back of the boat. The sound of the DeLorean from the movie will track with him on the waterside speakers until he gets to the bridge at the north end. The boat will duck safely under as the bridge erupts in pyrotechnics, kicking off the midnight fireworks.

On the night of the event, everything is going according to plan. The boat looks great, Doc Brown makes his lap and settles in by Central Park, waiting for his cue. Finally the big moment comes. From the south end we can hear the sound of the DeLorean firing up and flames burst from the boat's aft end. But instead of shooting out the back, they're just rising straight up...

Because the boat isn't moving. It's just bobbing there, up and down in the water. The soundtrack zooms up the lagoon, leaving the boat in its audio wake. The bridge on the north end blows up right on cue and the fireworks begin. And the boat sits there, in place, for the remainder of the evening. I go home, confused.

My confusion ends the next morning when I report to the Entertainment Offices. I find Tim sitting behind his desk, a stunned look on his face. We stare at each other a moment, then finally I ask, "What happened to the boat last night?"

Tim smiles. "I'll give you one guess."

Instantly, I know what happened. "Out of gas?"

Tim nods. We share a laugh and I tell him that shortly after Disneyland opened in 1955 someone found an unpaid bill for $10,000 in an executive's desk. When informed of the oversight, Walt Disney remarked: "Well, when you do big things, you make big mistakes."

Now that the Entertainment Department is unified, I grow more familiar with the actors-and-guides part of the operation. I start to hear grumbling from the actors about some of the company's policies. For example, until now I had no idea that the actors had to re-audition each year for employment, something we'd never done with the look-alikes. Since I'm no longer a part of front-line management these things don't affect me, but I'm flattered that people think enough of me that they would bring these issues to me and ask my advice.

Folks are starting to raise the idea of bringing the Actors' Equity Union into USF. Meetings are held off-site, union reps are talking to the actors, cards are being handed around and petitions are being signed.

One afternoon I'm summoned to the park administration offices where I'm introduced to a closely-groomed little man with slicked-back hair, a tight, shiny suit and wire-rimmed glasses. He introduces himself as a New York Labor Relations Lawyer who has been hired by USF to assist in the company's campaign to see that the studio remains free of any union involvement. "Mr. Schneider," he begins, "we asked the actors in the studio which members of management they relate to and apparently the person they feel closest to is you."

I'm amazed. "Really?"

"Yes, Sir. Have any of them discussed the union situation with you?"

"I've heard talk that there is some interest in bringing the union in," I answer honestly. "Some of the performers have issues that they feel aren't being addressed."

"And what do you tell them?"

"I tell them all the same thing: If you have a problem, take it to management. If they aren't solving your problem, you have to find someone somewhere who will."

He seems satisfied. "That sounds fair. Thank you, Mr. Schneider."

Shortly thereafter an announcement is made that there will be a new management team in Entertainment: a new show director, a new tech director and a new department head. I'm a little wary, since I've found that directing the stuff I've written allows me to rewrite as needed and insures that the original concept survives the production process. But since my job title is writer (and since I'll now be dealing with a production team unfamiliar with my prior experience) I figure there isn't much I can do about it.

A late meeting is scheduled in the Entertainment offices to introduce the new team. I'm the first to arrive and meet our new department head, who we'll call 'Wallice'. I introduce myself and, making conversation while we wait for others to arrive, I ask about his background. He tells me that he worked in entertainment tech support in a Reno Casino. Hmmmm… no mention of creative or managerial experience. I figure he's just being modest.

"What made you decide to get into theme parks?" I ask.

He answers, "I didn't know that's what I was doing." This will turn out to be our moment of ultimate bonding.

The meeting also introduces our new Technical Director (replacing Tim) and the new Show Director, both also from Reno. Afterwards, I'm unsure how this development will affect my work, but they seem very nice. Still no mention, though, of any theme park experience.

With Halloween on the not-too-distant horizon, I'm anxious to receive news of what I'll be working on. When I check in with Wallice, he assures me that he'll get back to me about it.

Weeks pass. We're now a little over two months away and I'm aching to script something. I find out through the grapevine that we'll be presenting a big stage show built around the characters of Bill & Ted. I ask Wallice if he needs me to work up some treatments for Bill & Ted and he says, "By all means." So I watch the films and fall in love with the characters; they remind me of a contemporary Laurel and Hardy. That night I fashion three treatments for Bill & Ted shows and submit them the next day. Two days later I find out that they've completed casting on the already-written Bill & Ted Halloween show. This is when I decide to stop waiting for any further Halloween assignments.

Halloween comes and goes without anyone knocking on my door. A week later I get a letter congratulating me on a highly successful special event and thanking me for my contribution to Halloween. I send a memo to Wallice pointing out that I had not been given the opportunity to 'contribute', and advising him against blindly copying everyone on any future form letters.

Even as I am being shut out of my own department, I'm developing a closer relationship with Jay up in the executive offices. Mr. Stein loves to develop show concepts and comes up with some nifty ideas. Usually this results in a one-and-a-half page treatment that sets up a concept, fleshes it out a bit, then stops abruptly. Then under the text I find this: '(need creative)'. I'm only too happy to oblige.

Writing for Jay presents its own challenges. When presenting him with a treatment, I'm always faced with the same issue: where's the <bang>? Jay always looks for that moment when the guest will be stunned, shocked, surprised or splashed with water. It gets to the point where I mark such moments in the text with a double asterisk and add a page at the end of each treatment labeled 'Jay's Bang List'. He seems to appreciate my thoughtfulness, though he isn't given to paying such compliments.

Many of the assignments Jay gives me are from his own mind; none of them come to anything, but they present interesting challenges.

One day he asks me, "Have you heard of this cartoon, *Ren & Stimpy*?"

I have to confess I have not. "Look it over. We're getting the rights to the characters and I'd like to put them in a street show or somewhere on the Nickelodeon Studios tour."

So I start watching John Kricfalusi's animated series *The Ren & Stimpy Show* on Nick at Nite and nearly bust a gut laughing. The stuff is brilliant... but too far out there for a family theme park audience, I think. Still, I'm a fan, so I dive in – and create a show set aboard a rolling puppet stage dressed as a giant space vehicle. The treatment is framed as a continuation of the episode *Space Madness* and starts with Commander Ren dictating an entry into his Captain's Log, and prompting an audience sing-along of the 'Log' commercial jingle.

The whole thing reads like an episode of the original... prompting this note from Jay, written in the margins of my proposal: "Is anyone going to want to watch this?!" I tell him the fans of *Ren & Stimpy* will probably love it, but everyone else will no doubt be as confused and upset as he is. The park winds up with a Stimpy walk-around character whose sole concession to Kricfalusi's creative genius is that his nose can fall off and be reeled back onto his face using a long cord.

My only complaint with the new regime is that I've been effectively shut out of writing for Entertainment. Most of my assignments now come from Publicity and Marketing, so I'm working on one-of-a-kind events, like grand openings and cross-promotions. For the grand opening of Fievel's Playland, Jay asks me to create a press event that will show off the new area whilst paying tribute to Give Kids The World, the charity that fulfills the wishes of terminally-ill children and their families.

Told that there will be dozens of these children at the event, I propose a very simple, short show since they (and the press) will be standing out in the hot sun while this is being performed. My brainstorm is to keep the kids behind the temporary stage in the shaded E.T. Adventure queue line.

After the executives speak, we'd bring up the music and then the characters, accompanied by dozens of Give Kids The World children (along with USF employees pushing the ones in wheelchairs), would gather onstage for a final picture. Very emotional, very short, very easy on the children and the press – and the youngsters get to be in the show!

I submit the script and am told very plainly that my job is done; I will not have anything to do with the staging of the event. Everything is handed over to our show director from Reno, so I turn my attention elsewhere until the day of the grand opening.

With the press gathered and the cameras rolling in the hot sun, Tom Williams delivers his dedicatory speech, the official from Give Kids The World offers profuse thanks to USF and the music starts… but it isn't the emotional *Somewhere Out There*; it's the rousing *Way Out West*. Out dance the *American Tail* characters by themselves – and they keep right on dancing. They do a long production number, completely ignoring the emotional moment set up by the previous speaker. As the number goes on I feel sorry for the dancers who are toiling in the sun for an audience of press and officials who couldn't care less about prancing mice.

Finally, they wrap the number to tepid applause; only then do the kids roll onto the stage to *Somewhere Out There*. It's a wonderfully touching scene – one which could have been so much more effective without the dance break.

Chapter 19
USF'S 'SANTA-TASTIC' CHRISTMAS (1993)

An excerpt of my letter to USF's Director of Operations of September 18th, 1992:

Since the recent reorganization, I feel as if I've been slowly shut out of the Entertainment Department. At last year's Halloween Event Post Mortem, Jay made it clear that he expected two things from me for Halloween 1992: 1) A duplication of the Bates Show (I've been told that this "would cost too much"); and 2) a Halloween Stunt Show.

I did five Halloween Stunt Show treatments of widely differing concepts. When the Bill & Ted concept was proposed, I submitted concepts to Wallice the week of August 9th. Wallice sent me a memo saying that he, Joanie and Michael had read them and wanted to discuss them with me. (I asked Joanie and Mike about this, and they said they'd never seen my treatments.) Then I heard auditions had been held in late August to cast the Halloween Stunt Show. I asked Joanie how this could be done without a script, and she told me that one had been written. To my query, "By whom?", she replied curtly, "Someone else." If my treatment was never wanted by the Halloween Producers, why was I asked to write one? If it was needed, but found wanting, why wasn't I asked to redo it?

I submitted the script for a Stunt Show Rain Demo the week of July 5th. At the time, everyone represented this as a matter of some urgency. Show Managers have still not received a copy of this script, nor any directions for implementing it.

Recently Wallice asked for four 15 minute stall-show scripts for Hitch, Post, Busters and Make-Up; he said he wanted them in three days. I shot him two scripts (Hitch and Make-Up) the week of August 23rd. To this date, despite my requests, I have received no feedback on my work, no one connected with these shows has seen the scripts, and no one has been told to implement them.

I did three different treatments for the Rocky and Bullwinkle New York Press Event, due to changing Guest Stars. All of them were enthusiastically received by Marketing, and the show that resulted was a hit with our New York Office as well as the Ward Family, who remarked on our own press reel that "... the writer had captured Jay Ward's sense of humor."

I did eight treatments of last year's Bates Motel show, and continued rewriting and polishing to the last weekend... three treatments for Elvira... thirteen for the Ricardos...

I have proven to Marketing and Publicity that I can rewrite my own stuff to suit whatever limitations or contingencies exist. That, while I make sure anything leaving my desk is as tight and polished as possible, I am not married to any of it, and stand ready to hit the ground running when someone needs a rewrite. Do I have to fight all-over-again to demonstrate this to my own Department?

✳ ⋅ ✳ ⋅ ⋅ ⁖ ⋅ ✳ ⋅.
✳

As a result of the above piece of whining, I am invited to attend a planning meeting for USF's first attempt at a major Christmas event, which the Marketing Department has dubbed 'Universal Studios' Santa-Tastic Extravaganza'!

All of the new management team are present, along with Joanie, a secretary who (I am slowly coming to realize) has become something of a creative force in the department. As Wallice runs down the areas in the studio, it's Joanie who explains to everyone what is planned for each section. "What do we have planned for Amity Harbor?" he asks

She replies, "Amity will be hosting Winterfest, a crafts village."

"And what will that consist of?"

Joanie has the perfect answer, "Oh, we'll give 'em some crap." I quickly write myself a note: Be sure to visit Winterfest.

There's some discussion of a ceremony on Hollywood Boulevard, with E.T. using his finger to light the big Christmas tree. I suggest getting a child out of the crowd to help him. Everyone seems satisfied with my contribution but I can't help feeling frustrated, knowing that I'll have no chance of following through on the project.

Then the subject turns to Santa Claus and how he's going to arrive. Everyone starts throwing in ideas – a parade float, a limo, a helicopter, the Bluesmobile. I pipe up, "Everyone does Santa arriving. But when you think about it, Santa's big moment should be when he takes off. Wouldn't it be amazing if he could leave from the studio for his trip around the world?"

Everyone at the table is suddenly quiet. Wallice asks the tech director, "Is that possible? Could we rig it so he flies off in his sleigh from the studio?"

The tech director answers (a little too quickly for my taste), "Sure, we can do that." No one asks any questions about *how* we can do that, and I'm too elated over having an idea of mine accepted to want to push the matter.

I quickly announce, "I'll work up a script for his blast off. We can treat it like NASA with the elves doing some technical cross-talk." No one argues with me and we go on to the next subject.

After the meeting, I quietly make the point to Joanie that the name 'Santa-Tastic Extravaganza' is a bit over-the-top and might be setting us up to disappoint some guests. She assures me she'll talk to Marketing about my concerns. A week later they announce the name of the event has been changed; henceforth it shall be called 'USF's Super-Santa-Tastic Extravaganza'!

So, on the Christmas event's second Santa-Tastic day, I walk into the studio to see the Extravaganza.

First, a stroll down Hollywood Boulevard. Much had been made in the meeting of the light design which would enhance the facades along the park's main thoroughfare. "Each building will receive its own treatment of decorative Christmas lights," was the claim, "that will light up in sequence leading the eye down the street to the moment we light up the studio Christmas tree." At the big moment, though, the lights all came on at once and are so small and dim they make no impression.

Then I turn toward Amity Harbor to see Joanie's crafts village. As I enter the area there is a large, lovely banner proclaiming, 'Winterfest'. I pass by the carnival games and spot one booth selling handmade crafts, and wonder, 'Isn't there going to be a craft-making activity for the guests?' I needn't have worried.

In the still-unused Jaws queue line there is a chance for kids to make their own Christmas tree ornament! Six big banquet tables have been set up, uncovered, in a circle. Within that circle stand three USF employees in their street clothes, each one supervising a plain cardboard box. One box is filled with red pipe cleaners, one box is filled with white pipe cleaners and one box is filled with green pipe cleaners. As a child approaches they are given one pipe cleaner of each color and shown how to twist them into a candy cane-shaped ornament.

And that is the extent of USF's Winterfest Crafts Village. Moral: if you promise "Oh, we'll give 'em some crap," you will give 'em crap.

Finally I cross the lagoon to Central Park to witness Santa's Departure.

An immense crane has been erected directly behind the Back to the Future show building. The top of the crane leans in close to the roof and peeks just a few feet over the top. From the crane a pair of cables stretches down the front of the building and out across the lagoon to the wharf at the foot of Lombard's Landing where the cables disappear into a makeshift garage placed facing the water's edge.

As the sun goes down, guests are addressed over the studio P.A. system by the voice of a Walter Cronkite sound-alike. I had figured since Walter was the voice of NASA on TV, it only made sense to start the show with him. I hadn't figured on the USF speaker system which sent the sound bouncing back and forth across the lagoon, making everything unintelligible.

Then Walter throws it over to Christmas Mission Control, from which Santa's elves will control the launch. Now, I thought everyone who had ever heard Alvin and the Chipmunks knew that when you do elf voices you drop your pitch, speak slowly and clearly, then speed up your playback. I was wrong. Neither the show director nor the sound tech knew to speak slowly and clearly, so the elf voices were unintelligible long before they were broadcast.

Then the magic moment. From across the lagoon a Super Trouper spotlight illuminates the garage doors as they swing open… and out flies Santa!

Santa is sitting in a small sleigh being 'pulled' by two plastic translucent reindeer (like you'd find on a neighbor's lawn, lit from within by a light bulb). As Santa cracks his whip and waves at the guests, which at this point are still on either side of him, the cable arrangement pulls him out over the water and up toward the top of Back to the Future – v-e-r-y s-l-o-w-l-y.

The guests are mesmerized! The children can't believe that they're seeing Santa in his flying sleigh; the adults can't believe that poor man is sitting on that tiny seat, strung between two cables and inching his way to the top of that building (and I can't believe I had anything to do with putting him there; suddenly I don't feel so bad about sticking Goofy out in those woods waiting for a train).

Santa whips and waves and waves and whips for what-seems-like-forever until he finally reaches the end of the cable far above the crowds. When the spotlight finally goes out, the sleigh is pointing heavenward at a 45 degree angle flush up against the top of the crane and the ride building.

The show is over at 9:30 p.m.; the studio doesn't close until midnight.

Strolling through the studio that night, I – and every other paying guest – stop every so often to turn toward Back to the Future to check. Yep… he's still there. That poor actor is still sitting waaaay up there on that cold, cold night, staring into the skies, trying to be as invisible as possible. And he's going to stay up there for three hours.

No matter how brilliant your original idea may be – and Santa's departure was a great idea (proved by the fact that Wallice bought it even though it came from me) – if you can't pull it off, change the idea to suit what is possible.

Perhaps a pre-landed sleigh and static reindeer on top of Mel's Drive-In; Kids could be escorted up stairs to the roof to meet Santa while he's on the job. Perhaps he arrives doing a slide-for-life from the top of that crane. Or his Sleigh is portrayed bent and broken in Kong's grasp in the ride (this is, after all, Universal… the same people who brought you *Nazarman's Chainsaw Massacre*)!

The point is if you're going to invest the time, money and effort (and most precious of all, your guests' credulity) in an idea, make sure it's going to work out the way you wanted. If not, change plans!

My last meeting at Universal is particularly satisfying.

A two-page memo from Jay Stein outlines his idea for the grand re-opening of the long-delayed Jaws attraction. The company has invested in the building of a ferocious-looking *Jaws*-themed truck that Jay wants to attack the audience and members of the press at the dedication event. The '(need creative)' question is how do we set this up without tipping the gag? I really like the idea because it is truly out-of-the-box thinking on Jay's part, avoiding all the Jaws clichés while focusing on the one thing everyone wants from the franchise – a good scare.

Jay's not asking for a treatment from me, though. He's called a property-wide board meeting in the big room up in the admin building… and the only two people he's invited from Entertainment are me and Wallice. Wallice comes by my office to join me for the walk to the meeting. As we travel, I get the feeling he can't understand why I'm being summoned to such an important gathering, especially when we're halfway there and he casually says, "Why would they ask you to come to this thing?"

"Gee, I guess Jay wants me there."

"Oh." We make the rest of the trip in silence.

The seats around the huge meeting table are almost filled. Wallice goes to the right, I go to the left and we wind up directly across from each other. The room continues to fill until it's standing room only all the way around the perimeter. After a long delay Jay finally arrives, takes his seat at the head of the table, turns to look right at me and asks, "Ron, what did you think of my idea?"

Before answering, did I take a moment to turn and relish the baffled expression on Wallice's face? You bet your ass. That's the part that was 'particularly satisfying'. As for the resulting event itself, I wouldn't be around to see it.

As preparations get under way for the Jaws event, the company holds a big awards dinner for the actors to convince them that they're loved and appreciated; and it works. The union is voted out. After having listened to the actors' complaints I don't quite believe it, but it's not my call.

Wallice is now free to take off on a two week vacation. But before he goes, he has to take care of one last bit of business. He walks into my office, shuts the door and sits down across from me. "Ron, I'm afraid we no longer have any work for a writer. I have to let you go."

I don't blink. "You've got plenty of work for a writer, you're just giving it to everyone else except the guy with the track record and the job title." We stare at each other. I add, "Thanks for stopping by." Wallice then gets up and leaves property for two weeks. I guess he's just bright enough to know how this is going to go over with the rest of the company.

All my old workmates are shocked, no one more so than the look-alikes. We hold an old-fashioned Irish wake in Finnegan's Bar and Grill, then I clean out my desk and split.

Moving on...

Chapter 20
FREELANCING 2 (1994-98)

I take my severance pay from the studio and buy my first personal computer.

While working as a full-time writer at USF, I'd been using a typewriter and had resisted learning to use a computer as long as possible. Now I sign online for the first time on Prodigy Classic and find a community of nationwide Disney Fans; a new family.

I wish I could find something online these days as much fun as the Prodigy Disney Fan community. We call ourselves Disnoids and enjoy online mad tea parties, masquerades, improvisational story sessions and glorious trivia tournaments. The toughest competition is a regular intense two hour event conducted on alternate Sunday nights by a studious fellow from Georgia, Josh Young. Unlike the rest of us, Josh's knowledge cuts across all fields of Disneyana, making for a challenge that is anything but trivial.

After a year-and-a-half, Josh retires and I offer to step in and take over the show. I have a great time creating challenging and entertaining quizzes for my online friends; however, it soon becomes clear that I've got my work cut out for me if I'm going to measure up to the high standard set by my predecessor.

Finally, I hit upon a plan. After a few competitions I announce that, "Two weeks from tonight... my next competition will feature a full hour of intense questions about *Mary Poppins*; so get out your video tapes, gang, and study up!" Two weeks later I start out with an hour of general trivia, but in the second hour I launch into the hardest, most nit-picky stumpers you can imagine. The crowd amazes me by shooting back the answers almost as soon as I post the questions!

Here, for your enjoyment and possible bafflement, are several of my own twisted Disney trivia questions from the old show:

RON'S PRODIGY DISNOID TRIVIA

1) In the 1937 classic, what's the first thing Snow White cleans upon arriving at the dwarfs' cottage?

2) According to the clowns in *Dumbo*, why don't elephants have any feelings?

3) Do the math: Dalmatian Pups divided by Old Men... plus Little Pigs... divided by Tweedles... leaves you with which hospitable group?

4) During *A Spoonful of Sugar*, how many lettered blocks jump up off the floor and into Michael's arms?

5) You might know what kind of handle Mary Poppins has on her umbrella; but what becomes of that parrot within the chalk drawing world?

6) What are the names of the two Disney characters who wield a weapon named Ol' Betsy?

7) In 1973's animated *Robin Hood*, while thinking about his lady love, what does Robin do with his right hand?

8) Besides Geppetto, who votes in favor of naming the puppet Pinocchio?

9) Thanks to Imagineering's policy of recycling faces from other attractions, what misplaced historical personality operates Gutenberg's printing press inside Spaceship Earth?

10) What is the oldest object in Disneyland, and who donated it?

(Answers can be found where they're always found – in the back of the book!)

Over the next eighteen months, I create tests on most of the animated classics, a healthy selection of live action movies and the various Disney theme parks. I also initiate a kind of 'comic trivia' called Figment's Corner, where I post open-ended remarks about Walt Disney and the Company. Contestants complete the statement in a satirical manner and their answers are judged on the speed, brevity and wit of their response.

Back when I was Dreamfinding, I spotted a job listing in the WDW employee newsletter looking for an experienced video editor. I immediately thought of my old friend from Universal Studios Hollywood, Jeff Palmer, who had studied video production in college and worked around the industry for years before winding up in media production at Chiat Day Advertising. I called him up, only to find he was already on the other line with Disney Professional Staffing discussing the job in question; *they* had called *him*.

In the years that follow, Jeff rises to the position of senior editor with Disney's post-production facility and helps direct many projects for the Company... even helping the Company win an Emmy for the WDW Christmas Day broadcasts. By the time I leave Universal, Jeff's created his own Orlando production company and he brings me in on the odd freelance job. We work together on the Chuck E. Cheese shows, the preshow video for *Doug Live!* for Disney-MGM Studios and the WDW 25th anniversary press event in Orlando Arena.

Between calls from Jeff Palmer, Steve Hansen and various other connections, the next few years are peppered with a variety of freelance projects. Some pan out and pay; most don't.

I only ever get one request from Universal for a freelance writing gig: The Florida Public Relations Association is holding their annual fundraiser. Each year they 'roast' some corporate big-wig, and this year their victim will be Tom Williams, President of Universal Studios Florida.

I get a call from the head of Marketing at Universal, asking if I'll help with the writing. He tells me that the assorted VIPs have all submitted their thoughts about Tom and it's fallen to him to create an entertaining evening out of what they've sent. Naturally, he's handed this chore off to various others in the organization but nothing's come back that's made him laugh.

Finally, someone tells him, "If you really need this to be funny, you should call that guy who used to write the shows at USF." By the time he reaches me, the event is a week away... so I quote him an exorbitant price and get to work.

Using some of the parodies I wrote about USF while working there, the inspiration of the submitted notes and my personal knowledge of Tom, I crank out the full evening in two days: eight different speeches roasting Tom and his closing rebuttal. I only find out the evening was a triumph when five of my jokes are reprinted the day after the event in the business section of the *Orlando Sentinel*.

And while we're on the subject, a word here about Tom Williams. I wrote a bunch of events while at Universal and most of them were hosted onstage by Tom, one of the world's Great Good Sports. For the dedication of *Beetlejuice's Rock and Roll Graveyard Revue* I set him up alone on stage with a very aggressive Elvira, Mistress of the Dark and Tom held his ground masterfully.

Today Tom oversees all the Universal parks, so hopefully he'll never be subject to that kind of abuse again. But if he is, watch him... Tom's a great guy, and I'm grateful I had him to write for.

Out of the blue, I get a call direct from SeaWorld Entertainment asking if I'd be available to pull some shifts two-days-a-week as Santa for the upcoming Christmas Season. This year they've invested in a whole new themed setting for Saint Nick; they're doing the Norman Rockwell version of Santa Claus.

This is something I find very exciting, because the Rockwell Santa is a <u>working</u> Santa, depicted in shirtsleeves studying a map of the world or in some other way preparing for the big night on Christmas Eve. I like that as it gives me something to play with.

I tell the nice SeaWorld lady that I'd love to come and play, and that I happen to be sporting a huge white beard at the moment, perfect for playing Santa. She claims to be delighted and we arrange to meet at the park the following day.

As I approach the employee gate, the SeaWorld rep lights right up, delighted with my appearance in general and my beard in particular. We drive over to the Entertainment Offices and all the secretaries are exclaiming, "Look, Santa's here! It's Santa!" I have my initial costume fitting and leave in a jolly mood.

A week later I'm back for a second fitting. There are more effusive greetings from the staff – "Hi, Santa!" – and then I sit down to sign my contract.

When I've finished writing my name, I look up to see a woman standing in front of me, glowering... and holding a white Santa wig and a beard. "Put these on." I try explaining that I thought I was being hired because I was the total package, that I have a real beard and putting theirs on top of mine is going to look really bad. "All of our Santas have to match exactly; put these on."

Only then is it explained to me that, since they schedule two Santas each day who alternate thirty minute sets, they have to look identical in case any guests walk through the exhibit more than once. So, figuring it's only two days a week, I honor the contract and show up on time for my first shift...

Where I find that the beard I am to wear has not been styled. It hangs down in a long, straight line. The other Santas' wigs and beards are beautifully styled and curled; not mine. I summon up what little hair-styling knowledge I have to make it look better, but without much success. And when I ask if there is a stylist on staff I'm told that she's on vacation till the end of the year.

Still I bravely step out on set, feeling truly uncomfortable but still trying to lose myself in the joy of playing Father Christmas (something I love to do, though I prefer to do it with my real beard)!

It's tough to enjoy talking to the kids, though, since there are none to talk to. The SeaWorld set-up is a photo-taking franchise. I'm supposed to sit in this lovely house with a sign out front listing the assorted prices for prints of 'Your Picture With Santa' which effectively means that the folks who have just paid to get into the park aren't going to drop the dough for a picture with me.

Finally, the frustration grows to be too much and I get out of my chair and stroll around the area. I talk to the kids and engage their parents and in this way I drum up some business for the photographer and make the nice folks at SeaWorld a little money.

Apparently, I also piss off the nice folks at SeaWorld because the next day I'm told that my Saintly Services are no longer required. Ho ho ho.

Chapter 21
VAN HORNE'S GRAND BUFFET
(1998-99)

Steve has married a wonderful woman from Alberta, Canada. She grew up in the small town of Canmore near the entrance to Canadian Rockies National Park. On a trip north with his new wife, Steve decides to move up there and start his own company producing events and convention entertainment.

Canmore is located next to Banff, a major ski resort and convention town, founded in the late 1800s by the General Manager of the Canadian Pacific Railroad (CPR), William Cornelius Van Horne. As he was carving a path through the Canadian Rockies for the CPR, Van Horne discovered a natural hot springs at Banff, and decided this would be an excellent tourist attraction to promote the railroad. He built the Banff Springs Resort, the first of the nation's Historic Hotels, and is credited with having invented Canadian Tourism.

As Steve is setting up his new business, he makes the rounds of the hotels in the area, meeting with local officials and the managers of the various resorts in Banff and nearby Calgary. He drives up the hill to the Banff Springs Resort and is intrigued by a statue of its founder, W.C. Van Horne, who, he can't help but notice, bears a striking resemblance to me. In his first meeting with the Banff Springs' Manager, Steve remarks, "By the way... That statue of Mr. Van Horne? I know that guy. I can have him up here working for you, if you're interested."

※ ⁂

As Steve gets established, he starts calling on me back in Orlando to send him treatments and scripts for his new company, Peak Events of Banff. The wide variety of themes they offer affords me the chance to stretch my creative wings and develop concepts set in many varied periods and environments. But the one constant idea, running through every email and conversation, is: one day I'll be coming up to Banff as W.C. Van Horne.

In the spring of 1998, I finally get the call I've been waiting for. This coming summer the Banff Springs Resort will present its own themed dinner show, *Van Horne's Grand Buffet*. They're going to turn one of their banquet rooms into a showroom offering an international menu. The show will consist of a small cast of characters that will circulate throughout the room, performing period songs and comedy six nights a week. With the support and sponsorship of the Canadian Pacific Hotels chain, Steve secures a temporary work visa for me to spend the summer in Banff and I'm off to Canada!

After sixteen years in Orlando, nothing could have prepared me for my first sight of the Canadian Rockies, or the glorious Banff Springs Resort Hotel. It's become cliché to refer to the Banff Springs as a 'Castle in the Rockies', but there is simply no other fitting description. It's a medieval castle with magnificent stonework carved from the surrounding mountains. The fittings and art work all reflect the period of W.C. Van Horne. The views on all sides are miraculous, the dining exquisite, the service impeccable and the welcome I receive is literally breathtaking.

After a quick lunch with a local historian, Steve and the manager escort me to my room. Because the hotel is located in a national park, it is required to provide housing for the entire staff; so across from the hotel there is a block of dormitories where the bellmen, waiters and managers reside. The vast majority share lodgings which sleep three and four to an apartment; I, on the other hand, have requested a place to myself, which they are only too happy to provide.

The three of us walk across the street from the hotel and up a steep hill alongside the adjacent convention center. At the top of this hill is a four story dorm; in we go... and up. "No elevator?" I ask. They both laugh. 78 stairs to the fourth floor. And the whole way, I'm gasping for air (what I meant by a breathtaking welcome) and I'm laughing because I can't believe this isn't some cruel joke. I wind up in a tiny dorm room on the top floor, sharing a bathroom with a member of the hotel service staff.

I resolve that in the coming months I will only make that climb once a day; staying in my room till midday then remaining downstairs in the hotel until after that evening's show. Still, thanks to those stairs I lose all kinds of weight over the summer!

The show is a simple affair: a grand piano, a couple of risers and a cast of four. Willie Joosen is at the keyboard... he's quite literally a musical genius. He keeps us amused during the medleys by spontaneously interpolating other melodies into the songs we're singing. The Chef character is a generic European Perfectionist and Romantic who oversees the buffet that occupies one end of the massive Alhambra Room. Tony Eyamie convincingly fusses and frets over the food line when he isn't singing or romancing the female clientèle. Our third cast member plays Lilly d'Valley, a touring operatic chanteuse W.C. Van Horne is hopelessly in love with.

Over the course of the evening, Lilly sings some opera as I sit by and stare adoringly... we do some period medleys of popular songs and a little Gilbert and Sullivan... and the Chef bustles around flirting with Lilly and exasperating me. Inspired by his circus background, Steve brings in a huge stack of white dinner plates, at least 40 in all, surreptitiously tied together in a flimsy stack; Tony turns this into an amazing comic routine trying to carry this between guests' tables through the crowded room. We space the tunes and comedy out over two hours by which time the room has turned – and, with a whole new crowd, we start repeating bits and songs till it's time to close.

W.C. Van Horne was a renaissance man – artist, architect, archaeologist, adventurer, amateur magician, musician, practical joker and visionary – providing me with tons of opportunity for creative interaction. And since Van Horne is to the Canadians what Teddy Roosevelt is to Americans, everyone everywhere knows who I am on sight. Even when I'm out of costume strolling through the adjacent village of Banff, people will stop and greet me as Van Horne. This immediate identification affords me a lot of extra fun.

Another of Steve's local projects is the annual Taste of Banff, a chance for area hotels and restaurants to show off their culinary offerings. Dozens of booths are set up in a huge white tent at the city center where townsfolk and visitors can, for a fee, sample the cuisine of the excellent local chefs.

The centerpiece of the weekend event is a competition between the major hotels, where celebrity judges pick a winner from everyone's best dishes… and there I am, front and center – town founder and Canadian Legend William Cornelius Van Horne! With all the bluster I can muster I take the stage and – while everyone around me are real celebrities – I can feel every eye on me; every little thing I do draws a laugh or a comment from the crowd.

The competition is sponsored by Grand Marnier Liqueur, and there's a bottle of the product displayed in front of every judge. Now friends, I don't drink; I don't like the taste of alcohol, and that includes the taste of Grand Marnier. But W.C. Van Horne was a man of notorious appetites and that includes a remarkable capacity for strong drink. So, without drawing undue attention to it, as the first dish is served up I pour myself a shot of Grand Marnier, silently toast the crowd and toss it back. And as each successive dish is brought up I repeat the ritual, stealing myself against the taste for the sake of the laugh. By the time the competition was over, I couldn't taste anything but the liqueur.

And I didn't want to.

One day, a special ceremony is held in the grand hall of the Banff Springs Hotel to celebrate the installation of Canada's new Minister of

Tourism. Many Canadian officials are brought to the hotel along with a ton of press. The hotel manager has the idea that I should crash the press event in character and assault the newly elected official in my capacity as 'The Man Who Invented Canadian Tourism'. He wants me to call the new Minister on the carpet and command that he invest a large part of the national budget in promoting Canadian Rockies National Park and the country's chain of historic hotels.

I'm a bit timid at first, but with the assurance that everyone will know who I am and what I'm about the second I arrive, I decide to really make an impression. Since there'll be no smoking at the event I light up a cigar and lurk outside in the back. After the Guest of Honor has started his speech I wait a few beats then bellow, "WHERE'S THIS YOUNG WHIPPERSNAPPER WHO'S TAKING OVER MY JOB?!" I burst in the back door and storm through the crowd blowing smoke in every direction.

I'm privately elated when, as they see who's making all the noise, everyone laughs and applauds in recognition. When I reach the stage the new Minister of Tourism is all smiles; he extends his hand and addresses me, "Mr. Van Horne! An honor, Sir!" He backs away from the mic and indicates that he's giving me the floor. I proceed to lecture him and all assembled on the proper care and maintenance of Canadian Tourism and charge him with looking out for my interests. With a warning that I'll be keeping an eye on him, I exit as I entered: to laughs and applause all around. Quite a thrill!

Fall comes to the Rockies and *Van Horne's Grand Buffet* closes... hopefully to be revived the following summer.

Returning to Orlando, I fall into a wonderful outdoor production of *Henry IV, Part 1*, playing Falstaff for the Orlando Shakespeare Festival; an association which will go on for years. The theater community in Central Florida benefits from all the theme park talent, assisted by the parks' willingness to adjust their scheduling to free their performers up for these outside gigs.

I make another new friend when my old Universal Studios boss

Mitzi Maxwell introduces me to her talented and charming husband, Alan Bruun, Artistic Director of the Orlando Opera Company. Our first show together is *The Fantasticks*. Upon our closing he grabs me by the shoulders and says, "Let's do more!" Eventually Alan moves over to direct at Central Florida Civic Theater and then to help create Mad Cow Theatre Company in Downtown Orlando. Over the next few years I'll follow him like a faithful puppy and we'll do ten glorious shows together.

*　·　*　．．*．．
*

Eight months after my return to Orlando the decision is made that *Van Horne's Grand Buffet* will run again in the summer of 1999! The only question is: Will the Canadian Government let me do it?

Getting a Canadian work visa for an American is tough; the government looks at it as taking a job away from one of its citizens. This is compounded in the case of an actor. It's assumed that one performer is as capable as another so Steve has to prove that he needs me, an American, to play this Canadian icon (who, it should be pointed out, was born in Chicago). He holds auditions in Calgary for the role, he acquires letters of recommendation from performing organizations he has worked with and he uses the influence of the Banff Springs Resort, the Canadian Pacific Hotels and the Canadian Pacific Railroad – organizations founded by William Van Horne – to plead my case.

It comes down to the wire, but at last – two days before we open – I'm back in the Rockies. One big difference: this time I'm treated by hotel management as The Returning Hero. Instead of being housed across the street, atop the hill and 78 steps up in the singles dormitory, I'm now immediately adjacent to the hotel and DOWN one flight, alone in a room meant for two... with my own bathroom and kitchen (and yes, I will put back on all the weight I lost the previous summer).

It strikes me that one unique feature of my career has been my track record of playing figureheads, characters that represent a place or an idea. King Henry at 1520 A.D., Prof. Spillikin in the Crafts Village, Womphopper at the Wagon Works, Dreamfinder at EPCOT Center and now W.C. Van Horne in the National Park, the town and the hotel he founded.

During my second summer I add the Canadian Pacific Railroad to the list. Steve and I make a pilgrimage to CPR's corporate headquarters in Calgary to meet with their board of directors. I walk into the lobby in character only to discover a huge, floor-to-ceiling photograph of Van Horne himself. The receptionist was surprised to say the least, "Mr. Van Horne, how do you like your picture?"

"It's not big enough."

Van Horne takes control in that meeting, much to the amusement of the men charged with protecting his legacy. They had recently invested thousands of dollars in restoring the historic rail cars of Van Horne's time, including his private carriage. The purpose of the meeting is to discuss the idea of CPR creating an historic excursion train that will cover some of the track laid by Van Horne in the Rockies, featuring the period cars and first class service with an appearance by W.C. Van Horne himself.

A week later, we are out on the railway with the board. They start in Calgary and pick me up in character an hour out of town. I barrel through the cars on a 'spontaneous inspection', winding up in Van Horne's private car; in his outsized bed with servant's quarters and working office. I rejoin the group later and regale them with stories of both my adventures on the line and in private life.

The following month, Steve and I fly east to Vancouver for a gathering of Canadian Travel Writers. I make a short speech at their arrival dinner, and early the next morning everyone boards the Rocky Mountaineer excursion train for a trip inland to Banff. Along the way I stroll between the two-story domed cars as Van Horne, reminiscing about my days laying the very tracks we're traveling upon.

I've been reading up on Van Horne's accomplishments for some time, studying photographs and historical accounts of his heroic effort to connect the country and drive Canadian tourism… but until this trip I have never personally seen the results (The only other train I've ever been connected with had only gone as far as Mickey's Birthdayland). With shades of the Disney Archives in 1970, here I am at the source of the legend, seeing Van Horne's life and landscape all around me.

This is a two day excursion, so I have to carefully space out the material I have prepared. I pad things out with some Van Horne-appropriate jokes and some Robert Service poetry, but basically it's like my training at 1520 A.D.; I speak a piece in the forward dome car then skip back to the second car and do it all over again.

At lunch we step into the dining car for a magnificent meal. Everyone else has a choice of entrées... but a special dish has been added to the menu in honor of Van Horne's presence on the Rocky Mountaineer: a recreation of his favorite meal. So there I sit, with everyone watching, as I swiftly consume two whole roasted chickens. Can't disappoint my fans!

At our overnight stop we are greeted as we disembark by a troop of Canadian Mounties in full mufti – complete with mounts! Everyone gathers for dinner at a locally-produced themed dinner show about the region's history, where I (as Van Horne) am introduced from the stage as a visiting dignitary.

The next day we are eastward bound again. When we arrive in Banff we are greeted at the train station just as the guests of Van Horne's era were, by large horse-drawn wagons which take us up the hill to the hotel.

We close out our second summer in the Alhambra Room and the rest of the cast departs. But since it's 1999, I remain in my little room across the street to wait and prepare for the Banff Springs' Millennial New Year's Eve Party.

Up to this point, all of my time in Canada has been spent in the summer months. But now this city boy – who has spent his entire life in either Southern California or Central Florida – is in for a hard, cold shock.

I sit up in bed one morning and look through the curtains at the foot of my bed. Normally I can see the dormitories across the street, but this morning they appear to be missing; all I can see is white. The thought occurs to me even before I go to the window for a closer look – *snow!*

Oh, I've seen snow before, but always on the ground; I've never seen snow falling from the skies. Like a shot I'm dressed and outside, afraid it will stop before I can get out there. I needn't have worried.

Today I discover how truly beautiful the Rockies can be... and how truly dangerous. My biggest problem is with momentum. You know how an object in motion tends to stay in motion and a large object in motion even more so? I was never so aware of my status as a large object as when I tried to walk on the icy sidewalks of Banff that winter.

Steve's plans for the New Year's event, titled *The Celebration of the Century*, could not have been more ambitious. We plan on producing no less than six themed parties in the Banff Springs Resort for the same night.

Every group of guests will have a table reserved at a medieval romp, an intimate jazz club, a '50s sock hop, a '40s dance club or a country-western hoedown. And each party will have its own dinner show with live music and atmosphere entertainment appropriate to the period. Then, after they've eaten and been entertained in their assigned room, everyone's invited to visit any of the other themes to enjoy the show there. Then everyone in every room will be led in a parade by Van Horne and his troop of bagpipers to the hotel's grand ballroom for the huge midnight bash with fireworks, guest artists and a full orchestra.

For the '40s dance club, Steve wants to recreate a live radio broadcast. I pen an original tribute/parody of *The Jack Benny Program*, in memory of my first drama teacher's father, Milt Josefsberg, a writer on the show. My only real challenge is that no one in the Canadian cast has ever heard an old radio program. So right up to showtime, I'm trying to coach everyone in the style of broad radio character-comedy of the period. It all comes together... for the second show, at least.

It's a bold plan which Steve and his team pull it off without a hitch. I get to host the evening as Van Horne before catching a flight back to Orlando later that week.

Chapter 22
TITANIC, THE EXHIBITION
(2000-06)

I'm back in Orlando in January, 2000 and looking for work. Coming off the holiday season, none of the big parks are hiring so I start making the rounds... and stumble into a small attraction in the Mercado Shopping Center on International Drive called *Titanic, the Exhibition*.

My experience as Van Horne serves me well here. They're looking for actors who can portray passengers aboard the ill-fated White Star liner while guiding visitors through a combination museum and re-creation-of-the-ship. I'm given a simple script to read from and am hired on the spot.

The management is a fun group... everyone is most welcoming and encouraging. Training consists of the entire cast pitching in to share what they know about the Titanic and her story, and I'm overwhelmed with photocopies of books and articles, personal stories and opinions. Apart from learning the facts and statistics of the ship, each actor is left to select and research their own character from the roster of passengers and to craft their own version of the tour. I spend days observing the others, jotting down notes and impressions, memorizing facts, wandering alone through the museum between tours and trying out ideas.

It's a wildly varied bunch… some are trained actors, some merely characters, and there are a few true authorities; but all share a passion for the story of Titanic. Then there are the 'regulars' – non-employees – who keep turning up; some arrive in costume, some with an attitude. Keeps things interesting.

After some time reading up on the ship, I finally settle on a real person to portray. An Irish shipyard worker, an engineer who was a member of the eight-man Guarantee Group: men who traveled on the maiden voyage as second class passengers to check up on the ship and make adjustments as needed. For the next six years, I will be Ennis Hastings Watson.

Management has worked out a rotation system that affords the guest a taste of several characters over the course of their one hour tour. The building is ideally laid out – a series of rooms that recreate the office of the owner of the White Star Line, the Irish shipyard where Titanic was built, the dock where passengers board the ship, a first class suite, the grand staircase, a third class hallway, a cargo compartment (complete with Renault Towncar), the ship's bridge and the deck at night (refrigerated, of course).

Scattered throughout are historic photographs, movie props, true artifacts from the ship and recreations. The tour is divided into six ten minute segments, with a different guide in each area, giving each group a chance at an encounter with a shipyard worker, a ship's officer and a first, second or third class passenger. Everything is carefully timed and coordinated, with groups being handed off between actors easily, creatively and — frequently — amusingly.

Over the ensuing years, the attraction goes through many changes. New management comes in and swaps things around; there are employee cutbacks and, while the basic show remains the same, the rotation changes. Soon the one hour tour consists of four segments of fifteen minutes each. Then three of twenty… then two of thirty… then each actor has the group from beginning to end.

Throughout my career of 'interacting' I have seldom portrayed a real person communicating a true story. *Titanic, the Exhibition* is a terrific laboratory for me; as with any other attraction you have the constant flow of guests, the chance to polish a bit of business, to judge the way folks of different ages and backgrounds react to what you're doing. Even more exciting is the range of the tale we are telling. People arrive expecting to hear of the disaster, forgetting that the sinking is only the last chapter of an amazing story.

There is the history of White Star Line, the talented men who built the ship, the hundreds of people on board... and the parties! It's really a happy, amazing tale until everything goes to hell. Tell it right and the disaster, when you finally get to it, is twice as effective because the audience has a greater appreciation of what was lost that night.

I quickly fall in love with the role of 'Historical Re-enactor' and set about trying to improve my tour. While the other actors seem governed by their own passion for the story, it occurs to me that the perfect tour would be one that varies with the guests' interests. I take a cue from the Titanic websites I find in my research; they each have a menu off to the side, listing different parts of the story, so the visitor can zero in on the aspect of Titanic that most fascinates them.

I construct my tour that same way. Over the years I develop about three-and-a-half hours of reliable, exciting material. There's the basic story of the ship and its sinking, the lifeboats, the numbers and the hard facts; the rest is special material about the different classes, individual passengers' stories, luxury steamships, the bizarre coincidences surrounding the legend, the many film adaptations etc. By drawing the guests into the tour, I can determine what they want to hear about and customize the tour to their interests while still telling the basic story.

There are a few actor/guides who take their roles too seriously. I am astonished one day to see a guest ask a 'crew member' where he can get some batteries for his camera. The actor grows indignant and declares that he doesn't know what a 'battery' is, "This is 1912!"

Thank heaven such nonsense is the exception. Most of the cast is totally focused on sharing the story with the guests... that is when we're not pulling pranks on each other. One actor likes to hide in the replica Renault Towncar we have in the cargo hold, featured in the James Cameron movie as Jack and Rose's trysting place. He'll wait until another actor comes through with a tour group, then bounce the car up and down and slam his flattened hand up on the back window.

When little Jimmy Trebowski, an elfish-looking fellow who plays an Irishman, comes strolling innocently through Joe Zimmer's tour group, Joe likes to grab him, pick him up, and dance around singing, "I caught me a leprechaun!"

The first thing the guests encounter after boarding the ship is a mannequin wearing a replica of a White Star Officer's uniform. Whenever I lead my group past him, I always salute and declare, "Permission to come aboard, Sir?" One of my fellow actors scares the hell out of me one day when he waits behind the mannequin and replies, "Permission granted!"

It's not unusual for us to have visitors to the attraction introduce themselves as being descended from folks with a connection to Titanic. On one tour I have a relative of White Star Line owner J. Bruce Ismay, the man who campaigned to carry only half the prescribed number of lifeboats and then got away safely in one of them.

One day a young lady tells me she's descended from a second class passenger, but the name she gives me doesn't sound familiar, so I grab a copy of the ship manifest and look him up. She admits she might have the name wrong, then says he may have worked on the ship. I ask if he might have been a member of the Guarantee Group and she says yes. I've got chills, but say nothing as I read off the list of eight names, leaving my own for last. When I finally read 'Ennis Hastings Watson', she lights up. "That's him!"

I tell her, "Darlin', I have terrible news. I'm your great-grand-uncle." Taking her through the story of the ship was a special thrill.

One of our Titanic actor/guides has a wonderful idea for an after-hours tour of the attraction which will tell 'ghost stories' about the ship. There are so many tales of precognition and coincidence about the sinking that one could easily fill an hour tour, so he writes up a first draft and presents it one night to the cast and management.

The only trouble is the man is not a very good writer; and his one hour tour stretches on for more than two hours and is filled with puns and long-winded, self-indulgent, stretches that try to set a spooky mood but communicate little information.

Ninety minutes into the show, the manager pulls me aside to quietly ask if I could do a rewrite of the material; can I make something manageable and exciting out of the concept? I tell him I'd love to try.

I pull together all the bizarre stories I can find. Then, to give the show some immediacy and a personal touch, I combine them with tales of the occurrences, real and imagined, that have happened in the attraction. The result is a pretty exciting one hour script. The following excerpt would take place on our recreation of Titanic's deck at night:

Ghost Tour Guide

In here, actors have heard phantom footsteps, even heard water hitting the deck, like someone wringing out a mop. One night a young man in an officer's uniform appeared standing there (point at the spot where an impressionable guest is standing), *then faded from sight.*

It's after 2 a.m. on the promenade deck of Titanic. Several hundred feet in that direction, people cling to the stern for their lives. Hundreds of miles beyond that, a little girl named Lizzie clings to life, slowly dying of consumption in Kirkcudbright, Scotland. With no one else available, Salvation Army Captain W. Rex Snowden is stationed at her bedside on what amounts to a deathwatch. Lizzie, tossing all night, drenched in sweat, suddenly asks him, "Can't you see that big ship sinking in the water?" Snowden assures her it's a bad dream, but she persists, "Look at all those people drowning. Someone called Wally is playing a fiddle and coming to you." Finally the little girl calms, slips into a coma and dies.

Captain Snowden later said, "I heard the latch turn in the door and felt a presence enter the room. Some hours later, the whole world was startled by the tragedy of Titanic. Among those drowned was Wally Hartley, its bandmaster, whom I knew well as a boy. I had no knowledge of his going to sea or having anything to do with any ship."

At an even greater distance – twenty-three years after Titanic – Seaman William Reeves is standing watch on a tramp steamer crossing with coal from Newcastle, England to Canada. He finds himself right here, in this patch of the North Atlantic, on a cold April night, no wind, no moon, nothing to see but stars.

Now, Mr. Reeves is not the panicky type. He's been at sea almost continuously for the past five years, serving on so many ships that he's long ago given up trying to remember the name of the ship he's on at any given moment. Bundled up and doubled-over, trying to stay warm, Mr. Reeves turns toward a bulkhead and sees a life ring, like this one, only this had the name of the ship on it: Titanian.

Mr. Reeves thinks of us. He turns to admire the flat calm of the sea, just as it was on that night in April, 1912 – and he recognizes the coincidence. And thoughts of coincidence bring to mind something his father had told him when he was a boy: that the date of young William's birth, April 15th, 1912, was also the date Titanic sank.

He scans the horizon, sees nothing but a little mist. And it occurs to him that the lookouts aboard Titanic had seen this very same view minutes before they struck. Without another thought, Reeves turns toward the bridge and shouts, "Danger ahead!" The man at the helm cuts the engine and, as the Titanian drifts to a stop, there appears a large blue iceberg dead ahead, near invisible in that still water.

If they hadn't stopped at that moment, they would've hit her for sure. More amazingly, sunrise revealed the Titanian was surrounded by ice. They sat there for nine days, waiting for an icebreaker to reach them from Newfoundland.

Since the original idea to have a ghost tour wasn't mine, I'm not surprised when the manager gives my script to the original actor to perform. But when I attend the public premiere of *The Titanic Ghost Tour*, my script has been cast overboard and the show is once again moving at a snail's pace. Guests are soon exhausted, groaning at his puns and leaning on the furniture to keep from falling over. After ninety minutes, the tour is only half done, so I sneak out the back door.

The Ghost Tour lasts another night or two, then – like the specter of a ship's officer on the deck at night – it fades away.

The success or failure of any themed experience can depend on many factors, the most ephemeral of which is people. Those who visit, certainly... but more frequently the people who create, operate and manage.

Through the six years I'm working there, *Titanic, the Exhibition* is a living laboratory where these four elements are in a constant state of flux. Business conditions and personalities conspire to swap out management teams… the occasional lack of clear hiring and performance standards result in uneven show quality… shifts in location, promotion and weather patterns cause similar shifts in guest interest and participation… and the content and structure of historical displays are subject to the whims of the market for artifacts and whoever holds the keys.

The situation is exacerbated – and occasionally enhanced – by the living nature of the story; by the authors, artists, enthusiasts and events that come along, frequently unannounced, to play on our ship a while.

There is the newly-published author who, while visiting our attraction promoting his book, makes a point of not only disagreeing with a performer's presentation but doing so passionately in front of guests. The amazingly talented actor who had made a living of portraying Captain Smith at conventions and events around the world who would pop in from time-to-time to address our tour groups. The silent creep who turns up every couple of weeks to lurk in the attraction for hours, disturbing the guests and asking the same questions he asked on his last dozen visits…

… And there's the ghost of William Thomas Stead.

Mr. Stead was one of the 1500 people who perished that cold night in the North Atlantic. His autographed portrait sits in a display case in our souvenir shop, a real artifact from the period. The woman who runs the shop is a psychic priest, a resident of the nearby spiritual enclave known as Cassadaga. Every morning she greets him, saying "Good morning, Mr. Stead," as she opens the shop. After I've worked at Titanic a while she shares with me the story of Mr. Stead, and – as my fascination with the old guy grows – I decide he would make a great second character for me to portray on the tour.

William Stead was a renowned social crusader in England in the late 1800s, and a major participant in the spiritualist movement. He wrote and published numerous articles and books about communication with the afterlife, and wrote two works of fiction which, many believe, predicted the events of Titanic's maiden voyage. These things, coupled with his pragmatic views on Christianity and man's responsibility to his fellow man, make creating a tour that reflects his thinking a real challenge.

What follows is the end of my Titanic tour, as presented by 'Mr. William Stead':

William Thomas Stead

"People ask, 'Where was God?' "They say it different ways. Children ask, "How could you do that? How could any man put his loved ones over the side and watch as those he loves — and his only hope of survival — float away in a half-empty life boat?"

"Well, that was our job, wasn't it? That's what we were there to do; our 'unpleasant duty'. If you're looking for God on Titanic, you need look no further than the faces and backbones of the men on that deck.

"Some folks don't think men today could do that; stand there — stone still and silent — and go down with the ship. And it's tempting to underestimate ourselves when being measured against legends. But we are common people, as they were... we cherish life, as they did... and when the last boat is gone and there's nothing left to be made of the moment but a memory, I believe our better self steps up.

"And when it's your turn, and you face that unpleasant challenge and do your duty, you're no longer just a child of God, you're his good right hand.

"I was thinking about what I'd say tonight, what I'd leave you with. This occurred to me: if mankind possessed and acted with the same compassion, the same wisdom and tolerance as our lord, his story would be unremarkable. And there'd be no Christians. Only Christs. Think about that. Dream on it. Act on it.

"I implore you — and those you love, work and worship with — don't be a Christian. Be a Christ. Do your duty. As we did. As I know you will. And may the one who watches over all hold you and keep you, warm and safe, in the palm of his hand."

Mind you, I wrote and performed this long before the company was acquired by a born-again gentleman who saw fit to scatter quotes from scripture around the walls of the attraction. My only aim then was to do justice to the spirit and memory of Mr. Stead in my portrayal.

I quote it here to provide an example of what I consider to be the true joy and potential of themed entertainment. We amuse people with our craft every day. *We can do more.*

(By the way, after years of greeting his portrait with, "Good Morning, Mr. Stead," our store manager claims that she was walking the darkened halls of the museum one night before closing when he shows up, wearing an evening jacket and a bright red vest. Mr. Stead smiles and says, "Good Morning," and then disappears.)

One night I get a call from Fred Franco, our lead Groucho from my days with the Universal Look-Alikes. He tells me that a week before Universal had suddenly laid off most of the celebrities, claiming that the guests had no idea who Laurel and Hardy, The Marx Brothers, W.C. Fields and Mae West were anymore. They were keeping Lucy and Ricky Ricardo, Marilyn Monroe and the Blues Brothers, but that was going to be it.

Fred invites me to the funeral for Universal's Look-Alike Program, a party being held that night at John McConnell's house; John was one of our Elwoods and had married Melissa Radley, our first Lucy Ricardo. All the Celebs will be there and Fred thinks I'll make a great surprise Guest of Honor.

It's a glorious evening, seeing these talented people again. I learn that in the ten years since I left off as creative supervisor they had twenty-five other supervisors, but none had lasted very long. The cast had taken to naming each one for their number; their current boss is 'Number twenty-six'. I've been reverentially referred to as 'Number one'.

John has set up headstones in his backyard, one for each deceased character. We all gather around the graves and I'm honored to deliver the eulogy for the USF look-alikes, recounting the glory days and paying tribute to those who made the program shine. I've always been proud of what we accomplished, but I'd never felt quite so appreciated.

Chapter 23
DISTRACTIONS: PIRATES AND FIASCOS

As I believe I've mentioned, I love a good themed dinner show. But since one can learn a great deal from the mistakes of others, here are the stories behind two shows I *almost* worked for – and learned much from:

During my time aboard Titanic, I go along one night to catch the show at *Pirate's Dinner Adventure*. My friend, Joe Zimmer, is working nights there, giving a wonderful performance as The Pirate Captain. It's an impressive operation, built around a full-scale pirate ship set. The evening has a great premise with lots of songs and stunts and humor, but here and there it loses focus; some little thing will suddenly drag on too long, or a bit will be repeated endlessly for no good reason. It seems obvious to me that what was once a tight, well-written script has been heavily influenced by a naïve and meddling management.

Joe invites me to meet with the show manager and offer my services as a script doctor to tighten and focus the show; not to rewrite, but to take out the 'improvements'. When I meet with the manager he claims to be all for anything that will help the show... as long as the 'fix' doesn't cost him anything. Since the actors are contractually obligated to two hours of rehearsal time before or after every performance, I figure that should be plenty of time to cut and paste, so his only expense would be my fee.

Over the next two weeks, I sit and watch the show with script in hand and plot out what to keep and what to cut. Finally, I have a clear idea of what I want to do and I set up a second meeting with the manager to lay out my plan. I tell him that I can tighten the show in two rehearsals (four hours total), cutting the dead moments and focusing the ones that have grown sloppy, and it won't cost him anything beyond my fee.

That's when the manager informs me, "You can't fix this show. These people won't listen to you; they don't know how to take direction. It's like with an orchestra: you can't improve the sound if the individual players are rotten. It's hopeless, so I'm going to have to say, 'No, thanks'."

Faced with his utter lack of respect for the cast, what can I do? I had spent time with these people; they were all behind me 100%. Watching their performances night after night had shown me that they were capable of anything I could throw at them. I felt they were trapped in a show that was being mismanaged and I sensed that they felt the same way.

The show has run profitably for years and will probably last many more; piracy is a timeless theme. And I've seen much better ideas more poorly executed...

I come back from a couple of weeks in L.A. to find everyone talking about a new dinner attraction opening near International Drive. All anyone seems to know is that the owner is an Englishman, newly arrived in the States, who's leasing the former home of a failed German Biergarten and is determined to open a new show to be called *Fiascos*.

Immediately I love the name and can't help thinking that, in a town full of horsie shows and hoop-de-doos, any show that could live up to the name 'Fiascos' might really clean up. So on my next day free from Titanic, I head over to hunt down the owner and find out what's going on.

The building is a mess, obviously a construction site... but where are the workers? Entering the lobby, the only person I see is a shabbily-dressed bum bent silently over a thirty-gallon metal oil drum as if he's being sick. Before I can ask him for directions, I realize he's a prop.

The main hall looks like a junkyard exploded. It's packed to the rafters with every conceivable type of cheap decoration and show prop. A recurring theme seems to be 'Stuff that Disney Sold for Scrap'; I recognize bits and pieces from the parks that haven't been used in years.

A voice draws my attention to the rafters where a young couple is busy rigging a trapeze. I call up, "I'm looking for the owner," and the girl points obligingly. Finally, picking my way through the hazardous mess of tables, benches, plastic greenery and faded banners I find a graying, balding old man in a dirty shirt sitting by himself, twisting some wires at a table covered with second-hand electric components. "I'm the owner; call me Joe."

Joe Weston-Webb is a 'promoter' from England. In his home country he is known as Grumpy Joe, an eccentric entrepreneur who races goldfish, shoots his wife out of a cannon and owns a catapult that fires chicken dung. He supports himself and his family with his invention of a portable, interlocking dance floor that he has rented and distributed around the world.

He also owned and managed a barge on a river in England that he rented out as a meeting place for corporate and private events. Its most unique feature was that the seating area was rigged to spring leaks on cue, surprising the patrons. And every time this 'emergency' cropped up, a member of the crew, in battling the hazardous condition, managed to fall overboard. Word of mouth on this turned Grumpy Joe's Party Barge into a smash hit. Building on this success, Joe expanded his grumpy empire, branching out into the dinner attraction business; first with a short-lived showplace in England, then – now, today – with a move to Orlando.

Grumpy Joe is planning a huge show this time with some impressive effects: a giant organ and bench will rise from the stage, carrying an organist on board. But the player's seat continues to rise until the musician is playing with his feet... then the instrument rises until he has to stand on his bench to reach the keys. Then the whole mess will seesaw up and down. Just when this gets tiresome, a nearby table (with dining guests seated around it) will get into the act, rising 10' off the floor.

At one point Grumpy Joe wants the kitchen to catch fire. On a whim, a decision is made to decorate the room for Christmas. Grumpy Joe bicycles into the room on a portable cart, making flaming crêpes; the cart catches fire. He's hired a waiter who does a mediocre Neil Diamond impression, a aerial act and a juggler, and is looking to hire a wait staff of misfits, since he is determined the service will be as much of a disaster as everything else.

And – while other dinner attractions might offer a choice of two or three selections for dinner – Grumpy Joe has a plan for presenting a menu of 150 different entrées to his guests.

Throughout this first meeting, my jaw is on the floor. I'm imagining this mess and picturing a success on the scale of 1520 A.D.; something that has to be seen to be believed. I can picture word of mouth carrying this show for years and on to other locations.

On the other hand, this old man might be nuts.

I start telling Grumpy Joe about my background, my experience with themed dinner shows and my enthusiasm for his concept and we quickly strike a bargain: for a set amount I will create a show treatment for *Fiascos* – a structure for his ideas. We set up a second meeting, where he will present me with all his ideas and a check for half my writing fee, with the other half coming when I present the finished treatment.

At our second meet, Grumpy Joe hands me a stack of 3" by 5" cards featuring his accumulated ideas for what should go wrong each night at *Fiascos*. As we go through them I'm considering which ideas might or might not work for the Orlando crowds and which ideas suggest characters or plot points for the evening. After he describes one gag, I make a remark about the type of character that it would work for; Grumpy Joe suddenly gets *really* grumpy. "There are no characters. This is not a show. There are no jokes. Everything has to be absolutely real."

I squeak out a timid, "But – "

"No buts! No jokes, no characters. This is not a show. <u>Absolutely real.</u>"

Our meeting ends cordially and I head home with my stack of ideas and my mind slightly boggled. Part of me thinks I should turn around and head back, return the check and tell Grumpy Joe he doesn't need a treatment since, if all he wants is a series of bad experiences, it's all there in the cards. The other part of me feels certain I can bring something to this project that is sorely lacking: showmanship, and a sense of place that can only help it become a creative presence in the Orlando market.

At this point I'm not sure what I'm going to present to Grumpy Joe when we meet next, but I am hopeful I can win him over by turning his random disasters into a long-running, profitable enterprise.

My treatment tells the story of two men: a fussy, fastidious Maître D' and a charming Seating Host. The Maître D' is (comically) demanding of the guests, trying to raise the cultural level of the evening, while the Host manages an eccentric-but-talented wait staff.

The Maître D' is trying to run a very high class restaurant; nothing is good enough for him. He's tough on everybody which leaves the Seating Host running around trying to keep the guests and staff happy. This would incorporate a lot of the disasters that Joe wants while clearly making the Maître D' the victim, instead of the guests.

While the guests are engaged in practical jokes the staff pull on the Maître D' (more of Joe's disasters), they are also entertained by little tricks and turns that hint at the fact that the staff is a lot more able and talented than their very strict boss suspects.

Halfway through the evening there's a mutiny and the Maître D' is tricked into participating in a magic trick which effectively removes him from the room. The Seating Host becomes the Showman Host presenting his wait staff as the talented group they really are and they take over the evening.

What follows is the epitome of the word 'Fiasco', but in a good way: wild, unpredictable, loud, funny and exciting. Everyone gets to show off their specialty (the talent they were actually hired for) and the show builds to an impressive finish, with even the Maître D' delighted (because the guests are)!

When I present my treatment to Grumpy Joe, he's livid; this isn't what he asked for. I try to explain my reason for adding structure to the evening but he won't listen. The decision is made to send me home without the second half of my writing fee and to part as friends.

Several weeks later, my pal Josh and I arrive for the grand opening of *Fiascos Circus and Magic Dinner Show* ('Where Dining Meets Disaster') in a state of sadistic fascination. We share a passion for bad attractions and lousy guest service, and from what I understand we're in for quite a night.

On the front of the building is posted The Menu: a list of over a hundred different dishes, every type of food imaginable from every country on the map. We're greeted by the dining host and asked what we want to order. I ask how this is possible (especially since I'm expecting the kitchen to burst into flames during the show). It's explained that the kitchen inside is hardly used; dinner orders for *Fiascos* are phoned in to the dozens of restaurants in the International Drive area and the food is delivered to the theater. I decide the meatball sandwich sounds relatively safe.

As we enter the lobby we are greeted by the sound of violent vomiting. The mannequin I had observed on my first visit, bent over the metal barrel, has been activated. What looks to be concentrated mushroom soup is pouring in long bursts from his mouth into the barrel to the accompaniment of synchronized pre-recorded puking sounds, as he heaves and hunches forward spasmodically. In a rather clever arrangement a small pump behind the barrel circulates the mixture from the barrel back up into the bum's throat so the cycle never ends. I am shocked... and mesmerized. So are a lot of people. At least Grumpy Joe had the good sense to place this display inside – AFTER we had ordered dinner.

We're ushered upstairs (into a space far too small to comfortably accommodate those present) to find Grumpy Joe overseeing a spirited goldfish race. He addresses the guests, explaining at length the struggle he's had to open on time and the problems he is having with American contractors and inspectors. Finally we're all led downstairs into the showroom (which seems only slightly more organized than the last time I was there).

Once everyone's seated, I can see there's been quite a good turnout for the grand opening. Centerpieces on the tables are deliberately cheap looking. Our waitress comes by and tosses a small plastic bag at each of us, containing plastic utensils, a napkin and packets of salt and pepper.

Grumpy Joe takes the stage with the Show's Master of Ceremonies (Joe Zimmer again; he left Pirate's only to wind up next door at *Fiascos*) and they introduce the first variety act.

The magician is okay, not terribly polished but adequate; the same can be said about the juggler. The waiters react enthusiastically to everything; the crowd less so. At one point the entire room is suddenly and quickly decorated for Christmas, then the decorations are hastily removed. The organist gets some good laughs. The singing waiter sings a couple of Neil Diamond hits, poorly. Grumpy Joe does his bit with the flaming crêpes cart. The aerial act is next, which (like everything else) is played as if things are not quite right. Then – at long last – the food arrives in tin trays with cardboard tops; each entrée is thrown down in front of the lucky guest. My sandwich is still warm, thank goodness.

Josh remarks, "I've seen enough," and leaves. I decide to stick around.

As the evening grinds on I take a look around the room at the faces and realize with a shudder that it's working. The crowd is actually charmed by the tackiness and random incompetence of the evening. The waiters appear to be having a good time, Grumpy Joe seems happy (well, happy for a guy known as 'Grumpy Joe') and the guests are smiling. Birthdays are called up onstage and one lucky celebrant receives the World's Least Surprising Pie in the Face. And it's over.

It worked. I'm not sure why, but the whole thing felt exciting and original, and the large crowd got swept up in it. It actually worked.

Two weeks later I'm back. Again with the meatball sandwich. Again with the mechanical Heaving Hobo in the lobby. Since the crowd is lighter the upstairs room is big enough to accommodate everyone, and Joe's greeting now seems longer than it did the first night.

Downstairs, the crowd is more obviously smaller; we're surrounded by a narrow buffer of empty tables. There appears to be fewer servers than last time and the energy in the room is down by about 15% from what it was at the grand opening. Still, it's the same show and the crowd, while hardly enthusiastic, laughs lightly and applauds in all the right places. I behave as any experienced audience member would, leading the laughter and applause whenever appropriate, eager to contribute to the evening's success.

It still works, but it worked better with the larger crowd and the excitement of opening.

A month later and again I'm back. No meal for me this time; Joe Zimmer comps me in.

Plenty of room upstairs. Grumpy Joe's monologue now goes on too long and is composed mostly of complaints about American business methods and the weather (we are entering hurricane season).

Downstairs the buffet between the audience and the walls is definitely wider. The wait staff continues to thin; the performers now participate in the distribution of plastic utensils. The juggler isn't evident this night. I'm still doing my part, laughing and applauding with gusto. The majority of the crowd is obviously British, brought in on a package tour. They seem pleased enough.

I start to wonder how long this can go on.

A few weeks later I'm upstairs listening to Grumpy Joe's Preshow Diatribe. Sitting across from me are four neatly-attired young fellows sporting trimmed beards and an easy-going manner. Every instinct of mine whispers, <Imagineers>.

They are laughing appreciatively at Grumpy Joe's whining, which confuses me until I imagine myself in their place. Unfamiliar with the history of *Fiascos*, they've heard of this new and different dinner show where everything goes horribly wrong and so they're here to see what's up. They're probably the first people from Disney Creative to venture forth and – Oh, My God…

They think this is a performance.

They think this is an actor *playing a role* and they're reacting to Grumpy Joe's sincere whining with laughter and applause, thinking this fellow must be the Lord Olivier of Interactive Performers.

When the party moves downstairs the four are seated front and center (at the secretly rising table, so I figure someone knew these were VIPs if not actually Disney folk). The show begins and they're right there, laughing at the haphazard décor and the service staff.

Then, slowly, The Dawn. As the evening proceeds I watch their laughter still and the smiles fade and the four of them come to realize, "Oh, my God. *It's real.*"

I sit at the very back of the room this night, alone at an empty table. The show is just horrid. The acts don't seem to care, the audience is entirely focused on the food and it feels like Grumpy Joe's dour mood is contagious. I become aware that even I am no longer laughing or applauding, an obligation I usually take very seriously. On the contrary, I'm sitting at the back of the room with my jaw hanging, a shocked look on my face (the same look as on the faces at the VIP table). Inside I tell myself to smile but I can't. It's all too awful.

The next day my friend Joe tells me that *Fiascos'* owner has banned me from the restaurant for making faces. I explain that I tried not to look so depressed but couldn't help myself; Joe is understanding but helpless.

The loss I feel passes quickly. I'm not sure I could endure another night, especially if the show continues to deteriorate the way it has been. At the same time, like driving past a particularly bad car wreck – or the sight of a mechanical bum throwing up into a barrel – I want to watch.

Months and months later...

One day at Titanic my pal Joe greets me with, "You'll never in a million years guess what next Friday is." I confess I'm stumped. "It's the one year anniversary of *Fiascos.*" Holy shit, I think.

"Holy shit," I remark. It's a tribute to my friend Joe's professionalism (and tolerance) that he's stuck by Grumpy Joe and the show all this time. And so, motivated by nostalgia and my emotional investment in the place, I formulate a plan.

I buy two dozen roses and sneak in the back door of *Fiascos* one hour into the anniversary show, find a hiding place behind a wall of plastic greenery and tuck myself in to watch the fun. It's the same lousy show; though everything runs smoother it's still an honest-to-Pete disaster, just like Joe described in our meetings over a year ago.

At show's end, after the birthdays have been disposed of, my pal Joe calls the boss front and center and informs the small audience that tonight is the one year anniversary. Grumpy Joe launches into his version of a 'thank you'-speech, explaining what a horrible time he had getting the place open, what with the American contractors and health inspectors and hurricanes…

By this time I've snuck around behind the stage. I creep up behind Grumpy Joe, tap him on the shoulder and present him with the roses. He smiles, puts his arm around me and introduces me to the crowd: "This is Ron; he's our favorite customer." Holy shit.

One week later, my friend Dan Carro is working at *Pirate's Dinner Adventure* as Duty Manager when he is summoned to the box office to deal with a crowd of unexpected visitors. A small mob has arrived without tickets or reservations, and yet they expect to be admitted to the next Pirate show. After a few questions, it comes out…

Fiascos closed that night forever. The manager turned the paid ticket holders away, sending them down the street to Pirate's with the assurance that their tickets for the former would be honored by the latter. After a word with *Fiascos*, Dan decides to honor the empty promise.

The Final Fiasco.

Chapter 24
MONSTERS, INC. LAUGH FLOOR (2006-09)

With the constant shifts in management and egos at Titanic, some days are inevitably better than others. The summer of 2006, however, marks a low point in operations. Conducting my tour is still fun – but practically nothing else about the place is. The new owner is readily available for a grin and a pat on the back, but has trusted the day-to-day operation to our Curator of Artifacts and his wife, who are better at dealing with the inanimate items on display than with live performers.

I start looking around at the surrounding attractions, hoping for another window to open. A Disney audition notice catches my eye for a new type of attraction, part of their Living Character Initiative. *Monsters, Inc. Laugh Floor* (MILF!) will be a live show featuring members of the computer-generated cast of the smash Disney/Pixar film – and some new personalities – performing stand-up comedy as part of their new mandate to collect laughter instead of screams to power Monstropolis.

Disney is looking for comic actors to assist the monsters in creating and performing this new experience for Walt Disney World's Tomorrowland, and I am selected! I sadly conduct my last tours of Titanic... then gleefully abandon ship.

In the fall of 2006, I'm 54 years old – twice the age of some of my fellow Laugh Floor Cast Members – and outrageously happy to find myself once more on the opening team of a new attraction. The Laugh Floor is a blend of all the things that make opening a new themed show a seat-of-your-pants experience: cutting-edge technology, live performance by characters from an established franchise, and real-time guest interaction.

About twenty comic performers are here to share their expertise with our monstrous cast, and almost that many other people are on hand to perfect the performers' interface and audience surveillance, polish the animation and projection system, and put the finishing touches on the décor and operations.

Opening has been scheduled for April 2007. We comic monsters are supposed to start work in early November 2006, leaving five months for us to work behind closed doors, mastering the system, perfecting our characterizations, and creating the material that Mike Wazowski and company will present. But a few weeks before we are to start work, Park management decides that it wants to preview and promote the new show during the upcoming press junket in December – *four months* sooner than scheduled.

So eight monsters are hired in October, a month earlier than planned. They will receive highly-focused training on the system so they can be ready to perform in December for the press. These brave individuals are quickly dubbed the Space Monkeys, since they will be 'launched' before the rest of us.

We of the second wave are brought on board in November, but will spend the first few weeks out of the way, playing improv games in a rehearsal hall across property.

When we are permitted to join our brother monsters on site, we are all mightily impressed with the new toy created by Pixar and Disney Imagineering. It needs a lot of work yet – bringing the animation up to snuff and tweaking the timing and placement of our show controls – but I can't help recalling my childhood dream of having my own Audio-

Animatron to play with. This is *much* better.

Our daily training resembles nothing so much as a day in high school.

Every morning we are greeted with a different rainbow-colored grid of scheduled classes where we are divided into groups of four and given intense instruction in the various aspects of the job *as the people who are training us imagine it will be*. Some of the material covered will be vital to know when we open. Some of it will be useless. But *all* of it is presented in deadly earnest.

Our instructors run the gamut from Imagineering technicians to writers and freelance consultants of many varieties. It occasionally feels like each instructor is trying to impress the others with how seriously he takes the work and how hard he is able to push us. Speaking for myself only, the most helpful and inspiring instruction comes from my fellow monsters (especially the Space Monkeys) and one Talkative Turtle who swims over from EPCOT Center's Seas Pavilion to lend a flipper.

When the December press event arrives, the door transporting Humans onto the Laugh Floor becomes operational. A few preview audiences are brought in each day to see a primitive version of the finished product. The screen resolution is only a fraction of what it will be in April, the animation is choppy and the scripts are almost verbatim those created by the Imagineering writers.

But the crowds laugh – and those laughs are captured in the massive yellow 'Laugh Can'; proof that, even in this primitive state, we're on to something good. The crowds are asked to fill out response forms at the end of each performance and, after a few breathless days, we're closed again.

Thankfully, Disney Operations comes to a preview performance and sees for themselves that we are definitely *not* ready to open, and we are now assured of spending the remaining three months of prep time undisturbed.

But the damage is done. The Disney Online Fans, tasting blood, have started posting reviews of our preliminary efforts. Their opinions are hopelessly uninformed and almost universally bad, since they cannot imagine that anyone but themselves cares about the quality of our show. We are trashed for the poor animation and the writing and especially for putting a Pixar show in Tomorrowland. In spite of repeated announcements at each performance that the preview is definitely *not* what the finished show will look like, they're certain that it will be no better. As if buying an annual pass endows one with knowledge of the future…

But our work goes on – this time with a lighter heart. We've made it through the worst. The pressure is off. We had our first dealings with the Human World and nobody was seriously injured. The Space Monkeys are properly lauded for having brought us through the first phase of opening and we are now blended into one team of monsters. There are even a few days where our army of advisors do away with the class schedule and we are invited to simply play with the show.

One particular afternoon is set aside for 'Monster Karaoke', where anyone in the cast can put the monsters through their paces, singing popular hits and showing off with no other objective than to make us all laugh. It's at low-pressure moments like this that the final show, and the true potential of the Laugh Floor, can be glimpsed. This is what it can be when all the managers and advisors and consultants finally leave the asylum and the inmates take over. We are all laughing – and the 'Laugh Can' practically fills itself.

April comes and the grand experiment goes public. Our full animation is dazzling, the crowds quickly warm up to us and we settle in behind-the-scenes to experience a new kind of teamwork. Everything blends perfectly between the individual monsters and most shows end with the cast relating to each other some funny incident with the guests or sharing a new discovery about the character interface.

Now when we arrive at the Laugh Floor the only schedule we have to face is our work schedule, showing who we'll be paired with, for how many shows and when. Since we've all come through the same ordeal and grown to love and respect each other's talent, every day is play time.

And as Steve Martin once sang: "The most amazing thing to me is… *I get paid for doing this!*"

When we aren't helping the monsters fill the 'Laugh Can', the MILF cast often get to spread our wings and play other roles in the parks. One day, just before the Magic Kingdom's 'Pirate and Princess Party', a brother monster mentions he's pulling duty in that night's parade on the Pirate Ship float, so I slip out between shows to see if I can catch him in action.

The park is jammed, of course, but I make it out to Main Street just as the Pirate Ship sails around the corner. I spy my friend in full pirate regalia, standing on the rail above the poop deck and clutching a rope hanging from the mast. I raise an arm to wave just as he turns and spies me. He shoots me a smile of recognition and salutes as he pushes off from the rail and swings out and across the deck to the far side of the ship.

In that moment I'm a little boy again, standing on Main Street and relishing a personalized wave from my favorite Disney character. I choke up and look around at all the other kids sharing this feeling. Some of them, like me, are in their fifties... their joy colored with gratitude that they can share this moment with their grandchildren. But I'm in a different space, simultaneously reliving my childhood and proud that – through luck, determination and many, many blessings – I've had a hand in crafting millions of such moments for the children, families, friends and fans I've touched.

Afterword

"Life's like a movie, write your own ending,
Keep believing, keep pretending,
We've done just what we set out to do... " –

-From *The Muppet Movie*, lyrics by Paul Williams and Kenny Ascher

October 1st, 2007

I'm back at Epcot for the 25th anniversary of opening day. The Company wasn't planning on holding any special celebrations to mark the occasion, so the online Disney Fans planned their own... and Disney had to scramble to catch up.

This morning there'll be a brief re-dedication ceremony at the Fountain of Nations, and I'm here bright and early to meet up with some friends. I'm dressed in my usual jeans and Hawaiian shirt, but underneath I've got a Figment Tee on and I'm sporting an Imagination baseball cap. For the occasion, the park's speakers are playing a collection of the musical themes from EPCOT Center's opening day attractions.

As soon as I'm in the park, I'm stopped by a family of strangers. The mother announces to the rest of the family, "This is the Dreamfinder!" and throws her arms around me. Everyone insists on having their picture taken with me. It really gets embarrassing, though, when I pose with her very confused-looking young children, who have no idea who the Dreamfinder is, who I am or why they should care.

I finally meet up with my friends in front of the re-dedication stage. They were smart enough to nab a bench in the shade of a large hedge and I join my old friend, Disney Archivist Dave Smith and Disney Intern Steven Vagnini. We commiserate over the early hour and our general exhaustion.

As the gathered mob mills about, I spot a couple of fans dressed in homemade Dreamfinder costumes, clutching plush Figment dolls. Suddenly the background music starts to play the opening scene from the original Journey Into Imagination and the crowd cheers. I get chills. Steven is beaming at me.

Afterward I dash off to meet up with Disney Video Guru Jeff Lange who has organized an historic tour of Epcot for his online fans and family. I've invited myself along as a contributor, thinking I might have something interesting to add about the old homestead, Imagination. When the group arrives I finally get to meet the Dean of Disney Bloggers, Jim Hill, whose writings (JimHillMedia.com) I follow religiously. We hit it off right away and I marvel at the depth and breadth of his knowledge of all things Disney. We spend the day touring the park with a core pack of fans, sharing stories, posing for pictures and answering questions. All day I keep being recognized and delightfully assaulted by fans of the characters. We end the evening in front of the Italy Pavilion watching a special edition of *IllumiNations*.

I'm thoroughly exhausted and drenched from the evening drizzle when the park-wide sound system once again launches into the turntable scene from 'Imagination'. Again, everyone around me cheers and I'm surrounded by people wishing aloud that Dreamfinder and Figment would return...

May 15, 2011

I'm back where our story started... Standing backstage with Figment in the convention center at the Contemporary Resort, watching a twenty-eight-year-old video of myself singing *One Little Spark* at the 1983 dedication of the Journey Into Imagination ride.

The blue suit I'm wearing may not fit the way it did long ago, but the characters are as comfortable as a pair of old pajamas. The last time I felt this nervous was the day of the dedication, not knowing what lay ahead – either in the show that morning or in my career. The difference is that back in 1983 I had something to prove; tonight I have something to celebrate.

The crowd of 2,000 D23 fans have already cheered the beginning of the video, with no idea of what's about to happen. My cue is coming up; my old phobia about the mic rears its ugly head. What if the sound tech misses his cue?

Two tiny wings, eyes big and yellow,
Horns of a steer, but a lovable fellow...

The video sound cuts out and my mic goes live. I can feel the crowd catch its breath as I step forward, singing:

He is my best imaginary friend,
And just like that we're back again!

No sooner are we on stage than the entire room is on its feet, cheering. I make it to center stage and look out at the crowd. There in the front row are Dean of Imagineering Marty Sklar, Figment's Daddy Tony Baxter, Disney Legend Bob Gurr, Archivist Dave Smith, historian Paul F. Anderson and many of the wonderful people who built Walt Disney World back in the '60s and '70s and EPCOT Center in the '80s.

Everywhere I turn, I see people cheering, weeping and running toward the stage. And (thank you, God!) somewhere out there one daring rebel has the sense to whip out his phone and videotape the moment for YouTube posterity.

And I stand there, beaming. It strikes me now, when I watch the video, that I can see Wally Boag's attitude. I'm totally at ease... as if they are the ones who suddenly surprised me.

When things finally calm down, I launch into the few jokes I created for Figment and I, then we step over to the piano to shake hands with Richard Sherman. He skips the dialogue we worked out in rehearsal, instead remarking that Figment hasn't aged a bit. I don't know where it came from, but I ad-lib, "Figment doesn't age. He ages *me.*"

What a thrill to sing the Imagination theme, *One Little Spark*, with its composer; then to step center stage and lead the crowd in a giant sing-along. When we leave together, Richard, Figment and I, the crowd again goes nuts and I practically float off the stage.

Backstage I'm overwhelmed with a tremendous wave of relief... and closure. Everything about this night seems to have bracketed and gift-wrapped the package of dreams and thrills that has been my professional life.

At that moment I want, more than anything, to thank the world for what it has given me in the preceding four decades. But when I get home and check online I realize it isn't necessary. Thanks to the opportunity afforded me that evening by the D23 team, my message of thanks has already been received and acknowledged by just about everyone. The online outpouring of gratitude for our little surprise – and affection for the characters – assures me that everyone got the message:

"Thanks to the Lovers, the Dreamers... and You."

APPENDICES

Appendix I
WALT DISNEY VS. THEMED ENTERTAINMENT

Themed Entertainment is an art. In my opinion it is the most challenging of art forms. This is for two reasons:

First, it is the one form of communication that has the capacity to embrace all other modes of expression – painting, sculpture, film and video, architecture, music, dance, writing, acting – all of these and all the rest. It presents them in glorious, harmonious concert where each one inspires and supports the others to tell a unified story.

And second, its ultimate expression exists solely within the personal experience of the audience. The result of the craft of theme is the physical, intellectual, emotional and spiritual changes it creates within the observer – or, more accurately, the participant. The Audience is the Medium.

The Themed Environment is a synthesis of elements that has a specific effect on the guest. As such it has always existed in its primitive form. While no one before Disney may have had the idea of sculpting a themed show, there have always been visionaries who have created environments with a specific focus; that focus would lead them to carve out the nascent themed environment.

In the early 1900s, visitors to the three major attractions of Coney Island, New York witnessed the perfect, living example of the evolution of a theme park. First came 'Steeplechase Park', an amusement area which featured many ingenious mechanical rides; purely physical experiences.

'Luna Park' came next; Luna being shorthand for Lunacy. Here, the individual ride often told a particular story, like Chicago Fire or A Trip to the Moon. The rides may have been themed individually, but the park as a whole was a mish-mash without any unifying theme. Guests were slammed from one new reality to the next. Lunacy, indeed.

Finally, 'Dreamland' was created. Here the rides and shows with their individual stories were united in an architectural setting straight out of the Arabian Nights. Though it was a cacophony of towers, monuments and extreme gingerbread, the whole of 'Dreamland' was a perfect unified setting for all these varied stories and adventures.

Walt Disney's genius was his drive to improve and refine whatever he touched. Even his very early personal artwork reflects this. The young Walter had two styles of drawing, a highly caricatured style which reflected the work of contemporary artists of his time, and a more photographic style, one that almost presages the use of rotoscope in his later films. He was striving to capture life in his art and thus couldn't be pinned down to just one style.

Whether it was in animated shorts, features, nature documentaries, travelogues, popular film, sound reproduction or amusement parks, every field Walt turned his hand to was improved by his influence and the contributions made by artists and technicians under his leadership.

Walt's ability to build a better – and more family-friendly – amusement place was most influenced by the fact that the people he used were storytellers. And since Walt and Company were most adept at telling stories through film and animation, they created environments that were, quite naturally, themed.

Their work since the '50s has revolutionized the amusement field and – if not actually invented – defined and perfected the themed environment. That's the good news.

The not-so-good news is that, as a result of its close association with the Disney style, the Art of Theme has for decades been synonymous with childish entertainment and simplistic storytelling. Even as the Disney Company employ a level of technical sophistication and artistic accomplishment unmatched in history, the image of the theme park as a Disneyfied construct has for decades stifled the further evolution of the form.

But salvation is at hand. Many of the Imagineers who have worked within Disney have now struck out on their own to explore the form on their terms. They have carried on the revolution Walt started in 1955, even as they study the work coming from WDI. And Disney itself continues to put its toe in the water, exploring new ways to push the envelope as far as they dare within their own corporate style.

The Art of Themed Entertainment is just beginning to evolve. It is an exciting time to be wearing a name tag.

Appendix II
FIVE KEYS TO GREAT THEMED ENTERTAINMENT

One of my earliest Disney memories is the Character Shows at Disneyland's Carnation Plaza Gardens, which I call the 'Where's Mickey?' shows because they all seemed to have the same plot: all The Gang is here, except – Where's Mickey?! Then they'd scatter to look for him, leaving Goofy, then Donald, then Chip 'n' Dale to do their specialties. Mickey would arrive in time to join everybody for the finale.

(With the '70s along came women's lib and 'Where's Mickey?' was replaced by 'Where's Minnie?'; finally in the '80s, Mr. Eisner put his hand in and we got the 'Where's Roger Rabbit?' show.)

Of course the *Golden Horseshoe Revue* at Disneyland was my favorite show in the park for decades, but *Show Me America* in 1970 really opened my eyes to what could be accomplished on a theme park stage; a book show with a full, live orchestra, Broadway-caliber talent and a script that told an original, coherent story.

The Dapper Dans and the Main Street Maniacs have always surprised and charmed. And in the '90s, Disney-MGM's Dick Tracy show was a landmark; not only for its production values, but for being a show based on a Disney film that dared to not recycle the same plot as the movie!

At the other end of the scale, EPCOT Center's *Splashtacular*, left me hot, sore and confused. Disneyland's ambitious *Snow White: An Enchanted Musical* was a beautifully-produced-but-wasted opportunity to involve us in the story we all knew and adored, and the less said about *Stitch's Supersonic Celebration* the better.

When theme parks dream big great things happen... about 50% of the time. (Remember that The Twilight Zone Tower of Terror at WDW opened the same day as Epcot's *Food Rocks!*) But looking back on the broad scope of live entertainment I've enjoyed (and the ones I've endured) a few elements stand out that the successful shows had in common. I call them the 'Five Keys to Creating Great Themed Entertainment', and I'd like to share them with you (and any Future Showmen who might be looking in):

#1 – DELIVER WHAT YOU PROMISE

Many years ago I visited Six Flags Over Georgia where I waited in a long, hot queue for their Jungle Cruise-style attraction. I was giving serious thought to leaving the line to find some shade and a cold drink, but as every boat returned, it was filled with cheering, clapping guests who apparently had the time of their lives on the ride, so I hung around.

When I finally embarked on my jungle adventure, I found the ride was a long, uneventful bore. The highlight of the whole experience was the moment just before the ride's end when our skipper announced, "When we come around this corner, be sure to cheer and applaud so the folks in line will think this is a great ride!" I would be tempted to condemn the park for lying to me about the quality of the attraction, but they never advertised the ride as being any good. All they really promised was that at the end I'd be happy... demonstrably so. And so I was, as I happily-but-cruelly perpetuated the gag.

What a show is called, how it's advertised and – yes – the other guests' reactions constitute a promise of things to come. We create certain expectations and if those expectations aren't met, if we haven't kept our promise, that's bad show.

When Disneyland's *Enchanted Tiki Room* opened in 1963, it was a perfect example of a show keeping the promise of its name. It was indeed an enchanted room filled with tikis.

On the other hand, when WDW's version was 'updated' to the *Enchanted Tiki Room: Under New Management*, all the 'New Management' did was complain about the original show. The title carried the promise of improvement – a change for the better. None was forthcoming. So not only was the promise broken, but those of us who knew and loved the original were confronted only with an Audio-Animatronic assault on Walt Disney's groundbreaking classic attraction.

When we were creating *The Blues Brothers Show* for Universal Studios Florida, our first version consisted entirely of the boys at stand mics singing next to the Bluesmobile. It was the Blues Brothers and it was a show. Promise fulfilled? Not nearly.

Even if the guests were only expecting to hear a few songs, we are a theme park where we are supposed to put you in the movies. By promising to deliver the Blues Brothers in such an environment, we have raised expectations. It now falls to us to create within the guests the sensation of being in a movie WITH the Blues boys.

Now look at the movie. John Landis' film is a series of relatively average situations that Jake and Elwood come into and violently change. They're single-minded, egotistical, delusional, disrespectful, rude and funny. They have a profound effect on those around them – offending, insulting, amusing and ultimately inspiring average folks to dance in the streets.

Now look again at the guests. They've seen the movie. They know these characters and they are there in anticipation of seeing the same kind of behavior and feeling the same deviant delight in their hijinks they felt in the movie theater.

Now look at the two previous paragraphs; that's the treatment for *The Blues Brothers Show*. Everything you need to include to fulfill the guests' expectations is listed right there. So instead of announcing "The Blues

Brothers!" and starting the medley, we meet those expectations. We keep that promise by creating a situation, something that involves the guests' presence. We set up a premise: a need, an adversary and a crisis...

A lone saxophone is heard and a young man (Willie) rounds the corner in cook's garb, playing for his own enjoyment. His wife (Mabel) meets him at the apartment door and they perform a song for the crowd (*Stand by Me*). Willie tells Mabel he's got a date to play a gig in Chicago with Jake and Elwood, but she refuses to let him go...

THEN sneak in the music (*The Peter Gunn Theme*). If you've done this right, the guests will turn and smile, because the Bluesmobile will just be rounding the corner. The Blues Brothers hop out of the car and introduce themselves to Mabel.

So now they start singing, right? Wrong. Park management might tell you they should start singing and even some of the guests might be ready for a song, but we're on a Mission from God; we're building an emotional moment that will exceed expectations and engage the guests in a way a mere medley never could.

Now there's a scene. The Blues Brothers plead for Willie's release, Mabel self-righteously objects and Jake proceeds to work his magic: whining, conniving, pleading and pouting while Elwood stands by, stoically backing up everything his brother says.

NOW there's a song... from Mabel. Wait – WHAT? Why aren't the Blues singing?! Because we're still building that moment.

Remember the scene with Aretha Franklin in the diner when she sings *Think* to her husband, backed up by three diner patrons? There's a magic moment in that song that we're going to recapture; it's the moment when Jake and Elwood are suddenly up off their stools and dancing along to the number. It's funny because: 1) it's unexpected; 2) they're deadly serious; and 3) it's wonderfully choreographed, shot and edited. So (while we're using a different song and a different situation) we're going to borrow that bit while pushing the scene forward.

I'll change the song to help the audience see the moment through new eyes. I don't even use an Aretha Franklin song here; I borrow an 'angry attitude' song from *The Wiz* (*Don't Nobody Bring Me No Bad News*) that conveys the same message as the original scene. This keeps the audience with us and in the moment as opposed to thinking back to (and making comparisons with) the original.

After Mabel sings (with the Blues Brothers as back-up) the scene continues: there's a desperate come-to-Jesus moment and finally Jake and Elwood have to prove themselves. The vamp for *Soul Man* begins... and now the guests aren't just ready, they're primed. The songs we were going to throw at them now have a purpose and an emotional context... in essence, we've placed the guests within the framework of the movie. And when, at the end, Jake invites the guests to join the cast in a street dance, there won't have to be any, "Aw, come on! You can do better than that!" whining from the stage. The guests will jump in and line up and rock the street because, after all, aren't we all in this movie together?

We promised the Blues Brothers. We have delivered on that promise.

Nomenclature is one of our most powerful tools in creating magic. What we choose to call the show forms a pact with the audience, setting up expectations. While in the park, the guest has a million decisions to make, and to an unfamiliar visitor using a map or guide book those decisions are made based on nomenclature: when choosing between Space Mountain and Dumbo The Flying Elephant, which seems a better investment of my limited time and effort?

Calling it *The Blues Brothers Show* promises a certain experience. By anticipating and exceeding expectations, we can keep that promise. It's always easier to identify bad nomenclature after the fact. Any guest filing out of the studio after USF's first Christmas Event knew for a fact that 'Universal's Super-Santa-Tastic Extravaganza' was bad nomenclature; it made a promise no one could hope to keep. (The blame for this kind of misjudgment lies not only with the originator of such blather, but with the manager who approves it and believes the guests won't be disappointed.)

Keeping our promise to the guest is the biggest reason to see that a show or attraction is properly maintained. Repeat visitors, especially, expect to see the same show they saw before with all the effects and elements operational.

Every attraction has a Moment of Maximum Anticipation; that feeling the guest has before the show actually begins, before they've even entered the venue, when they're relying on you to keep the promise made by the show's name and premise. Before they step inside, they are still free to believe the seats will be comfortable with a good view of the stage, the show will be funny or dramatic or nostalgic, everyone in their group will be enchanted and they'll leave happy that they invested in the experience.

Then the process of tearing into that anticipation begins: the seats are metal benches instead of comfortable recliners, the view is obstructed by the man in front with a child on his shoulders, the animation is out-of-synch or broken, the jokes are poor, the climax is disappointing or the rest of the family are sorry they came.

Some things we can't help; and some folks will always have unreasonable expectations. But the quality of the writing and the maintenance of the show are things we can and should make a priority.

One more note: shows evolve. Deadlines shift, limits are reset and budgets get cut. These influences will inevitably affect the final product, as will the unavoidable effects of a long run. And since the craft of themed entertainment is Dealing Creatively with Operational Reality, it is the responsibility of the producer to continually check the work-in-progress, to make sure the result delivers on its promise. As changes dictate, adjust your nomenclature and promotional content to match what your guest is actually getting.

#2 – DON'T WASTE MY TIME

To the guest, the only thing more precious than money is time. They have only so long before the park closes (or the children implode from hunger, heat or fatigue) and there are hopefully too many rides and shows to choose from; if they invest part of their day in your efforts, you'd better provide something that starts 'paying off' in a hurry.

There are a great many ways we waste the guests' time; some have become second nature. The most obvious is the show opener that begs for an unearned enthusiastic response. "Are you having fun today?" The guests respond with some cheers. "Oh, come on! I said, ARE YOU HAVING FUN TODAY?!" Repeat until the show director has beaten the crowd into 'enthusiasm'. If this happened once a day it would be one thing, but the guest spending a week in Orlando gets this in every show at every attraction for seven days.

Even more pointless is the current variation on the "Oh, come on!" routine: "Everybody make some noise!" USF's 2011 *Blues Brothers Christmas Show* began with a cast member commanding, "When I say 'Blues', you say 'Brothers'!" These are contemporary clichés that drag the guests out of the story we're telling and add nothing to the experience but mindless noise.

The worst offender I've seen is a certain piracy-themed dinner show that divides the crowd into four teams before the 'Big Competition'. The show host asks each group, "How will you cheer for your champion? And how will you boo the other sides?"

He proceeds to make the rounds of each section with these questions multiple times, back and forth, round and round... apparently deaf to the fact that the standing, enthusiastic cheers he got the first time around are dwindling to apathetic sighs; and all this before anybody has done anything worth cheering for. By the time the competition begins, the crowd has been effectively drained of any enthusiasm whatsoever.

You can bet that the first time this was performed the actor made the rounds of the room once, and the crowd's response was fine. But the actor reacts to the high of the noise and the cheers and his position and then one day he goes around a second time. It's like a drug... and the performer goes on chasing that high over a long run and the bit gets longer and who is there to call him on it?

At moments like this, I can often spot someone from the ranks of management standing off to one side, similarly pleased with the moment while not giving too much thought to what the guest may be experiencing. Moments like this must be watched for and controlled throughout the run of a show.

Involving the guest in the show is a wonderful thing if that involvement comes naturally and if the show doesn't come screeching to a halt for those who aren't taking part. Otherwise it can be viewed as a terrific waste of time.

At Fort Liberty, we had four points of direct guest interaction built into the evening. Each was clearly connected to the attraction theme and advanced the story being told.

For the first, the waiter deputized the man nearest the aisle to supervise food distribution for the table. Born of necessity, it served to cast the guest in a role in the Cavalry theme and promoted similar interaction among the others at his table. At the end of the evening the guest was cheered by his tablemates and presented with a grandly executed certificate for 'Honorable Service'.

Our next participation moment came after a medley of country-western love songs when the band broke into a spirited instrumental. Cavalry Soldiers are a naturally rowdy bunch. Combine that with a young, healthy wait staff liberally serving beer and wine... and the men of Fort Liberty had no trouble finding female partners eager to take the stage and dance with their waiter. This involved only the women (generally the family member most willing to participate), built quickly and ended before it became tiresome; and it set up what would follow.

Main Course service started with a medley of Western Themes from TV and the Movies. After the food had been distributed and everyone had a chance to eat for a bit, the Fort Commander would put the call out for New Recruits. The wait staff would encourage small children to step onstage for inspection and close-order drill; no one would be coerced (at least not by our staff). The bit was long enough to draw the kids in... the inspection process was built for comic interaction with the Commander, thus keeping those without a kid onstage entertained... and the drill made for a nice photo opportunity for the parents. It also, I noticed, gave the parents a breather to have the kids onstage and away from the table; they could eat and drink in peace.

Having had the women and children onstage made it easier to drag a few of the Daddies up for the show finale, a comic recreation of Custer's

Last Stand. Every man selected wore a Cavalry uniform overlay and no one had to portray the Indians since we had a family of real American Natives in the show. It also helped that this was toward the end of the evening when the beer and wine had loosened up the 'troops'.

In this way, everyone that wanted to had a chance to shine, many guests got to see their family members onstage and pictures were taken (and shared with the folks back home) that showed us off to advantage, properly publicizing the attraction.

Meanwhile, back on the high seas – the piratical dinner show finishes with a massive attack on the pirate ship, using all the men in the audience as mutineers and all the children as British troops, thus clearing the house of all but the women. The sheer number of people involved means that *no one* has a chance to shine... and at the show's climactic moment almost the entire audience is onstage where they can't see what's happening. Meanwhile, management is patting themselves on the back for getting such a large part of the audience involved.

Another way we waste time is by repeating ourselves. When creating material for a franchised character there is a strong tendency to re-use dialogue and bits of business that the guests have already seen spoken or enacted by the original.

Stage adaptations of film material, particularly based on animated films, are everywhere nowadays... and some wonderful work is being done there. Guests love to hear the songs they remember and parents enjoy taking their kids to see their favorite characters live and on stage.

But the stage adaptation can only hint at the magic of the original. A singing teapot in a movie, brilliantly animated, becomes a dancing crate onstage; spectacular effects are replaced with painted flats and the limitations of the live venue are emphasized. The audience is relegated to the role of detective, deciphering what's what and who represents who, based on their memory of the original.

If we must cater to the guests' expectations, it can't hurt to keep in mind that these characters have a life beyond the original story; they surely have other tales to tell, tales they'd love to share and which are better suited to the strengths of the current medium – thus building on prior friendship and deepening the experience for everyone.

#3 – MAKE ME LAUGH

For many years David Letterman started his late night show on NBC with a monologue that seemed cool and detached, which led to a muted response from his studio audience. More recently the monologue has been consistently better received and is now punctuated with regular bursts of applause. What has changed?

Today David comes out before each taping and answers questions from the audience, something he was loath to do at first. He then starts each broadcast with a reference to someone he just spoke to (and who is then picked up on camera). In spite of it usually being a remark at the questioner's expense, the fact that he has shared that 'inside joke' means that everything that follows becomes a 'Joke Between Friends'. The response throughout the show from folks in the studio is stronger for that connection.

* ⋅ ∗ ⋅ ∗ ⋅

Every themed show should have a laugh. Laughs draw people together, and a *good* laugh demonstrates the artist's affection and respect for the audience.

Note that this section is not called, "Make me groan"; the word I use is *laugh*. A laugh is, by definition, not a groan. A laugh from the audience tells the performer, "I am sincerely and spontaneously enjoying myself". A groan says, "Please don't do that again". As much as some writers may choose to believe different – these are <u>not</u> the same.

As you may have guessed from the above, I am not a fan of puns. Puns are notorious groan-motivators. Try watching any broadcast of NBC's *The Today Show*. The writers are constantly sprinkling their on-air copy with puns, which the cast dutifully read and then apologize for. Why? Because puns call for an apology. (With one exception: EPCOT Center's *Kitchen Kabaret*. It made no apology and needed none.)

There are three types of humor: Jokes Only You Laugh At, Jokes You and Your Friends Laugh At and Jokes Everyone Laughs At. Which kind do you think go over best in a theme show?

If you said 'Jokes You and Your Friends Laugh At', treat yourself to a Mickey-shaped ice cream sandwich.

'Jokes Only You Laugh At' are everywhere. Writers put them in scripts all the time and so do actors (especially over a long run when they're getting bored with doing the show as written). By their very nature they exclude the guest and so must be watched for and removed promptly.

'Jokes Everyone Laughs At' might appear to be the best type for the themed show (which is, after all, aimed at pleasing everyone). Good examples of this type of humor can be found in the animated shorts produced by Disney Studios in the '30s, '40s and '50s. Those films were beautifully drawn and animated... but the humor has not aged well. Even the Disney Channel has started running severely-edited versions of their own classic shorts in an effort to wring laughs out of their old product.

'Jokes You and Your Friends Laugh At' get the best response in a themed show because they rely on a common context that connects the audience and the actor. It says, "I'm sharing this because we have a common perspective and experience." In this case, the common experience is the themed reality, so each bit of humor has the effect of subtly reinforcing the guests' involvement in the story being told.

This type of humor acknowledges and references the themed environment. It ricochets off the guests' own thoughts and comments on the characters' feelings the way one friend shares his troubles and victories with another. It's a privileged communication, inclusive and private at the same time.

Contrast the Disney shorts with those produced by Warner Brothers during the same period; the Warner shorts are not as beautifully drawn or animated as Disney's, but they're still every bit as funny today as the day they were made; funnier, in fact. The Warner artists built cleverly on our prior knowledge of their characters' personalities – but there's more at work than that.

The men who created the Warner shorts worked out of a rundown little studio known as Termite Terrace. They endured together the poor working conditions and whims of management, a unifying experience to be sure. They survived because of their respect and affection for each other and their work, and this was manifest in their product. The cartoon shorts they made were not, as Disney's were, produced for The Audience... they were produced for each other; in other words, their friends. They were trying to make each other laugh.

This resulted in a product that respects its audience; so today we laugh at Bugs and Daffy in a way we don't at The Mouse.

A final note... In his book on writing for television, author Carl Sauter includes a glossary of film terms in which he defines 'cute' as "I don't like it." So if you show your material to someone whose opinion you respect and the best they can muster is "It's cute," you'll know what they mean.

Mind you, they're not being insulting. What they're really saying is, "I don't like it, but I expect other people will." A lot effort and expense is invested in material that has been deemed 'cute' by managers and producers; it's stuff they themselves don't care for but that they imagine the guests will enjoy. (How else can we explain *Stitch's Supersonic Celebration*? or *Toy Story - The Musical*?)

Sometimes I feel management believes that guests will like something simply because the Company *thinks* they should. People don't work like that. People like things that surprise them, move them or make them laugh. Since the odds are that you're a people, you have within you an excellent and pretty accurate way of judging what they'll like. But you have to be honest – even ruthless – if you're going to use it.

If you're writing comedy and find yourself thinking, "That's good" or "They'll laugh at that", they generally won't. But if you laugh out loud when the joke first occurs to you, that's a virtual guarantee of laughs down the road. If you don't laugh – *out loud* – when you think of it, odds are they won't laugh when they hear it.

#4 – SURPRISE ME

When I was writing treatments for Jay back at Universal, he liked me to identify and list each project's 'Bang' moments – those times when an audience would be consumed in fog or sprayed with water or subjected to some loud, startling explosion. This is one – very primitive – way of defining 'surprise'.

But here I'm defining 'surprise' as anything that challenges guests' expectations.

My friend Alan and I had a weekly date to watch the TV series, *Fringe*. At the end of every season, faced with another cliffhanger, we'd speculate about what twists the show had in store the following year. We both loved the creative challenge; at the same time we both hoped we'd be wrong. We wanted the writers to go on surprising us the way they had all year. They would have let us down if we had been able to guess what they were up to.

We've all had those moments when we know the next line of dialogue or can guess the end of a TV show ten minutes into it. There is an immediate flush of pride that comes with being one step ahead of the author... but there is also, if we're honest, a subtle sense of disappointment. Because we want to be surprised.

Challenging expectations helps the guest focus on the story; it keeps them listening, open to your creation, and so tuned in to what's happening around them that they can relax, free to participate spontaneously, creatively and unselfconsciously.

A theme park's live stage version of a film will almost always regurgitate the plot of the original; while the same movie will often be followed by a direct-to-video sequel that takes the story and characters in a new, exciting direction. The sequel-on-DVD – no matter how moving – is then considered a grab for more money. BUT if the same extension of the original story were to debut LIVE in the park, it would be greeted as an original and highly creative surprise.

The 1990 Dick Tracy stage show, *Diamond Double Cross* at Disney-MGM Studios, was the perfect example of this. It was ALL surprises: the staging, the choreography, the masks, the songs (not to mention the extreme speed and efficiency with which the story played out). Most surprising of all, though, were two things: 1) the plot was not a rehash of the movie; and 2) the new plot was a true, well-developed mystery.

The simple fact that the story was original and well-written kept the audience focused and engaged throughout. If the story had been a re-telling of the movie, we might have enjoyed the staging and execution, but we wouldn't have had the same thrill of discovery (and the producers wouldn't have kept the promise inherent in the subject matter).

Here are a few subtle, simple ways to raise the level of surprise in a themed show:

When developing your story, let the characters drive. They'll always make more interesting and unexpected choices than any 'author'; don't be afraid to let the characters seize the keyboard or pop their head through the fourth wall and run the train a while. (I had one hard-and-fast rule when meeting the guests with Figment: whatever question they asked about him we would answer the opposite of what was expected. This then left it to me to explain away the illogic, which was an interesting challenge.)

In staging the live *Snow White: An Enchanted Musical* at Disneyland, the Company chose to simply recreate the film onstage. Technically it was wonderful, but it was, after all, the same story with the same dialogue and a total lack of the surprises of the original. What if the writers had instead chosen to embrace our prior knowledge and make that a part of the experience?

How much more exciting it would have been if the Dwarfs seized control of the moment to engage the audience in a give-and-take sing-along performance of *Heigh-Ho*. We all knew the words and were already singing in our seats; the Dwarfs could have reached out to include us.

By choosing idiosyncratic language, the audience gets more than the facts from the dialogue; they get the mood, they gain insight into the characters and they are gifted with clues and language they can use to involve themselves in the experience.

The words need not be ones familiar to the audience. Veteran

Imagineer X Atencio, when writing for The Haunted Mansion and Pirates of the Caribbean, used lots of phrases unfamiliar to our ears. He chose them, not only for their meaning, but for their sound and rhythm, and they became sonic markers which helped isolate and distinguish moments and characters in the spectacle around us.

Don't be afraid to shift the point-of-view of your writing to the guest. By suddenly acknowledging them and their feelings, or even having characters voice the audience's perspective, you draw them in tighter to the story. They should feel that the show wouldn't be happening if it weren't for their presence and participation; at the same time, that participation needs to be inspired... never demanded! (In the 2011 Muppets movie, the most memorable and funny moments come when the cast on screen talk directly to us or make reference to the fact that they are in a movie. Far from taking us out of the story, it actually makes us feel closer to the performers.)

If the story you're telling is well known, find a new path to get where you're going. Disney's TV series *Once Upon a Time* is brilliant at this. They've taken the plot points we've grown up with and forged new connections and backstories that enable us to feel for the characters in new and potent ways. Even Walt chose to have Cinderella's glass slipper shatter before she could put it on!

If your show is a walking tour, provide a creatively-staged rest area, or an unexpected ride in an exotic vehicle. If it's a musical revue, introduce a brief dramatic moment or, if it's a comic show, a touching wrap-up that is then undercut with an outrageous finale. If it's a holiday-themed medley of old standards, rewrite some of the lyrics to satirize the theme.

By the way, not fulfilling your promise to the audience is not a surprise. It's like the old gag of telling someone they'll have their palm read, only to cover their hand with red paint. Shoot for the polar opposite – give them <u>more</u> than you've promised; now that would be a surprise.

#5 – MOVE ME

The fifth key to writing for the Theme Park Guest is where 'Operation' becomes 'Art'; where rides become adventures. This is the ephemeral something that Walt stumbled upon in 1955 and has contributed to every breakthrough success themed entertainment has enjoyed over the last half century. It is the appeal to and engagement of the guests' emotions.

I don't suppose any guests would claim to have been 'moved' by Disneyland's bicentennial musical attraction, *America Sings*. But the show was so brilliantly designed, programmed and executed that audiences would break into spontaneous applause at the conclusion of each automated performance.

Who were they clapping for? The technicians and artists who weren't there? The attraction host? The robots? I contend they weren't clapping for anyone else. They were giving vent to the feelings that had been generated within themselves by the act of investing emotionally in the experience.

A 'willing suspension of disbelief' has been the hallmark of the arts throughout history. A great painting invites the viewer to place himself imaginatively within its borders. Great music lifts the listener out of his plane of existence into another world. Even the simplest creation, well executed – a child's electric train layout, a brilliant cloud-filled sunset, the exceptionally-maintained garden of a neighbor – can inspire our heart and imagination far beyond its own reality.

But the themed show asks for more from the guest than a suspension of disbelief. Any stage show or movie can be a hit if we are willing to forget that it's a simulated reality. Themed entertainment asks us to invest *ourselves* in the story. In other words, the true attraction is not 'The Haunted Mansion'; it's '*Your Experience of* The Haunted Mansion'.

How does the attraction designer or show writer invest his creation with the power to engage a guest's emotions? Care-fully. Anyone who has experienced the outstanding themed attractions of our time can't help but notice that someone must've <u>cared</u> a great deal about what they were building.

Be real. Remove any impediments that might come between your audience and the underlying emotions of your story. For instance, it is hard to empathize with characters who are pre-recorded and obviously 'mouthing' their dialogue; the fact that they are 'canned' objectifies them.

The characters' reactions to a situation must appear natural and sincere; if they get over-excited or laugh uncontrollably at something mundane or that the guests don't think is funny, they can appear foolish and unsympathetic.

Guests are reluctant to express enthusiasm if they feel it is expected of them; they will hang back and avoid any reaction, not wanting to appear foolish or to feel used. One dinner show I worked in had a neat little scene between two of the supporting characters that built to a duet of a '50s classic rock song. Seeing these characters bond and sing together became a reliable show-stopper early in the run.

But as the weeks wore on the two performers began to play the scene – not for its emotional reality – but for the response they'd come to expect from the audience. The guests stopped responding because the actors were no longer playing the action; they were playing the result.

I discovered in my work with Figment that it always paid to approach the guest with slightly less energy and interest than they were displaying (this was especially effective when meeting very young children, or teenagers who considered themselves too mature to deal with a puppet-wielding wizard). If I came on too strong, children would react with fear and teens would just stare. But a laid-back attitude, one that said, "It's up to you how to react, I have no expectations," freed them up to play. I could then respond to them with a little more enthusiasm and interest... which would serve to lift the energy of the whole exchange.

At *Titanic – the Exhibition* (now called, *Titanic The Experience*) visitors have a chance to explore the ship and all of its story; not merely the disaster, but the design, construction, social atmosphere, various classes of accommodation and operations of the ship. In the beginning each room is brightly lit, full of music and sound effects. We use humor, broad movement and interaction with and within the tour group to tell the story and establish the festive mood that was prevalent on Titanic's maiden voyage.

Toward the end, however, the rooms get darker and (predictably) colder. The guide's tone grows more somber and the pacing slows. Information that came tumbling out in an entertaining and objective stream now slows to present, step-by-step, the choices made by the crew and passengers that night. The results of those choices are explained clearly and without emotion. The guests are now in a darkened room that recreates the deck of the doomed ship, complete with fiber optic stars and wave effects; *Nearer, My God, to Thee* plays softly in the background.

Whereas the guide held center stage in each previous room, he now stands among the group, letting his voice and the atmosphere hold focus. There are benches at either end of the room where one might sit alone and reflect on the story being told. The effect of all this is to isolate the guest, to turn their thoughts inward and to invite them to put themselves imaginatively on the deck of Titanic on that tragic night.

It is the desire for this emotive experience that has set theme parks apart from amusement parks. It is the reason families seek out and pay more to visit Disney, rather than the more accessible and thrilling Six Flags operations.

Finally – leave room for the guests to express their feelings. When the *Country Bear Jamboree* debuted, it was standard procedure for the host to hold off on their closing spiel to let the guests applaud at the end of a performance. As the attraction continued to run for years, these exit announcements started to creep up until today when they come right on the heels of the show's last line, effectively killing the audience's opportunity to express themselves.

But decades later, it's a tribute to the show's creators that, whenever the guy at the mic will pause to allow it, the crowd still breaks into spontaneous applause.

Appendix III
WORKING WITH LOOK-ALIKES

Show producers love look-alikes because they appear easy to do and come with a built-in history and emotional identification with the audience. But these 'assets' form ongoing challenges for the creative director and the performer.

ON CASTING THE LOOK-ALIKE

Finding the best possible celebrity impersonator to fill the part relies on the auditor's knowledge of the character, and his skill at recognizing and developing those qualities in the performer. Often an actor will not know which role they're right for, and may pursue one role when they are naturally more suited to another.

Talent and audition time are too limited for auditors to sit back and wait to be shown what they want; they must proactively seek and explore the relationship between the needs of the role and the skills of the performer.

Casting the look-alike usually starts with a high-profile casting call, where auditioning talent is invited to arrive in costume and perform some song or classic bit in character. A subjective judgment is made based on: 1) the auditor's knowledge of the character; 2) the actor's physical resemblance; and 3) the accuracy of the performance/audition. Let's examine these one at a time:

AUDITOR'S KNOWLEDGE of the character must be based on a physical, emotional and intellectual familiarity that comes only through study of their life and work.

Biographies and autobiographies provide insight into the character's objectives and methods. Casting a look-alike calls for the study of source films and videos, with a strong focus on physical presence, style and speed of reaction, mental process and emotional investment in situations. The star's vocal pattern should be isolated (usually on an edited audio recording), studied and memorized so that it can be recognized, critiqued and developed in the performer.

PHYSICAL RESEMBLANCE is commonly held up as the Holy Grail of casting look-alikes; but a borderline resemblance can be enough to recommend a performer, if they can recreate the spirit, intellect and presence of the original.

Chaplin's timing and balletic style is so distinctive that recreating them becomes more important than the performer's resemblance. And a pretty young woman who can make every man feel like a powerful, sexual being makes a more reliable and valuable Marilyn Monroe than the clone who must rely on a subway grating and an aerated skirt.

PERFORMANCE ACCURACY is rarely more than an indicator of the amount of study the performer has already done. Because we are casting a living character, who will interact rather than recite, the auditor must look beyond the prepared material and draw out the performer's knowledge and identification with the role. When the auditor shares his love and knowledge of the part, the tense and foreboding audition can become a creative experience for all involved. By playing with the performer, you will find the natural style and connections that make for good casting.

This collaborative approach to auditions prevents the cattle call atmosphere that oppresses and stifles the actor. But it pays another, more valuable, dividend when filling positions for an ongoing stable of look-alikes – it cultivates future talent. A knowledgeable auditor will spend time with each actor – praising their efforts, analyzing their successes and honestly-but-gently illuminating their shortcomings – always with an eye to the next audition.

Careful guidance of aspiring look-alikes encourages further work that may pay off for the producer in filling later vacancies. Once the actor is hired, there's usually precious little time for training and refinement; it makes sense to challenge (and thereby test) the performer's ability to refine their own performance at this preliminary stage.

ON TRAINING THE LOOK-ALIKE

Coaching the performer is an ongoing process that will typically continue well into the run. For this reason, the freshly-cast look-alike needs an enthusiastic third eye, endlessly critiquing and refining... helping them establish an understanding of the relationship between what they are doing and how it is perceived.

Two tools are invaluable in beginning this process: a studied, collaborative immersion in the character's work, and an original script. The director and the performer watch and listen to everything they can, focusing myopically on their star... dissecting and discussing every nuance of the performance... and drawing inspiration for how these moves and ideas will eventually intersect with the audience.

The original script takes all this out of the realm of talk and theory, and gives the performer a powerful insight into the living character. This cannot be done as well with a 'classic bit', as the focus there is on re-creation. The original piece forces the actor to create as the character. Reference to the classics is important, but by bringing a new piece to life, the look-alike steps closer to breathing life into his new role. Specific, accurate choices will always result in a stronger performance.

Recreating Groucho Marx would appear at first blush to be a simple task. Most people do it by waggling their fingers in front of their face and sing-songing "That's the most ridiculous thing I evah hoid!" No one questions who is being imitated; in fact, this impression has, over time, become the international symbol for 'Groucho Marx'. But a higher standard is imposed when one dons the swallow-tail coat and greasepaint mustache and tries to pass as 'The One, the Only – Groucho'.

When meeting Groucho, the audience expects more than a mere allusion to a broad caricature; they hope he'll react to them in the same manner he did to Margaret Dumont and the situations found in the Marxes' films. All the irreverence, the insolence, the verbal and intellectual skills are expected of the imitation; or the guest walks away disappointed.

This situation is complicated by the fact that most stars commonly impersonated by look-alikes are known for more than one specific film or time period. In imitating Groucho, for example, one could choose to recreate:

... the wild, early Groucho of Broadway and the east coast films;

... the sharp, energetic shyster of the Marxes' golden years;

... the older, slightly-caricatured Groucho of the later films;

... the Groucho with the real mustache from the lousy movies;

... the wisecracking host of *You Bet Your Life*;

... the still-vital-but-aging star of the one-man concerts;

... or the quiet, old man-in-the-beret who walked the streets of Beverly Hills in his late years, insulting lucky fans because he felt he owed them the experience.

Each manifestation of Julius 'Groucho' Marx has its own style, energy, wit and vocal pattern. Depending on the audience members' age and experience, any of these might be perceived as the 'real' Groucho – when in fact they all are.

Which Elvis are YOU familiar with – Ed Sullivan's or Las Vegas'? Which Marilyn – the pin-up girl or Sugar from *Some Like it Hot*? Which John Belushi – the effusive Bluto from *National Lampoon's Animal House* or the stoic Jake of *The Blues Brothers*? Which Dick Nixon, W.C. Fields or Moe Howard would you recognize as the 'real McCoy'?

Audience perceptions of a star's 'real' personality are further colored by other imitators. Ed McMahon's relatively weak W.C. Fields was better known than the real scoundrel; good as it was, Dick Van Dyke's Stan Laurel pales by comparison to the real thing. On the other hand, Robert Downey Jr.'s breathtaking recreation of the little tramp went largely unappreciated by those who had never seen Chaplin's films.

ON WRITING FOR LOOK-ALIKES

Ask, "What will the celebrity do when they meet the audience?" and 99% of producers will proudly respond:

"Marilyn can stand on a subway grate and have her skirt blown up... Lucy Ricardo can walk around with a bottle of Vitameatavegamin and act drunk... Laurel and Hardy can push a piano crate up a flight of stairs!"

There are two powerful reasons why these are bad ideas.

First, their respective fans know exactly how Marilyn looked, how Lucy lost it and how Stan and Ollie wrestled with that crate. By presenting a mere rehash of those bits, you are inviting the audience to compare the performances; the look-alike can only come out second best.

The guests are hoping for a *personal* experience with the star, one which appears to grow organically out of their input, the setting and other real circumstances. When you impose this famous-but-inappropriate behavior on their experience, they feel cheated.

And second, when Marilyn's skirt was blown up in *The Seven Year Itch* we saw it through the frustrated eyes of her companion in the film; the same action repeated endlessly as a photo opportunity becomes merely crude and mechanical.

Lucy's gradual descent into an alcoholic stupor came as the climax to another scheme to break into show business; out of that context, it's pointless.

A review of Laurel and Hardy's performances in *The Music Box* reveals that the comedy owes much to the editing, camera angles, sound effects and structure of the short film; elements that are virtually impossible to recreate in a live performance.

"Ah!" says Mr. Producer, "But the audience *expects* the star to do these things!" Wrong! If that were right, then every episode of I Love Lucy would've built to the Vitameatavegamin bit.

We don't expect the bit... We expect the *behavior*. Through hundreds of episodes, we've come to know and love this woman, so we tune in to see how her naïve, star-struck and single-minded behavior will get her into trouble *this* week. 40 years ago, it resulted in her drunkenly pitching Vitameatavegamin. But we're here with her today... What is she gonna do now?

The person writing for look-alikes inherits the creative freedom (and responsibilities) of the original author. They must hang on to that spirit while creating new circumstances and behavior, separating the characters from the specifics of their prior lives and freeing them to grow and live in new situations.

In the movie, we saw how Beetlejuice reacted when Lydia Deetz and family moved in on his territory; but we're not the Deetz's. How will he react to *us*? Director Tim Burton chose to make the Deetz's dance to *Day-O* (and since then every Beetlejuice look-alike has been singin' and dancin' to Harry Belafonte). Imagine, though, that you are the new writer for Beetlejuice – what other bizarre, improbable music might he employ to freak out an audience (the way we freaked the first time we saw the movie)?

The look-alike Jake and Elwood are not performing in the same situation as the movie. If we're meeting the Blues Brothers on a cruise ship, on a New York street or in a foreign country – these things should affect their attitudes and inspire new hijinks, or we're not doing right by these great characters (or our audience).

LOOK-ALIKES IN THE LONG RUN

As time passes, look-alikes need more guidance, not less. A strong positive response from early audiences must not stop the performer from developing greater subtleties and new material. If there is no creative mentor, watching and constructively advising, the look-alike becomes complacent and stops growing.

Because of the intense long-term identification with a particular personality, it is helpful to realize the effects the job can have on the performer, and vice-versa. Experience with a wide variety of personalities has revealed that successful Marilyn look-alikes usually share the charms and foibles of the original; they are sensitive and emotionally labor-intensive. Oliver Hardys are gentlemen, Stan Laurels are perfectionists, Jake Blues are con artists, and W.C. Fields are sweet souls hiding under a cloak of misanthropy.

This helps explain how a creative and temperamental talent can commit to portraying a demanding personality for years at a time. It suits them, as it did the original. On the other hand, boredom and repetition can erode the performer's efforts in ways he or she may never realize.

The talent who has kept a straight face as Jake Blues for several years can become bored, and start incorporating the 'takes' and attitudes of other Belushi creations. Marilyn will borrow bits and quotes from other characters – Mae West or Judy Holliday – that may be too forward or cerebral for the innocent Ms. Monroe. The frustrated Chico may get tired of bad puns, and lapse into Groucho's realm of quick slams and sexual innuendo.

The creative director mustn't wait to correct these situations when they crop up, or he or she will have a hard time getting the successful performer to see where they're slipping. It makes more sense to caution the actor from the beginning to watch for these tendencies, and to draw the differences clearly and emphatically from the start of training. Thus, when unwanted change starts to filter into the performance, all concerned can easily identify it and nip it in the bud.

Appendix IV
IMPROVISATION IN THEME PARKS

People are the same all over. Given any particular stimulus, guests will react one of the same four or five ways every time. Whether it's a broad physical type, a location, an event, a musical cue or a type of costume... through life experience people are conditioned to respond in a particular way. And knowing only their own life experience, people are unaware of this preconditioning and thus believe that their reaction is unique.

Hardly a day went by at Spillikin Corners when someone didn't ask me, "Hey, Professor, sold any snake oil yet?" This question would follow me for the next four years, and each person who said it believed that they'd conjured the thought themselves.

I had four standard responses to this cue. I might smile and wink at them, I might speed up and slink away guiltily, I might raise a 'shushing' finger to my lips or I might ask, "Are you ailing, Sir?" If they answered in the affirmative, I'd launch into my pitch, using the guest as an example of a customer-in-need. In every case the guest was sure their remark to me and my response was exclusive between us, and that they had a brush with a true medicine pitchman.

Did I ever get tired of hearing the same question over and over, and the necessity to answer it each time as though it's totally clever and original? Yes... until I realized that this was the job. This knack for responding to – and tolerating – repetition was the very thing I was being paid for. And if I was going to turn what I was doing into a career that would sustain and fulfill me, I had to become better at it than anyone else.

It is fashionable today to put every auditioning theme park actor through a series of improvisational exercises, in the belief that this skill is a prerequisite to scripted performing in the parks. Improvisation is certainly a component in the creation of interactive shows, but there is little room for it in themed performance.

In a club atmosphere, patrons pay to see improv artists grapple with the parameters tossed from the audience. The show is about the performers' mental and verbal agility, and the laughs come from watching the team onstage making a cohesive reality out of the scraps they're given.

But a themed show is not about the performers; it's about the guests' experience. It's about their intellectual and physical reaction, their emotional identification with the hero and their personal investment in the story. The moment the performer's skill becomes the subject matter, the guest is taken out of their private experience and is back behind the fourth wall – a mere spectator – when they should be the star.

A themed show is not improvised because it does not stand alone. It is a scripted experience that contributes to the story being told in the setting. It should give the guest a personal experience of the time, place and genre we've carefully created around them.

It falls to the writer to keep the focus on the guests' point-of-view. Each beat of the show should provide more information, advance the plot or deepen the characters – thus encouraging the audience to invest themselves further in the experience. Any time spent 'treading water' becomes a waste of time, because the guest is left waiting for the next remarkable moment to come along.

In writing the theme park show, we create the cues the audience will respond to and we anticipate their responses. Then we open and throw what we have in front of the guests – and the real writing begins.

We let the guests show us what we have... what works, what doesn't and why. We spend a lot of time listening and watching to learn their thought processes and patterns, which will suggest new, more successful, sophisticated and involving bits of business.

And, ideally, we do this with one finger on the keyboard – ready to rewrite – and one on the delete key; no material is sacred.

To create the illusion that the guest is a participant in the show, to enable them to participate freely and spontaneously, the performers must appear to react spontaneously to their input. This definitely calls for improvisation while the show is being created and polished. But over the long run, improv becomes less and less vital, being supplanted by acting skill, timing and a good memory.

So every teenager would put their hand in Figment's mouth to get him to bite it.... and every person who met Laurel and Hardy would tell Stan to scratch his head like in the movies... and every guest on camera in the *Monsters, Inc. Laugh Floor* would hold two fingers up behind the head of their neighbor.

The performer faced with such mindless repetition can't call attention to the guests' lack of imagination, and mustn't appear to react to the cue the same way every time – even though he can't be expected to improvise a different original response every time.

Instead, the performer cultivates a variety of spontaneous responses to the guests' input. Once he has learned the four or five ways the guest will interact with the stimulus he offers, he uses his practiced answers carefully, switching them up, cycling through them and keeping them fresh for each group.

Not to say that there won't be natural opportunities to play in new, unprepared and exciting ways... but the goal in themed entertainment is most often consistent perfection rather than constant innovation.

Improvisation is, by its very nature, risk-taking. Sometimes you're golden, sometimes you bomb; that's the game. In an improv show you pay your money, gambling that the show will be great; if it dies, you're only out $15 and, besides, you knew what you were in for.

But in a theme park the guest has paid $14 to park and $85 to get in... and they want a guaranteed experience. We can't gamble with their satisfaction; we have to deliver every time. So we let the guest improvise, spontaneously contributing to the limit of their ability, while we 'spontaneously' respond with one of our own pre-written, guaranteed come-backs, thus insuring a first-rate show every time – a show in which the guest has the starring role.

No, we're not audio-animatrons; but we must offer that same artistic consistency even while delivering a level of interactivity and sophistication that an audio-animatronic figure can't.

Appendix V
NOTES ON NARRATION

Back in the day, if you wanted to laugh at a truly funny narration at Disneyland, you didn't hop aboard an African launch – you caught a Keel Boat for a ride upriver. Maybe it's because the approved narration was looser, or the pace was slower... or there was less chance of an operations manager hiding in the bushes to monitor your mouth... but the guys who piloted the Keel Boats were funny; and most of it was attitude.

A good ride narrator will let you know he's real and alive by the way he conveys immediacy in his spiel. He can take a phrase he's said a million times and twist it ever-so-slightly so you listen to him and think about what he's saying and actually react.

You might think this is a terribly difficult stunt to pull off, but really it's not. It does, however, take a conscientious effort to invest yourself in the job, to be there mentally when you're spieling, thinking and caring about what you're saying and – just as importantly – what the guest is hearing.

And while I'm belaboring the point, I'd like to say a few words about 'Theme Park Inflection', a pet peeve of mine. It's the nasty habit that spielers and tour guides develop of emphasizing the prepositions in a sentence (is, does, of, was, will, etc.) instead of the nouns they're actually talking about. A few examples:

"Coming up on the right IS the home of the Seven Dwarfs."

"You've parked your car IN section D as in Dumbo."

"Your Mother-in-Law WAS struck by a parking lot tram and WILL be limping for the rest of your visit."

Try a few. It's fun.

I believe this annoying habit is born of the spieler's need to inject some life into a speech they've delivered too many times. It's an easy habit to fall into… particularly if you're working with dozens of Cast Members with the same bad habit and a management team who mistakes such delivery for effective communication.

For the guest, though, Theme Park Inflection effectively communicates that the person talking isn't really there, isn't thinking about or feeling what they're saying and is only talking to be heard (not understood).

And now a word to Cast Members everywhere who unwittingly employ Theme Park Inflection: Stop it.

Being able to recreate the sound of the Dreamfinder got me my first recording job with Disney. While I was in the recording booth at Studio D, I carefully messed around, just a bit, to let the people I was working with know that I was capable of doing more than the one voice. Since these were the same people who would be seeking voices for future projects, they'd remember my versatility; this led to more work.

Back at home, I was always practicing my cold reading skills so I could pick up any kind of copy and quickly give an intelligent reading. That skill, along with being pleasant and flexible and being able to take direction got me a lot of voice jobs through the years.

If you wish to be taken seriously as a voice actor for the parks, it's vital that you develop a proficiency in cold reading. I have always enjoyed reading aloud, something I inherited from My Sainted Mother who read aloud to me from an early age. In my bathroom I have a small library of reading material: scripts, magazines, newspapers and books, both fiction and non-fiction. Pardon the mental image – but while others might be silently cogitating in the bathroom, I'm usually reading aloud.

The most important thing in narrating for the parks is to develop a warm 'real' delivery. Too many performers start by over-modulating their voice, developing a vocal pattern they think will give their reading life and energy. Listen to them for any length of time and all you hear after a while is their inflection; like Charlie Brown's teacher – a rhythmic pattern with no content.

Instead, think of your audience as a close friend who's sitting next to you in a moving car. Speak warmly and intimately, and focus on communicating the ideas in the copy rather than the words.

Appendix VI
SUMMING UP

In my teens I would see Jack Benny, George Burns or Groucho Marx on *The Tonight Show* talking about their days in vaudeville and burlesque, and it seemed that sometime during every appearance they'd say something like:

"There's no place nowadays for a young performer to go to learn the craft. In vaudeville we might do four or five shows a day and travel the country perfecting an act, but today there's nowhere an actor can get that kind of experience."

Listening to them, I couldn't help feeling I'd missed my time; that I should have been born 60 years sooner so I too could have been a part of that magic. But I think I've gained that same luxurious experience many times over – in the themed parks and restaurants where I've performed in front of millions and millions of wonderful people (and hundreds of drunks).

Every performer I've worked with has gained valuable experience on the stages of these attractions. The long, long run of a show gives an artist the chance to explore their craft, their audience and their skills as a performer. I recommend it.

An interviewer is asking me about the wide variety of roles I've played. After listening to me describe each one, he asks, "What is it that made that work?"

I've never thought of looking for something that each project had in common, but under his questioning I begin to see a pattern, a unifying quality – respect. The truly successful projects I've seen or participated in were all based on...

<u>Respect for the Performer</u> – The desire to give the talent, backstage and onstage, all the technical, moral and financial support they need to do the job.

<u>Respect for the Audience</u> – The desire to challenge and inspire as well as amuse, and to give the guest nothing less than the quality of experience you'd expect if you were in the audience.

<u>Respect for the Source Material</u> – The desire to be true to the story you're telling, its characters and its themes... understanding that only by being faithful to the original can you hope to bring those same qualities to the guest experience.

<u>Respect for the Medium</u> – The desire to realize, with every project, the full potential of the themed experience: to give each guest a personal relationship with the story and its characters.

Theme parks around the world are very much alike. They've all bought into one blockbuster franchise or another. They all have their simulators and 4D movies, their stage revues and record-breaking coasters. They all strive – to one extent or another – to treat the paying customer as a 'guest' and to keep the grounds clean. And they all seem to have strolling animated characters and Streetmosphere.

It may appear that the future of the industry lies in technology, but don't be fooled. What is 'exclusive' in one park today will within months be popping up down the road in a competitor's new attraction.

But the well-crafted live themed show can only be generated with the participation of the audience. The guest vividly recognizes with each interaction that what is happening is uniquely theirs. That is where the future lies and where the potential for great things may be found.

ACKNOWLEDGMENTS

The first bow must go to Jim Hill (of JimHillMedia.com) who started this whole thing with his comment back in 2007; after hearing me speak about my career at an NFFC meeting, he remarked, "That's a book." Jim has been an enthusiastic booster of this project all along, even before there was a project to boost.

Then to Josh Young, a manly fellow who started as one of the Prodigy Classic Disney Fans and has grown to be a dear friend and supporter... thanks for your insight, humor and guidance.

My entire family has always been extraordinarily patient with my Themed Obsession, but I still marvel that My Sainted Mother, Bea Goodman, has stood by me, as thrilled with every step in my career as I ever was. Mom, I owe you – and love you – more than I can possibly express.

Alan Roy Josefsberg was my first Drama Teacher and an encouraging presence all my life. I still miss him and will always take comfort in the friendship of his beautiful wife, Vickie, and the FARJ Memorial Menagerie.

Love, as well, to all my teachers, mentors, counselors and classmates who helped me find my own way to this bizarre place; especially J.R. McCloskey, Norman Mennes, Sanford Robbins and Donna Tollefson from the L.A.C.C. Theatre Academy.

Thanks to everyone who assisted with the production of *From Dreamer to Dreamfinder*: Jeff Heimbuch and Lou Mongello for valuable guidance; Jim Hill, Josh Young and Audrey Marie Brown for reviewing the manuscript; Dan Carro for the cover design, Joshua K. Harris for graphics, Gina Johnson for photo retouching, and Larry Nikolai and Ron Logan for their contributions; Hugh Allison for his brilliant and thorough "fact checking and/or proofreading" (ably assisted by Eva Maler); and Leonard Kinsey at Bamboo Forest Publishing for turning the whole thing into a real boy – er, book.

Professionally I want to acknowledge the wonderful people who gave me a chance to play in this profession and occasionally got to play along with me as well; especially Stuart Adelson, Bob 'Bubba' Allen, Walter 'Sonny' Anderson, Tony Baxter, Peter Bloustein, Wally Boag, Barry Braverman, Alan Bruun, Fulton Burley, Danny Burzlaff, Dan Carro, Robert Earl, Mitch Evans, Ernie Guderjahn, Steve Hansen, Amy Henry, Keith Kolbo, Frank Lamping, Ron Logan, Mitzi Maxwell, Mark McConnell, Neil Miller, Sharon Miller, Monica Mitchell, J. Paul Moore, Neil 'Poppy' Morgan, Gary Paben, Jeff Palmer, Ellie Potts, Ronnie Rodriguez, Dave Russell, Mike Schweitzer, Billy Scudder, Steve Skorija, Dave Smith, Stephen Stanger, Jay Stein, Bryce Ward, Sarah Whitten, Tom Williams, Terry Wines, Steven Vagnini, Joe Zimmer, and the Rev. Danielle Morris.

And many, many thanks to the Grand Prix pit crew, the Animal Farm staff, the Wenches and Conspirators of 1520 A.D., my L.A.C.C.T.A. classmates, my fellow USH tour guides, The Firesign Theatre, Handpicked and the citizens of Spillikin Corners, Magic Mountain's Rainbow Circus, Poppy's Stars, the Jim Gibson Band and the Womphopper Seaters and Sales Staff, the Dreamfinders, the recruits of Fort Liberty, the Big Mountain family, Gladstone's Talented Traveling Troupe, the USF Celebrity Look-Alikes, the Banff Springs Hotel staff, my Titanic Shipmates, the M.I.L.F. Monsters of Comedy and the patient staff at Golden Corral.

And to you, Dear Reader, and the hundreds of Dreamfinder Fans who've inspired me this past year to get this thing published and done – eternal love and gratitude. Keep Dreamin'....

ANSWERS TO RON'S PRODIGY DISNOID TRIVIA

1) The front window (to look inside)

2) They're made of rubber.

3) Dwarfs (99 Dalmatian Pups divided by 9 Old Men = 11, add 3 Little Pigs = 14, divide by 2 Tweedles = 7 Dwarfs)

4) None (Eleven blocks jump up into Jane's arms; enough to spell 'Mary Poppins'.)

5) It turns into a flamingo.

6) Davy Crockett and Trigger (a buzzard in *Robin Hood*)

7) He stirs his dinner.

8) Pinocchio

9) U.S. President Andrew Jackson

10) A petrified tree; donated by Mrs. Walt Disney.

www.ingramcontent.com/pod-product-compliance
Lightning Source LLC
Chambersburg PA
CBHW021045090426
42738CB00006B/196